"The U.S. Center might well be one of the most important, if not the most important, movements in our generation, perhaps our century." --**Olan Hendrix, formerly U.S. director of SEND International**

"I know of no comparable organization doing as much for the cause of world missions, and particularly for that of unreached areas. Africa Inland Mission is fully behind the program of the U.S. Center..." --**Peter Stam, U.S. Director, Africa Inland Mission**

"Nowhere in the world is there an equivalent space devoted to the cooperation of mission agencies together. Nowhere else do you see people from 70 different mission boards working together." —**Edwin L. (Jack) Frizen, Jr., Executive Director, Interdenominational Foreign Mission Association**

"The Center is an invaluable resource for locating target groups of unreached peoples, evaluating current mission methods, exploring creative strategies, and motivating young people to global involvement." —**Colin McDougall, Association of Church Missions Committees**

"The U.S. Center for World Mission and the ministry of Dr. Ralph Winter have been pivotal in providing me with a broadened perspective of the task of world evangelization. Perhaps as no other single agency, the Center has polevaulted the Church into a new era." —**Jack W. Hayford, pastor, Church on the Way, Van Nuys, California.**

"I give my enthusiastic support to Dr. Ralph Winter, whom I have known, admired, and held in high esteem for more than thirty years." --**Bill Bright**

"I heartily endorse and support the United States Center for World Mission. Let's join hands together and make this a success for the advancement of the Kingdom of God throughout the world." --**Billy Graham.**

WORLD CHRISTIAN SERIES*

Concerts of Prayer
  David Bryant, Regal Books

Eternity in Their Hearts
  Don Richardson, Regal Books

From Jerusalem to Irian Jaya
  Ruth A. Tucker, Zondervan

The Hidden Half
  Samuel Wilson & Gordon Aeschliman
  MARC Publications

I Will Do a New Thing
  Roberta H. Winter, William Carey Library

In the Gap
  David Bryant, Regal Books

Journey to the Nations
  Debra Sanders, ed., Caleb Project

On the Crest of the Wave—Becoming a World Christian
  C. Peter Wagner, Regal Books

Operation World
  Patrick J. Johnstone, STL Books and
  William Carey Library

Perspectives on the World Christian Movement
  Ralph D. Winter and Steven C. Hawthorne, editors
  William Carey Library

Shadow of the Almighty
  Elisabeth Elliot, Harper & Row

Take My Life
  Michael Griffith, Inter-Varsity Press, U.K.

The Small Woman
  Alan Burgess, Servant Publications

Today's Tentmakers
  J. Christy Wilson, Tyndale

Touch the World Through Prayer
  Wesley Duewel, Zondervan

Wanted: World Christians
  J. Herbert Kane, Baker Book House

William Carey, A Biography
  Mary Drewery, Zondervan

*(Missionary Education Movement, Mission 2000,
  1605 Elizabeth St., Pasadena CA 91104, 818-797-1111)

I Will Do

A New Thing

THE U.S. CENTER FOR WORLD MISSION... *AND BEYOND*

Roberta H. Winter

William Carey Library

PASADENA, CALIFORNIA

Published by
William Carey Library
P.O. Box 40129, 1705 N. Sierra Bonita Avenue
Pasadena, California 91104
Telephone (818) 798-0819

Printed in the United States of America

Unless otherwise noted, scripture portions appearing throughout this book are taken from the *Living Bible*, Tyndale House Publishers, Wheaton, Illinois and are used with permission.

Library of Congress Cataloging-in-Publication Data

Winter, Roberta H.
   I will do a new thing.

   Updated ed. of: Once more around Jericho, c1978.
   Includes bibliographical references.
    1. U.S. Center for World Mission. I. Winter,
Roberta H. Once more around Jericho. II. Title.
III. Title: New thing.
BV2360.U553W56   1986   266'.023'7306   87-14731
ISBN 0-87808-201-8

CONTENTS

FOREWORD

(to *Once More Around Jericho*, 1978)

It may sound funny, coming from me, to say that I am surprised and excited by this book. I knew my wife, Roberta, was working away at it, but I didn't pay much attention. She didn't ask me many questions. It was completed before I saw a page of the manuscript.

When I finally sat down to read it, I was really impressed. I could never in the world have captured as she does the moods and moments of the stranger-than-fiction true account she relives so lightly and yet so passionately.

But this is not just an exciting story, inviting you to be a spectator. It is a gauntlet thrown down, we believe, from Heaven: God is asking sincere, believing Christians in America to stop in their tracks and to reevaluate the way of life to which they have gradually become accustomed in the last twenty years.

Our garages are bulging with things we may have never really needed. Our schedules are bulging with nice things that do not dramatically help the world's helpless. Our menus are bulging with food that makes us overweight. Our bookstores are bulging with books on the abundant life—for *us* in *America*. Our churches are bulging with Americans who have been drinking in blessings for years. (Some say that 80% of all the trained Christian workers in the world are in America.) We are vaguely proud of our past achievements in missions.

But today, new, hard questions are being asked.

Today it is suddenly clear that we are not well enough aware of what has been done in missions to be suitably impressed by either the amazing successes of the past or the amazing scope of the unfinished task in the future.

When our people talk these days about missions at all, the first subject that often arises is the delightful possibility that the new Christians overseas can finish the job by themselves. Well, all right! The presence of the overseas church, this "new fact of our time," must be taken into account.

Yet, if there is any validity to the vision this book describes, it is the awesome fact that a large number of the world's non-Christians—about five out of six—live in communities or social strata within which there is no culturally relevant church from which evangelistic outreach can be made unless, in fact, outreach to these people is "missionary" outreach which crosses the barriers that compartmentalize such people. This presents a disturbing limitation to what any church, anywhere, can do. Our home churches are not effectively reaching through such barriers, nor are the overseas churches effectively reaching through such barriers. It is as though the number of missionaries in the world working in new fields has suddenly shrunk, instead of being increased by virtue of the help of the overseas church.

I spell this out in some detail because the massive concern and effort and excitement which my wife describes is utterly senseless apart from this single amazing insight. Everything else flows from there.

Perhaps you, too, will be caught up in the flow. Don't resist. This book is talking about the highest of all priorities.

Ralph D. Winter
June, 1978

FOREWORD

(To *I Will Do A New Thing*, 1987)

I wrote the foreword to my wife's book, *Once More Around Jericho,* in June of 1978. Since then much more has happened which needs to be told. Still, those early years are integral to understanding what has happened since. The new chapters could not stand alone, yet when merely added to the former, made the book unwieldy and long.

Consequently she has spent more than a year in revising, editing out, adding to. That earlier book was slimmed down to make room for sixteen new chapters and covers twice as many additional years. As before, it is 100 percent my wife's work.

This time, however, it carries a new tone which reflects a balancing new optimism. Back then, as my foreword suggested, we were mainly heading into the wind, trying to be faithful to "the amazing scope of the unfinished task."

Now, eight years later, we possess, breathlessly, a major additional insight: that we are in the final stages of a countdown to the End of History. We once thought of the task remaining as immense and challenging. Now we see it as amazingly do-able by the year 2000. Ten years ago we spoke of 2.5 billion unreached individuals. Today, we speak in terms of *merely* 17,000 unreached people groups. We didn't realize ten years ago that there are 150 times as many Bible believing congregations in the world today as there are groups still to be reached.

We—the believers around the world—can finish the job! We really can!

This perspective is "new." But the dynamic unfolding of this greatest *New Thing* is still ahead, in fact just around the corner. It is what God is about to do. But you will have to read this story to understand.

Ralph D. Winter
January, 1987

PREFACE

The events recorded in the early chapters of this book were told about in *Once More Around Jericho* and its later update, *The Kingdom Strikes Back.*

So much of the book this time is new--at least half of it-- that I have chosen a new title, *I Will Do a New Thing.* This title goes beyond what God is doing with the U.S. Center for World Mission to the larger world of global mission and the approaching "End of History."

Trying to explain the U.S. Center for World Mission has always been difficult. Now, more than ever, its larger context is crucial. God is doing something new in the world of missions, and the Center's role is potentially more significant than ever.

The vision of the unreached peoples is not unique to us, though we have more people working full time on that problem than any other organization anywhere else on earth. Certainly, the concept cannot be said to be "new." Twice before in modern history, at the turn of the last two centuries, the vision of the unreached captured the attention of the Christian world and resulted in massive new outreach, the first time to the coastlands of the world and then, around 1900, to the interior of each continent. For our generation, however, the concept of the specific unreached "peoples" is new. Such peoples, the new focus, may be touched in Los Angeles and Munich, not just in Papua New Guinea. Once more, God willing, a new wave of concern will mobilize the church worldwide so that we may finish the task of the Great Commission by the year 2000.

As one mission agency among many, our methodology is new. We work on three fronts at once: mission research, mission mobilization and mission training. Many departments and autonomous offices have come into existence on campus to aid in one or more of these fronts. This is why some have called the USCWM a *Missions Pentagon.* It is amazing what you can find out here: staff workers speaking 40 different languages, backgrounds in 70 different missions, etc.

According to *World Christian* magazine, which for a number of years occupied several suites of offices here, "David Bryant has compared the Center to the town, Rivendale, in Tolkien's *Lord of the Rings*: the place where visions can be born, where fragile dreams can become reality, where battle plans can be laid for great battles ahead, and faith renewed in ultimate, inevitable success."[1] This is the dream the Lord has placed on our hearts. This is the dream which is becoming reality.

Since the publication of *Once More Around Jericho*, I have often been asked why my quotes are from the *Living Bible*. Although I use many different versions and in some ways actually prefer the *New International Version* for Bible study, still it is the *Living Bible* which, more than any other translation, speaks the language of my heart. It has been my daily devotional companion for ten years now. Its words have comforted me, condemned me, and guided me precisely because they were too clear to be misunderstood and ignored.

Many people have helped me with this book. My special thanks go to Dr. Kenneth Cashin, recently retired from the School of Engineering at the University of Massachusetts. As a volunteer on staff, he spent months meticulously going over this manuscript, checking for typos, misspelled words and inelegancies of expression. He is the proof reader *par excellence.*

I am also very grateful to Ron Saito for the beautiful

cover design, which so well symbolizes our hopes and dreams as well as the property which we claim in the name of our Lord.

Many others read the book in manuscript form and made helpful suggestions. I am especially indebted to John Holzmann and to Tricia Johnson, who spent months on the preliminary revision, and to my husband, without whose help the book would have been full of many factual errors.

As the author of this book, and cofounder of the USCWM with my husband, I should perhaps apologize for my "over-loyal" comments about him. He is not perfect, as I am not. Nevertheless, I have never known him to be other than single-minded in his determination to fully obey the Lord, even when the costs have been high. Forgive me if I seem too uncritical of him. I'm just trying to relate things as I see them.

The years of the founding of the USCWM have not been easy years, especially for our younger staff who, as a rule, were inexperienced in spiritual warfare when they came. It would have been much simpler for them to have joined long-established organizations and to work in settled positions under seasoned management structures. Here, they didn't even have the benefit of a single experienced manager until Art McCleary came in 1983.

Many who came intended from the first to stay only two years, yet stayed four before finally going to work overseas among an unreached people. We are still very grateful for all their help.

Ralph and I are especially grateful, however, to those who felt called to stay and help. They could see that unless the battle of mobilization were won here, the battle of evangelization could never be won there. They gradually had to give up their own plans in order to embrace as their own the struggles, plans and dreams which originally we bore quite alone. But they have carried enormous responsibilities for their age and are growing into impressive maturity.

It is to these wonderful, forgiving, patient, godly younger staff that I therefore dedicate this book. May God richly use them to bless the world is my prayer.

1. "United States Center for World Mission," *World Christian*, March/April, 1983, pp. 20-22, P. O. Box 5199, Chatsworth, CA 91031.

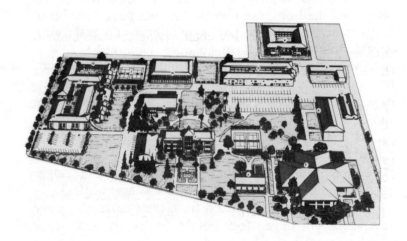

1

JULY 1974

"LET THE EARTH HEAR HIS VOICE"

I leaned forward in my chair, trying to catch some of the words of the language spoken by the girl with the long blond braids seated in front of me.

"Maybe she's Swedish," I thought, "or Norwegian." All around me people were listening through earphones as the message given from the platform was being translated at the same time into French, German, Spanish, Chinese, and Japanese, their native languages. The girl and her companions were all dressed in black. There were two women—the girl, and an older woman; the rest were men. The young girl was obviously the interpreter for the group.

"Finland? Hungary? Yugoslavia? Austria?" My mind kept clicking off all the European countries from which a blond girl so dressed could have come.

There was a pause in the meeting as the speaker on the platform sat down, and I leaned forward and tapped the girl on the shoulder. "Excuse me. Would you tell me something? What country do you and your friends come from?"

"We're from Romania," she answered.

"Romania! Oh, I'm so glad you came!" I sank back in

1

my chair. Even from behind the Iron Curtain, then, they had come. And we were all here to worship the same Christ and to discuss together the task of worldwide evangelization.

I looked about the room with its multiplicity of earphones, the bank of translation booths off to one side, and the colorful assortment of national costumes visible everywhere. Clearly the gospel could not have reached so far without surmounting a jungle of language barriers. Yet I wondered if anyone would believe my husband when he told them, come Saturday, that most of the language and culture barriers were *still* to be crossed!

My husband, one of the Congress speakers, had been asked to deal with precisely that subject—cross-cultural evangelism. He called it "the highest priority."

We were seated in the big hall at Lausanne, Switzerland, there for Billy Graham's International Congress on World Evangelization. Two thousand seven hundred participants from all over the world were there, and many had brought their wives. The great convention hall was crowded. From the back rows those on the platform seemed almost toy figures moving about. Yet, astonishingly, high above the speaker's head a huge screen depicted on closed circuit television every gesture and facial expression of the one speaking.

Ralph knew many of the people, so many, it seemed to me, that out in the central lobby we couldn't walk more than five steps before he was greeting or being greeted by someone. Some were friends—mission executives or evangelical leaders from other parts of the United States. Others were his former students—missionaries and national leaders from India, Africa, Taiwan, Australia, Germany, Latin America and Singapore. By now he had had more than a thousand in his classes at the School of World Mission of Fuller Theological Seminary.

Some weeks before the Congress, his address, and all the others, had been sent to each delegate. From the flurry

2

of responses which had come back, we knew his address would be controversial. All the delegates were involved in evangelism, but almost all worked exclusively with their own kind of people. Few were working cross culturally, and of these, almost none were working among unreached peoples. Yet the remaining missionary task was huge!

Saturday was the end of an exhausting week, with another yet to go. Some of the delegates had joined their wives on a bus trip to L'Abri, Francis Schaeffer's world renowned Center. Any other time I too would have liked to go. But . . .

Even so, the hall was mainly full, and I prayed as I sat near the front that the Lord would use Ralph's words to convict the hearts of those present.

Ralph's address[1] was one of only two or three that had scheduled responses from the platform. His responders were three well-known mission leaders working in different areas of the world. Their comments were written responses to Ralph's pre-conference paper which they had received weeks before. Since the address Ralph was about to give continued where that earlier paper left off, at his suggestion all three "responders" spoke before he began. Two were a bit critical of his first paper. One had missed his point completely and the other assumed that if we appeal to strategy, we ignore the crucial role of the Holy Spirit.

I was troubled by the criticism, especially of the second. "It is true," I thought, "that in relying on a specific strategy we may be relying on man's best wisdom without reference to the Holy Spirit. But it does not have to be this way. The scriptures show that God often gave detailed plans as to how He wanted something done. Isn't that strategy? I do hope this man's negative comments don't confuse people so that they will fail to understand the importance of what Ralph has to say!"

Then Ralph began to speak, backing his statistics with diagrams on the video screen high above his head. He

3

responded first to those who had preceded him and then commented on some of the pre-conference letters he had received. Several from India and Africa had written: "We are able to evangelize our own countries. The day of the missionary is past; we don't need missionaries any more."

Obviously they too had missed his point. How could he make them understand? "If you are like most evangelists, pastors and missionaries, almost all your efforts are spent bringing nominal Christians to a real and vibrant relationship with Jesus Christ. Even when your church does evangelize people from a totally non-Christian background, are these not almost entirely from within your own cultural group?

But what about those others, maybe even in your own country, who do not speak your language or who belong to a different culture, tribe or people? *That* is where the main, *unfinished* task lies. Almost no one is even *trying* to reach them.

"Do you realize that in India alone there are 500 million unreached people, mainly hidden behind caste barriers? And what about the 600 million Muslims, 800 million Chinese, 100 million tribal peoples, and many other unreached people groups scattered around the world?

"Even supposing every church in the world were to reach outside its doors and win everyone within range—people who speak the same language and come from the same culture—do you realize there are so many other untouched groups that, even then, five out of six of the non-Christians in the world would remain unevangelized?"

The figures were too staggering. Ralph's words were like a time bomb that had not yet gone off. Yet I knew that his information was accurate, as accurate as anyone's could possibly be. I had been with him through the years when he was amassing those statistics. He had drawn on the most reliable sources, and because of his graduate degree in mathematical statistics, he knew how to analyze the data. Yet we both realized that many at the Congress would find it hard to believe there was so much yet to be done—*beyond new barriers!*

I glanced around to see how those near me were reacting. With a sigh of relief, I saw they were listening intently, with apparent understanding and increasing conviction.

"Nominal Christians need to be truly saved," Ralph was saying, "and I'm all for the kind of evangelism that brings such people into a personal relationship with Christ. Even more crucial, perhaps, is winning the non-Christians who speak our various languages and are from our own cultures. All too often we have really neglected them.

"But if you are asking what evangelistic task must have the *highest* priority today, then without question we must refer to those who have never had a chance to hear the gospel in their own languages and cultural settings. Of 2.8 billion non-Christians in the world, these number 2.4 billion—over half the population of the world. Despite all the wonderful mission work across the years and the outreach of national churches everywhere, there are still *2.4 billion people beyond the range of present efforts of any existing church or mission.*"

I could hear the sharp intake of breath from someone behind me. Glancing back, I could see that he looked astonished, unbelieving.

On the platform, his face now televised on the screen high above him, Ralph put it more vividly. "If every one of us had stopped on his way to this Congress and won a *million people* to Christ, we could have disbanded this Congress. The job would have been done. But each delegate here would have had to win one million people. That is the size of the unfinished task!"

Ralph wrote that message for the participants, but God meant it also for Ralph (and for me). Was his role only to be that of "a voice crying in the wilderness," pointing the way?   Or did God intend for him to set a personal example?

That was the question which, almost two years later, launched us on the greatest adventure of our lives.

---

1. This address was printed in the Congress compendium *Let the Earth Hear His Voice,* edited by J. D. Douglas and published by World Wide Publications, 1313 Hennin Avenue, Minneapolis, MN 55403. It is also available as a separate pamphlet entitled "The New Macedonia: A Revolutionary New Era Begins," available from William Carey Library, 1705 N. Sierra Bonita, Pasadena CA 91104.

2

"THROUGH THE VALLEY OF THE SHADOW"

(Psalm 23:4)

We were back home in Pasadena. From the crowded halls at Lausanne, Switzerland, we had gone by train and ferry to England, visiting a couple of European missionary headquarters on the way. I had talked until I was hoarse selling books on missions that second week in Lausanne. Then, on the train through Europe, I had picked up a terrible cold while sitting at an open window to escape the cigarette smoke strangling the atmosphere. All this time, by doctor's orders, I had been taking large amounts of thyroid medication in an effort to reduce two nodules on my thyroid gland which he had discovered just before we left. Now he recommended surgery.

I looked forward to the "rest" that surgery would involve, yet somehow I felt reluctant and ill at ease with the whole idea. "You, a nurse, afraid, and it isn't even major surgery!" I chided myself. Still, uneasiness lingered, and I recommitted my life and future to the Lord.

At first the surgery seemed uneventful. The nodules were benign, for which I praised the Lord. The surgeon didn't even seem alarmed that I could only whisper. "That is probably due to the large metal tube the anesthetist put in your throat," he told me. But he seemed increasingly concerned when my voicelessness persisted three days, a week, two weeks, three weeks. And I was getting desperate.

It was the beginning of the seminary school year and, as usual, faculty and students were invited to an opening banquet. I went with Ralph and quite by accident (or Providence) sat beside a seminary friend who had recently had problems with his voice. He advised me to see his specialist, whom I called the next day.

I was well—perfectly capable of driving the 45 miles to the doctor's office in Santa Monica. And though I couldn't speak, I could whisper. So I went. Alone.

I didn't know whether to be impressed or dismayed by the showy display of autographed photos of movie stars which covered Dr. Hans von Leden's walls. "Are they a status symbol for him, or is he really a capable laryngologist?" I wondered.

But when he examined me, I was impressed by his thoroughness—and totally unprepared for his diagnosis.

"You either have a bruised or pinched nerve, in which case your voice will soon return. Or the surgeon accidentally cut your laryngeal nerve. Your right vocal chord is paralyzed."

I leaned toward him, whispering as loud as I could: "If it is cut, will it grow back together?" I should have known better, but my mind refused to accept the alternative.

"If it is cut, there are two options," he matter of factly explained. "If we can get it before three weeks are out, we can sometimes splice it together. It is too late for that. Sometimes, very rarely, in three out of one hundred cases, the left vocal chord alone will compensate for the right. If this happens to you, your voice will return suddenly after about six months. But don't expect that. It happens very rarely. There is nothing we can do. Nothing but wait."

I was stunned as the truth dawned on me. I might never be able to speak again! I might always have to clap

8

my hands to attract attention, or touch the grocery clerk on the arm, or pull my husband over to my lips as we travelled the freeway. I might never be able ever to sing again.

Tears filled my eyes. I looked at him, then choked out a whispered, "We can pray."

I was fairly sure this man was not a Christian—in fact, he was probably Jewish—but I couldn't restrain myself. "There is a greater Physician who made me and can heal me. I will go to Him."

I stumbled out of the office and down the stairs, hoping I would meet no one who would wonder at the tears raining down my cheeks. The long drive home during rush hour traffic was a nightmare. I couldn't see well because of the tears, and I worried about the safety of driving in my condition. Yet I had to go home. God's angels must have been very close to me that day.

For some time I had been praying that the Lord would make the Bible more precious to me. I had read the Bible all my life, but I sensed that it didn't seem so precious to me as it did to some others who had newly come to it later in life. Disciplined obedience on my part was necessary, I knew, and thus I had reread sections of the Old and New Testaments. But for some time, I had tended to shy away from the prophetic books since their interpretation was, I thought, subject to so much speculation. Yet of late I had been impressed that obedience required reading these books also. I had completed Daniel and Revelation and was halfway through the Book of Ezekiel, where I had left my marker that morning.

It was a relief to find myself alone when I got home. I wanted to tell Ralph, but not yet. I had a battle to fight with God. Throwing myself on the bed, I cried and prayed and then reached out for my Bible. For lack of any other idea, I started to read where I had left off. And the words leapt from the page as if God himself were speaking, "On the day of his coming your voice will

9

suddenly return to you" (Ezekiel 24:27).

"Oh, God, could this be for me? Dare I claim it?" I searched feverishly for the context. Did it mean (for me) when Christ would return? Whose coming? *Suddenly!* That's what the doctor had said. If my voice were to come back it would come back *suddenly!* "Oh God, you must mean this for me. Otherwise why would I see it when I wasn't hunting for it—when I didn't even know such a verse existed?" And my heart became calm and trustful again.

The next months were "toughies." Various pastors and friends prayed for me, but I could sense they didn't really believe God would heal me. Even those who specialized in praying for the sick wanted to warn me against all possibilities. "You know, your verse says, 'On the day of His coming.' "

I knew they meant well, and I knew that true faith was not a conjured-up feeling that God would somehow honor. My faith at times was strong. I would assure people that whatever was God's will was okay. I knew I was in His very loving hands. Yet on the way home from such a public declaration I would break down in tears at how long it seemed and how difficult to be patient.

God gave me those months because I needed them. I was unable to rush out and manage this or that; I couldn't make myself heard. Little by little I began to understand the rock of security that the Bible is meant to be, and mine became underlined throughout in pinks, yellows, and greens of felt-tip markers. Every morning I tried my voice, hoping to find that this was my "suddenly" day. And every day I again cried to the Lord, reminding Him of His promise, yet assuring Him that I'd serve Him no matter what. He'd just have to show me how. I constantly prayed that no matter what happened, my attitude would be a testimony for Him and that I would not be resentful of the surgeon who should have been more careful. I wanted especially for the non-Christian doctors to know of God's power—that He is real!

By the end of January, I began to notice a slight difference. The left side of my throat was very weary at times, and I would stretch my neck to relieve the tension. Then the whisper became a bit louder and every now and then would crack into a real voice for a moment. Day by day there was a bit more voice until, in about three weeks, I was talking again. How I praised the Lord! Even the Jewish doctor said, "Well, I guess God has done a miracle for you. Your right vocal chord is still paralyzed, but you'll get along okay."

As I look back now, I see that God had me, and our whole family, in training, making us ready to trust Him wholly. If we had been able to do something—*anything* —we would have done it. But there was absolutely nothing we could do except wait and trust and pray.

That lesson was invaluable. We learned that God looks over the daily affairs of man. That He cares what happens, even to us. And that, to Him, our growing stronger in faith is far more valuable than anything else.

Not my voice, not our financial security, not our position—*nothing* is to be compared to the value of learning to depend on Him. I needed that lesson for what was to come.

3

THE TWENTY-FIVE UNBELIEVABLE YEARS[1]

Ralph and I met almost by chance in 1951, just as I was graduating from nurses' training. He had come to speak at the chapel which the few Christian student nurses had organized. In spite of very different backgrounds and the pitfalls of courtship by mail, we were married in five months.

He was different from all others I had dated. He talked about the world and about strange people in strange places. He spoke of dreams. Goals for the future. Unfinished tasks. He had a way about him of seeing sides to issues that I never imagined existed. And I was fascinated.

I was also drawn to him by his open honesty. From the first he referred to certain personality traits he had which, he said, seemed to irritate some people. "I have a reputation for being somewhat a 'son of thunder,'" he told me on our second date. I remembered the reference to James and John but couldn't quite imagine this soft-spoken, intellectual type wanting to call down fire on an unrepentant village. So I waited for an explanation.

"I guess what I mean is, when I'm convinced of something, I go all out. Some accuse me of being sort of a fanatic." He paused, watching me. Still I waited.

"One summer," he went on, "my mother was terribly embarrassed when I concluded I should no longer wear dress clothes, not even to church. I felt it was somehow wrong to spend money on such things when people elsewhere in the world were starving. I still feel that way, but now I see that if the only message church people get from such action is that you're weird, then you've lost the point. So now I wear dress clothes like everyone else, but only as a uniform. I still don't believe it's right to spend a lot of money on them. I guess this fundamental willing-ness to be different—to do things that others may not understand—is very much a part of me. I don't know if I'll ever change there. And I guess most girls would find it difficult, therefore, to marry a guy like me." Again he looked at me somewhat quizzically.

I had other questions I wanted answered: "What are you going to do with your life?"

I was impressed that he was beginning studies for a Ph.D. in linguistics and anthropology, but beyond that? "Are you going to be a teacher, an engineer (He had an engineering degree from Caltech.), a pastor (He had attended seminary two years.) . . . ?"

And I threw out *my* challenge which had often stopped a relationship in its tracks: "I'm going to be a missionary!"

I watched for his reaction. "I really don't know what the Lord wants of me," he responded. "John Wesley said, 'The field is the world. God has no geographical boundaries.' I know I'm ready to do anything God asks me to do, but I don't know what that is. People keep insisting that I make up my mind. But I'm waiting for God to show me, and in the meantime, I'm doing what seems best."

We had only one month to get to know each other before he went back East for graduate studies. I was willing to drift along in our relationship, but he plunged into a thorough research. He talked to a mutual friend about me; he checked out my theology, my reputation, my Christian commitment, my scholastic ability. He even gave me oral math quizzes as we sped along the freeway—which I promptly flunked, every one.

13

I was learning many things about him, too. A mutual friend, also in nurses' training, obviously admired him, yet admitted that his unusual and unexpected conclusions sometimes irritated people. "He is an innovator," she said, "sometimes far ahead of others in his thinking." And she was right.

He told me of the experimental class in Biblical Greek which he taught at Pasadena (Nazarene) College, the one I had attended just a few years before. He told me of the program he initiated which eventually sent many Christian English teachers to Afghanistan (then, as now, a country closed to missions). He told me of his boxes of file cards of New Testament Greek vocabulary he intended to use for producing a series of reference tools for seminary students and biblical scholars.[2] And I noticed that even his conversation was unusual: at times brutally honest, at others extremely diplomatic.

We were married that December, just after Christmas. Three days later we flew to New York state.

It was, in many respects, a cross-cultural marriage. I had grown up an Arminian in theology (Nazarene); he a Calvinist (Presbyterian and Congregational). What to me were unintentional "mistakes" were to him "sins," intentional or not, if they were contrary to the known or unknown will of God. I had to learn to sing Presbyterian hymns instead of Nazarene gospel songs. Being in the East for the first time in my life, I had to wear a hat and gloves to church. Even the English spoken there was different. Once in the middle of the night, when I told Ralph I was cold, instead of throwing another blanket over us, as I expected, he responded with a local colloquialism, "How about that!" which set us both off into peals of laughter. It was a period of adjustment but we were together and in love, and we knew the Lord had chosen us for each other.

After Ralph graduated from Cornell, we went to Princeton Seminary where he accepted a student pastorate

14

in a little, historic country church. There our two older daughters were born. And I saw in my husband a gentleness and patience which before had not been quite so evident.

Up to this time I had alternately worked and studied, auditing Ralph's classes, doing research for his doctoral dissertation and studying one summer at Wycliffe's Summer Institute of Linguistics while he taught. Now, suddenly, I was housebound with two lovable but very confining babies. I wanted the babies, and I wanted to study, but it seemed I couldn't do both.

Fortunately for me, Ralph was also frustrated. With a Ph.D. in linguistics, he didn't expect trouble in that area. Yet his first week in Hebrew class was his last. "I just can't take it," he complained. "I'm never going to be able to sit in that class for a whole year! The way Biblical languages are analyzed and taught is terribly out of date. No wonder pastors-to-be learn to hate Greek and Hebrew and rarely ever use them again. But they are required courses. What am I going to do?"

Typically, he started looking for other academic options and gained permission to study Hebrew on his own. If at the end of a year he could pass the comprehensive Hebrew exam, he could skip the regular class.

That year he faced a demanding schedule. Besides going to school full time and pastoring a church, he worked every Saturday to supplement our meager income. Hebrew was completely forgotten until six weeks before the comprehensive was to be given, and then Ralph began to panic.

I volunteered, "If only I didn't have the babies, I could study with you." (How I would enjoy that! I had studied French and German with him for his doctoral exams, and I knew he hated studying a language by himself.) When his parents learned of Ralph's crisis, they paid for someone to take care of our two babies for six weeks while we studied

Hebrew together in the church office next door. That exposure to Hebrew enabled me later to help with his second-year Hebrew exegesis homework while I fed our youngest at 2:00 AM. Still later, I worked on *A Contextual Lexicon of Genesis* which he co-authored with Dr. Charles Fritsch, one of the Hebrew professors. I enjoyed the mental stimulation again, even though house work suffered.

I enjoyed even more the sense of "partnership" with Ralph in his tasks. To me, "helpmate" has always implied helping wherever needed—at home, in the office, in research. And during that period I needed the sense of working *with* Ralph, not just *for* him.

In 1956, we went as missionaries of the United Presbyterian Church to work with Mayan Indians in the highlands of western Guatemala. We were fortunate to be assigned to work with an older couple who had a great love and understanding of the Indian culture and saw the missionary task as all encompassing. They had pioneered the work among a group of 250,000 Indians, being joined much later by several couples in another mission three or four hours away, and by a single nurse who ran the clinic they had started.

During those years we were involved in the development of a number of crucial projects: the Theological Education by Extension (TEE) movement (which now enrolls perhaps 100,000 students around the world); a nationwide rural adult education program offering a government sixth-grade diploma; the formation of the first junior high school in our town; the establishment of several small industries (actually tentmaking ministries for Indian young men in seminary); the formation of a credit union; the establishment with two other families of the Inter-American School for missionary and Guatemalan children who needed to prepare for higher education in the U.S. later on; and even collaboration in the founding of an evangelical university.

16

Although he delved deep into educational and developmental programs, Ralph was still convinced that the only real answer to man's need was the change of his heart by the Holy Spirit and his incorporation into a continuing body of believers, the Church. By comparison, all other approaches were incomplete and essentially impermanent by themselves. An article to that effect which he wrote caught the interest of a man who would loom large in our future, Dr. Donald McGavran.

Toward the end of our second five years in Guatemala, largely because of his effort in the TEE movement, Ralph was named the Executive Secretary of the Association of Theological Schools in Northern Latin America, and in that capacity became personally acquainted with the seventeen Latin American nations north of the equator. When we went back to Pasadena on our furlough in 1966, Dr. McGavran of the newly established School of World Mission at Fuller Theological Seminary asked Ralph to teach a course on Theological Education by Extension.

It was a heady experience to work with Dr. McGavran. We had known of him for some time through his writings, and had admired his insight and courage in trying out new ideas in mission strategy. Now Ralph had the rare privilege of working at his side and learning from him directly.

We had finally agreed to teach in Pasadena six months each year, and were preparing to return to our work in Guatemala, when in a brief space of time Dr. McGavran twice came close to death. He was past the age at which most men retire, but was so energetic that he seemed indestructible. The entire permanent missions faculty at that point consisted of Dr. McGavran and Dr. Alan Tippett, a well-known and capable missionary anthropologist, now retired. Dr. McGavran insisted that Ralph stay on the faculty full time, and at first we vacillated, trying to know the will of the Lord. It soon became obvious,

17

however, that to pilot missionaries through a master's dissertation, the so-called "major advisor" needs to be around all year, not just six months.

So we stayed at Fuller for ten years. Ralph became a full Professor of the Historical Development of the Christian Movement as well as lecturer in Theological Education by Extension and various strategy and statistics courses. To him this was ten years of learning about all parts of the world in the present and in the past. God has truly done marvelous things, starting with that little band of twelve apostles!

Although in Guatemala we had seen the wonderful changes that the Gospel brought into a community, we were surprised at Fuller by Dr. McGavran's exhuberant conviction that we were in the sunrise, not the sunset, of missions. Like others, we had heard plenty of the bad news of the world, as reported in the newspapers. At the School of World Mission we were privileged like few others to have access to the *good* news, the wonderful news that God was no liar: that as He promised, His gospel was spreading and growing, often out of control, all around the world.

Missionaries who came to Fuller for training brought with them tales of revivals sweeping across many countries, of whole people groups coming to Christ, of the gospel growing underground in the face of fierce opposition, of new advances into nations and peoples never yet reached. We discovered that Sub-Saharan Africa would soon be over 50% Christian, and that Korea was the forerunner of a dramatic turning to Christ in Asia such as had never been seen before. We knew most people never heard such good news—certainly not from secular media! A hopeful thought began to flicker in our minds: "Is it possible that the church worldwide, if mobilized for action, actually has the muscle to *finish* the job Jesus gave us to reach all nations?"

The thought remained submerged for many years.

There were many gaps—many things still needing to be done to get the gospel to all the world, and we remained busy while at Fuller trying to help with some of them.

When Ralph had gone from a degree in engineering to anthropology and linguistics, people asked why he had left engineering. They always seemed a bit confused by his answer: "I didn't; now I'm a social engineer!" Then when he went to seminary after getting his Ph.D. in linguistics, his answer to such questions became, "I'm a Christian social engineer." People would laugh and ask, "What on earth is that?" And he would explain, "It's a person who looks for the gaps in the social structure of the Christian cause and tries to fill them."

In a very real sense this has been Ralph's chief calling.

If no one seemed to take the initiative to get self-supporting Christian teachers into Afghanistan, he would.

If no one studying biblical Greek took the time to work on the method of Greek teaching, then he would.

If a system of theological education were needed that would train real leaders where they were, without tearing them from their jobs and families, then a Christian social engineer should design such a plan. He and another missionary engineer-turned-anthropologist, Jim Emery, did just that. TEE was the result.

If a publishing house specializing in low-cost, high quality books on mission strategy were needed, as the faculty at the School of World Mission believed, then a Christian social engineer should design one that could operate in the black and get its publications to missionaries all over the world. The William Carey Library came into being.

If students making decisions at the Inter Varsity Missionary Conference at Urbana needed a missions educational follow-up program to maintain their vision and inspiration, then a Christian social engineer should design one. Such a course should be spiritually challenging and help them ascertain God's call for their lives. At the same time it should give them fully accredited university credit which would be transferable even to secular universities. Ralph's design became the SIIS (the Summer Institute of International Studies).

More than a professor or a missionary, Ralph is really a Christian social engineer. If to John Wesley " the field is the world," to Ralph "the task is as big as the need, whatever that is." His assignment was teaching and research, and he did that faithfully, curtailing outside speaking engagements far more often than the other professors realized, lest his teaching suffer.

And I worked alongside him, doing research for his classes, helping prepare lessons, grading papers and helping him in his writing.

But of what value is the planning of strategy if the bridge collapses for want of a span? Of what value is teaching if the cause of which one speaks is weakened for want of a missing link?

I looked forward to weekends, hoping for times to relax. But weekends were filled with engineering projects —Christian social engineering: first the formation of the William Carey Library publishing house and the Church Growth Book Club, then the formation of the American Society of Missiology and the development of its journal, *Missiology: An International Review*. Later, after the Urbana Conference in 1973, Ralph established the Summer Institute of International Studies.

Sometimes I felt that such engineering was as much *fun* to Ralph as a football game was to others. He worked hard, on his own time, and he loved it.

All the other projects, once set up and running, could be turned over to others to operate. But this new one would be too big and risky. For months Ralph tried to bury himself in his work. Wasn't it enough to do? But the cause of the unreached continued to beckon. He had almost a hundred missionaries in his class, and over and over tried to persuade one or another to join him in this new challenge. But the months passed, and still no one responded. Gradually Ralph became increasingly burdened with the conviction that God expected *him* to do something about it. Alone, if necessary.

He felt that to attack the problem adequately, a large, multifaceted mission center would be necessary. A huge amount of research would have to be done. Students would need to be motivated and trained. Most difficult of all—and a job that very few were attempting—the church nationwide needed to be mobilized. The church had to be awakened to see the size of the task—both the complex and simple aspects. There was a large task still to be finished; yet it could be done—in our generation—*if everyone helped!*

Ralph's dream for a center for world mission was big and not at all sure of success. It couldn't be done just on weekends and after hours. It would take someone's full time—and more.

Ralph knew he could not possibly found such a center on his own. But there was no way around it. Whether he found someone to help or not, he had to move, even if it meant sacrificing his own plans and security and leaving a job he loved.

It was a very difficult decision. And here we faltered . . . for seven long months.

---

1. This chapter title comes from a book by the same name written by my husband and published by the William Carey Library, 1705 N. Sierra Bonita, Pasadena, CA 91104. It discusses the advance in missions between 1945 and 1970. A condensed version appears as the last chapter in Kenneth Scott Latourette's seven-volume *A History of the Expansion of Christianity*, published by Harper and Row.

2. Two of these tools are *The Word Study New Testament* and *The Word Study Concordance*, companion volumes usable by both laymen and pastors. They are available from the William Carey Library, 1705 N. Sierra Bonita, Pasadena, CA 91104, and from Tyndale House.

4

MAY 19, 1976

"IS THERE ANYTHING TOO HARD FOR ME?"

(Jeremiah 32:27b)

"If you need a million dollars, or two, forget it! You'll never raise it. But if you need ten million, then I think you can find the money you need. "Dale Kietzman knew what he was talking about. For some years he had been one of the top executives in an organization specializing in helping Christian agencies in management and fund raising. "Small projects just don't attract attention," he said. "They don't provide enough of a challenge. People respond best to big ones."

"Ten million! You've got to be kidding!" the others laughed. Ralph also was astounded but thoughtful. "What's more," Dale continued, "you can raise that kind of money without tapping any of the seminary's sources."

For two years at various times the School of World Mission faculty had discussed the need for a large building close by, a sort of implementing annex, which could carry forward some of the mission strategies suggested by their research and teaching.

It could house, they hoped, a major mission research library. They all still grieved over the fact that Fuller had lost its bid to buy Yale's Kennedy School of Missions library, one of the two best mission libraries in the world.

22

It had been sold instead to a school not really interested in missions. Now, however, the other library, really the better of the two, was possibly available, especially to a neutral type of center.

Some months before they had begun thinking about buying a small college campus that was up for sale a few miles away. It had several large buildings, but could house retired missionaries as well as everything else they had earlier envisioned.

They thought of the Association of Church Missions Committees, located just a few blocks away. Two years before several of these professors had helped launch that organization, but now it was rapidly outgrowing its office space. Its work was crucial in mobilizing the churches of America for a new thrust in missions.

They had planned that the center would house the editorial offices for certain key mission publications as well as provide a number of significant services for mission agencies, such as computerized research. Also, they hoped, the new center would have space for significant mission conferences.

Could that dream ever become reality?

5

JULY 1976

"IF YOU BELIEVE . . IT'S YOURS"

(Mark 12:24)

"Hal-le-*lu*-jah!"

Most of the graduating seminary students merely accepted their diplomas, shook hands with the president and the chairman of the board and went back to their seats. But Erik Stadell, from Sweden and a missionary to Greenland, turned to the audience, raised his diploma high and shouted, "Hal-le-lu-jah!"

Everyone laughed. Everyone loved Erik. His faith was vibrantly enthusiastic and he obviously loved his Lord. But in day-to-day matters, it was difficult to take him very seriously. He was too mystical, too unrealistic.

Ralph and I also wondered what to think about him. Tall and gangly with a Pinocchio nose and a puckish smile, he seemed the opposite of the dedicated scholar, the competent mission leader. His English was good, but a bit unusual. His mannerisms seemed overly animated, exaggeratedly enthusiastic—"different," yet in a lovable way.

As we came to find out, however, Erik was far more than what he seemed. For several years he had prayed that the Lord would send more laborers into His harvest. Increasingly, he began to be burdened with the necessity of

24

setting up a new mission agency for Swedish candidates. It was a big step to take, and he didn't know how to go about it.

Ralph was the faculty mentor for Erik's master's dissertation. Ralph, also, had never set up a mission agency, but by that date he had been involved in the incorporation process of a number of organizations. When Erik told him of his burden, Ralph looked at him and wondered. But he also remembered how improbable a leader Hudson Taylor had seemed to the older missionaries of his day. Perhaps God was in this. But first Erik would have to work out all his plans on paper.

Erik was delighted when Ralph encouraged him to write of that dream and the practical way in which God might accomplish it. Could he set up a new Swedish mission board? How would he work out the legal papers? How could he attract and train candidates? While he wrote up the details for his dissertation, he began to carry them out in reality, praying all the while that God would send him twenty Swedish missionary candidates by the next summer.

We were not the only ones amazed when by July he had his first contingent of candidates, ready to begin their training in Pasadena. He asked Ralph to come and speak to them their first night of classes, and I went along.

I was a bit bemused as I sat in the lounge of the former girls' dorm on the Pasadena College campus, where those Swedish students were housed. Did Erik have what it took to start a mission board? He seemed so much a dreamer. But when that meeting began I saw an Erik I hadn't known existed. This man had charisma; he was dynamic, forceful—a tremendous leader! The young people from Sweden all responded to him with obvious deference; they believed in him; they trusted him to hear from God and to lead them.

Erik had his own dreams, and they were large. But at one point his and ours converged.

Two years before, he had come with his family to Pasadena, supernaturally led all the way from Greenland to a school he hadn't even known existed. Housing was found for him in one of the vacant houses bordering the Pasadena (Nazarene) College campus. The college had recently purchased a new, larger campus in San Diego, and workmen were busily moving furniture, disassembling offices, and vacating the premises. Erik noticed the activity and started asking questions. He had been praying for some time that the Lord would provide property somewhere which would be utilized solely for world missions, "perhaps even for a new world mission center." And here was a 17 1/2 acre campus, vacant. Could this be God's answer to his prayer?

About the same time Ralph and the School of World Mission faculty had also begun to realize the need for a mission center of some sort. Their dream was not less huge, and it too seemed impossible.

Some years earlier, Pasadena College had built a small prayer chapel at the heart of the campus. As Erik dreamed, he began circling the campus in prayer claiming it for the cause of missions. One day, a workman, also a Christian, saw him standing praying by the prayer chapel, and asked him if he would like to pray inside.

"I went in and a burden of prayer came over me. I prayed all day and into the night. My wife sent my children looking for me, but I told them I couldn't leave—not yet. I prayed there for a week before the Lord let me leave," he told us almost four years later.

Before moving, the college had a sure offer to purchase by a group which wanted to start a Christian college. Now that the Nazarenes were gone, this offer fell through. Others made bids, over 100 organizations in all, but something always happened to prevent the sale. Meanwhile, Erik was praying that somehow the Lord would hold this campus for missions.

August 10, 1975 was a blistering hot day, as most

days in August are in Pasadena. Erik and his family had been invited to spend a few days at a friend's cottage on the beach at San Clemente, and this seemed the perfect day to go. They all looked forward eagerly to a swim in the cool ocean. Neither Greenland nor Sweden had prepared them for this climate.

Erik watched his family race to the beach, but felt somehow he couldn't follow them. Not yet. He still had something to settle with God.

His diary of prayer for that day records that the Lord impressed him with this verse: "Thou shalt speak and say before the Lord thy God" (Deuteronomy 26:5). And he went on to claim the campus in Pasadena: "Before the face of the Lord our God we both speak and confess that the campus of Pasadena College is consecrated for world missions and can never belong to any other purpose."

He later told us that peace immediately settled over his soul. He dashed to the water and frolicked joyously with his family.

There were other times and other prayers about the campus, and Erik wrote in his thesis:

"Never before in my life have I experienced that a prayer *must* become a reality as the prayer that (the) Pasadena College campus will be used for the purpose of world mission. In the name of Jesus Christ, I know that this miracle is predestined by God Himself. Written at Pasadena College, Wednesday, December 10, 1975."

The preceding summer the Lord had begun, quite independently, to lay this same burden on Ralph.

6

AUGUST 1976

DREAMS

The faculty of which Ralph was a part was scattered to the winds. The dean was at a conference in South Africa, the former dean in India, one faculty member in Illinois, another in Nigeria. I had often complained that year after year Ralph was gone almost all summer long on one trip or another, speaking or teaching here and there. But for some reason, Ralph was home for most of July and August that year. And the Lord was talking to him.

That evening when he spoke to the Swedish students, Ralph remembered the words of the other faculty members several months before when they had discussed using the Pasadena College campus as their mission implementation center.

"It costs too much."

"It's too far from the seminary."

"Maybe the administration won't approve."

During those intervening months, Ralph had become more and more burdened about the 2.5 billion unreached. It seemed to him that nothing was being done but talk about them—only talk! And he became increasingly frustrated.

Unbeknown to me, Erik every now and then would mention the campus to Ralph. And one day in July, at his urging, we walked all over it with him. We were impressed by the number of large buildings, quite well kept.

28

"Roberta, I had hoped to wait until the faculty were all home to discuss my burden with them. But most of them are gone until September. I tried to talk to one, and even discussing it seemed to make him very uncomfortable. Yet I feel so strongly that God wants us to buy that campus and start a center that will stress the unreached peoples. I just can't shake this conviction. I can't wait any longer. I've got to move."

In those next few days, Ralph began contacting Point Loma College officials one by one, trying to find out the terms of purchase. Although the board of trustees had had many offers, they still seemed eager to hear him out, even arranging for him to meet the Executive Council at once. Ralph's proposal to them must have seemed preposterous; they knew we had no money. Yet in a very strange way God seemed to be overseeing the entire situation.

"The Lord must have sent you," one board member told him privately afterwards. "We are at an impasse. We must sell. We desperately need the money to pay for our new campus. Yet the only good offer we have right now besides yours is from a cult known as the Church Universal and Triumphant (also called Summit Lighthouse). Our constituency is up in arms about it. Either we split the Nazarene church in this area or we split the college board."

Almost immediately we began negotiations with them. Ralph knew that his demands would seem to them to be quite unreasonable. "But," he told me, "if they accept these terms, we will know that God is in this. These conditions will be our fleece. Anyhow, I don't see how we can do anything else, under the circumstances."

Gideon's fleeces were not very reasonable either. If they had been, he would have doubted that they were truly God's guidance. Never, in all my relationship with Ralph, had I known him to resort to fleeces; ordinarily he didn't believe in that kind of guidance. But this time was different. Because so much was at stake, we needed more than just our strong convictions. We needed for God to make his way extremely clear before we dared go ahead. We were told that the college board already had in its hands an unsigned rental contract with Summit which included the statement "with the option to buy." Various people hinted that they had the money necessary. For the college board to deal with us instead would be a miracle in itself. But for those men to yield to our terms as well was next to impossible. Only God could bring that about!

7

SEPTEMBER 1976

NO TURNING BACK

It was past midnight when we left the restaurant. Ralph's hand gripped mine tightly as he said, "Well, Roberta, I guess we've crossed the Rubicon. There's no turning back now."

It had been a quietly determined, but tense, two hours. We had struggled for months with an issue we were asking the president of the seminary to understand in minutes. And we sensed that he was disappointed in us. His questions implied that he felt somewhat betrayed, abandoned in midstream. And we were the culprits.

It was the first week of the fall semester. All the professors and students were back on campus. The registration lines at last were dwindling, the orientation programs completed, and the student body picture taken. After their return, Ralph had talked several times with various members of the School of World Mission faculty about what God was saying to him. Nevertheless, when he came to his final decision, it was like jumping off a cliff.

Fortunately, that semester Ralph was on a sabbatical leave from teaching. To resign his professorship at this point, we felt, would create less disturbance than at any other time. His earliest scheduled class was three months away, and he offered to teach his main course at that time.

"I must admit," he told the other professors, "that this project may very well fail. But I am overwhelmingly convinced that God wants someone to try it. No one else seems willing, so I guess I'll have to."

He didn't need to remind them of the hundreds of millions of people beyond the range of any existing church or mission. They knew the facts as well as he. As a faculty, they were proud that the church was growing around the world, its leaders often inspired by the classes they themselves taught. But those completely unreached —the cultures where no church had as yet been established—were rarely on the agenda of studies. The problems of occupied mission fields seemed big enough without asking for even greater ones further beyond.

It was extremely hard for Ralph to decide to leave his teaching job. He had enjoyed working with these men. Moreover, as a full professor in a prestigious seminary, he had professional standing and was often asked to serve in important ways around the world. He had contributed a great deal to mission thinking and was warned by one that if he left, all his talents would be buried in fund raising.

Also, the economic sacrifice would be significant. At the seminary he had the financial security we needed with two of our four daughters still in college and another about to finish high school. Our oldest daughter had just married, and I knew wedding expenses would follow in just a few years for the others.

We felt we were turning our backs on both honor and security, and to even contemplate such a step was painful. Our salary would stop almost immediately. And what if we fell flat on our faces? We would become the laughingstock of all who knew us. Some might accuse us of egomania: "Who do you think you *are*," one asked Ralph, "to speak for the 2.5 billion unreached people?"

We knew also that there would be no road back. No school wants a has-been on its faculty, especially one who has very publicly tried something and failed.

I worried about the finances. Could God take care of us? Yes, I knew He *could*. But *would* He? How could I be sure?

"How can we know for certain that it is God who is leading and not just our own foolish dreams?" I agonized. (Ralph had already settled it for himself.) "If I can only be *sure* God is guiding this way, then I can trust Him to take care of us.

One day in prayer, I felt God tell me, "I will take care of you as well as you have ever been cared for. You will not lack anything you need."

My heart at last was at rest. With the words "When God guides, He provides" on my lips, and with my hand in Ralph's, I stepped forth into the unknown.

8

OCT. - DEC. 1976

"IF YOU ASK ANYTHING IN MY NAME . . ."

(John 14:12)

Ralph, his secretary, Prudence, and I stood in the entrance way and looked at "our building."

The previous month, the Church Universal and Triumphant (or *Summit*, as it was more commonly called) had moved onto the main portion of the campus. Erik Stadell and his twenty Swedish missionary candidates had been very discouraged when they were told they had to move out of the dormitory they had occupied for only two months in order to make room for Summit. They were even more discouraged when they came to know more about the group which had rented all but three of the buildings on campus.

Summit, we learned, is an Eastern mystical group which reveres Buddha, Krishna, and other so-called "ascended masters" and practices chanting and meditation. We had heard that its adherents were well-behaved and nicely dressed—not at all the hippie or drug-culture type of people. Also, we heard that though they were mainly Americans, their religious philosophy was basically Hindu. According to several large newspaper articles, Summit leaders spoke openly of their intention to buy the campus.

Hundreds of Nazarenes in the area were convinced, however, that this campus, which God had given them sixty or more years before, was still to be used to bring men to a saving knowledge of Jesus Christ. After long days and nights of continual prayer, Erik's little band was also convinced that somehow God had special plans for this place. Our own guidance up to this point, though completely separate from theirs, seemed to "fit" amazingly.

For more than a month Ralph talked with college officials about the possibility of buying the campus as a center for world mission. He insisted that in order to raise the funds we would need, we had to have an office on the campus somewhere. After the cult moved in, Erik's group was housed in the only building which was physically separated from the rest of the campus. This building was just across the street to the north. It was this building, a former dormitory, that the college officials offered to us.

Besides office space, we had several additional requirements.

Several months before, the college officials had begun selling some of the houses surrounding the campus. They still owned 84. Ralph told them that before we would even consider buying the campus, we must be guaranteed that they would cease selling the houses and hold them for us. He felt that the campus would not be financially viable without them, and they agreed. He told the officials that the earliest we could make the down payment on the houses would be a year after completing the one for the campus proper. They would have to be willing to wait that long.

Also, he said, "the people who will be working with us will need to rent some of those houses. They cannot afford to wait years before they come up on the waiting list (which we were told had a hundred names). We need to be able to say, 'We need that house,' and get it. Can you agree to that?"

"Yes."

"And," Ralph continued, "we expect to have a number of other mission organizations moving in with us. We will need space for them. The rents must be reasonable. In fact, we ourselves need some free space so that we can give all our energy to raising the money for the down payment. How do you feel about that?"

"That also can be arranged!"

Like Gideon with his fleeces, we were amazed as one by one all our demands were met, most graciously. We had the free office space—two large rooms on either side of the lobby in which we now stood plus three other smaller rooms just across a small corridor.

We were also given 4000 square feet of other office space at a low rent for the organizations which we hoped would join us. If we grew as fast as we dreamed, very soon our mission research department would have to expand across the street into the science building, not rented by the cult because of all the labs. We could also put research offices into the beautiful library building, unavailable to the cult because of government restrictions on its loan.

As we stood there looking at "our space," I had to smile. All the dreams the faculty at the seminary had dreamed of could be fulfilled right here. There was ample room for a graphic arts division as well as for film and photography, both so essential in interpreting missions to local churches. There was room for computerized mailing list management service. And for graduate university departments dealing with literacy and translation, with community development overseas, with teaching English, and especially with special studies relating to the major blocs of mankind still beyond the reach of the gospel. God had answered our requests more than abundantly! And He had done it so graciously!

Before we had even moved in, word got around that we had space to rent. Almost immediately various mission organizations began calling Ralph. "Could I rent some office space?" each would ask. Some needed so much space Ralph had to turn them away. Others didn't quite fit the necessary qualification of serving other mission agencies. In a matter of weeks there were six organizations besides our own on campus, as well as many internal projects which we ourselves were directing. All but one were housed in the building north of the main campus, just across the street from the cult.

We had many things to do to get started. We had to file the articles of incorporation, set up rules for membership in the Center community, organize a governing board, and decide which group should join us and where each should work.

Then there were other questions to decide. Should the various organizations on campus be entirely separate entities? No, we decided not. We should work together as a missions community. Then, what about our accounts? Should each organization keep its own set of books? Or should there be one general accounting office which would serve everyone?

Some things we decided to do together— for example, mail and duplicating services. Other things each organization did by itself—for example the organizational accounts. I can't say things ran smoothly all at once. (Do things ever run smoothly in a new organization?) But we were off and running, and the Lord began adding more organizations to our number as the weeks went by.

On the staff of the main organization, the United States Center for World Mission, we were only three: Ralph, Prudence and myself.

Ralph and I both wondered if, under the circumstances, Prudence would stay with us. We desperately needed her help, but she was aware that our salary had now stopped. Where would we find the money to pay her? How, even, were *we* to live?

Again the Lord proved faithful to His promise. At the suggestion of one of Ralph's former colleagues at the seminary, one local church picked up our full support for November and December—and even now continues with part of it. Bill Bright, the founder and director of Campus Crusade and a long time friend, for an entire year gave us a sizable amount each month out of his personal work budget to help with our office expenses.

We began asking churches which knew us well for personal support. But it was already October, and we knew that many would have already allocated their mission money for the next year. I thought Ralph was crazy when he sent several special delivery letters to pastor friends of his saying "Help!" Some replied right away. "Of course. We'll be glad to." Others said, "We're sorry, but you're too late." Some didn't answer at all. But the Lord provided anyhow.

In a matter of days we had our incorporation papers from the State of California. We were moved in, somewhat comfortably, and began to work.

But it would be some time before the Lord sent the staff we so desperately needed.

9

JANUARY 1977

"I SIGNED AND SEALED THE DEED"

(Jeremiah 32:10)

"How much money do you need?"

Ralph sucked in his breath and replied, "Ten thousand dollars." At that point ten thousand seemed enormous! We were still struggling to pay Prudence's salary, the rent, the lights and the phone bill.

Mr. Ottomoeller took out his checkbook, and we watched in amazement at God's grace and timing as he wrote out the check. Morris Watkins, a member of our governing board and director of All Nations Literacy Movement, one of our member organizations, had brought Mr. Ottomoeller to Ralph's office that Saturday morning on thé off-chance that Ralph would be there. Now, suddenly, we had enough money to bid for an option on the campus!

Just after the turn of the century, the property that would become the Pasadena (Nazarene) College was purchased by a group of godly ministers and laymen. They wanted to establish a school to train young men and women for the Lord's service, especially as ministers and missionaries. In 1946, the largest building on campus, the auditorium, was built. It became the scene of yearly "camp meetings" or spiritual retreats and celebrations. All across the front of this building stretched an old fashioned "mourner's bench" at which people would kneel and, in tears, confess their sins and ask God's forgiveness and the infilling of the Holy Spirit. That building, so sacred to many, was still the scene for spiritual exercises—but now in the name of Buddha, the "ascended masters," the "great white brotherhood," Lanello, Krishna, etc. Where strains of "Amazing Grace" once floated, now came chants of "I AM..."

Composed to a large extent of Christians formerly associated with the college, the neighborhood surrounding the campus was distressed and incensed. "How could the college rent to them, a non-Christian cult?" they asked, a note of betrayal in their voices. Their protests were loud and long, and were sent to all levels of the denomination. When they learned of our offer to buy, they all breathed a great sigh of relief.

Others, less friendly to us, also learned of our move. Just a few days after we first spoke to the college authorities, the cult submitted legal papers requesting a two-year lease with an option to buy the campus.

It was a great temptation for the Point Loma trustees. They badly needed to sell the campus. Their new campus near San Diego had cost millions more than they could hope to get from the Pasadena property, and the interest on their mortgage was high. Moreover, they felt that as the college trustees, they had to be responsible stewards of their assets. The Pasadena property had been on the market for three years. More than 100 offers had been made, yet one negotiation after another had broken down. They doubted that we, so very few, and with no great, well-known organization behind us, could raise the money. Yet they knew that the wrath of the Christians in the area would fall on their heads if they sold to the cult. It was an agonizing time for them as well as for us. Nevertheless, after extensive deliberations the board finally compromised by signing the lease presented by the cult, but crossing off the statement, "with an option to buy."

We found out what was happening from a member of their board, a godly, elderly realtor deeply troubled at the presence of the cult. He warned Ralph, "You must get an option immediately."

"An option?" Ralph asked. "What is that?" Obviously our education in real estate had just begun. "How much will it cost?"

"Usually, on a piece of property this size, at least $150,000. But I think that if you offer even $15,000, it will be accepted. Our board is in a shambles right now over the presence of the cult. But move fast! I'll give you the first $5,000," he added.

And then on Saturday, Mr. Ottomoeller walked in. We learned later that his gift to us that day was the largest he had ever given, even to his close friend, Morris Watkins, on whose board he served. We immediately sent a check by special delivery, calling ahead to tell the college officials that it was on its way.

But then the see-saw began.

Several on the board were shocked that we would presume that $15,000 could possibly be enough to hold the property for us. Still, when the Executive Council of their board met, it voted to give us the option on the basis of the $15,000. The cult found this out, and then offered $75,000, we were told. And the college board went into special session to decide what to do.

Almost by happenstance, we learned about this meeting and immediately went to prayer. We really didn't know what to do. By then several young people, alumni of the Institute of International Studies program, as well as several retired people had joined our staff. As a group we covenanted to pray earnestly that God's will would be done. And Ralph wrote a carefully worded letter to the board which he hand delivered to their meeting the following Friday.

In the letter, he admitted that the cult had more money

41

than we did. "But," he reminded the board members, "our potential constituency is the whole evangelical world of some 40 million people. According to the newspapers, Summit claims at best only about 30,000 followers."

It was a rash claim to make since we still had no mailing list nor any money coming in. We hadn't even begun to ask for any because we felt we first had to get the backing of well-known evangelical leaders who would vouch for us. Later we were told that if Ralph had not written as he did to the Point Loma board, we would have lost the option. But his letter caused them to reconsider, and they finally decided to confirm the decision the Executive Council had already made—namely, that the option should go to us.

A few days later we received their letter confirming these facts and asking us to prepare a legal document with the option agreement.

It seemed that all was in order when several days later the college lawyer met with ours and went over our document line by line. All we lacked was the signatures of the college officials.

But then, once again, nothing happened. One week went by, then two, and the signed agreement still hadn't come. Understandably, we were very puzzled.

"Whatever is happening," we asked our friend on their board.

"Well, someone seems to be keeping the cult leaders well advised," he answered, "because they have now offered $1 1/2 million as an immediate down payment!"

We were stunned! We didn't have money like that! Even if we should receive an immediate response, it would take us some time to inform those 40 million evangelicals about our cause. Most of them had never even heard of us. We had no mailing lists. Professional fund raisers had told us it was impossible to raise that much money in six months. Now it was possible we would need it in days!

In spite of our dilemma, we had a certain peace. We truly believed that the Lord had led us here. He knew our situation. He knew how impossible it was for us to solve our problems in our own strength. The problem was His!

A number of the staff and several concerned college students fasted all that weekend. We didn't know what would result. We knew the college really needed the money. And their board knew we had none. Only God could find the answer.

On Monday, our financial adviser, one of the retired volunteers, came to our noon prayer time beaming.

"Listen to what the Lord said to me over the weekend," he said. "I was praying earnestly on Saturday, much burdened about our situation and not knowing what we should do. All of a sudden a scripture reference came to my mind. I hadn't the least idea what it would say; it was not a verse I had ever memorized. I just knew that the Lord said to me, 'Look up Jeremiah 32:10' and I did. Just listen to it."

And he read,

"'I signed and sealed the deed of purchase before witnesses and weighed out the silver and paid him.'

And further down, in verses 16 and 17, it adds:

'Then after I had given the papers to Baruch I prayed: 'O Lord God! You have made the heavens and earth by your great power; nothing is too hard for you!'

I have been walking on air since Saturday," he continued. "God is going to give us this campus. I just know it. Let's just trust Him and wait."

10

MARCH 1977

STAN PETROWSKI

Months had passed since we moved to the campus. We had been working diligently, building the organizational structure, seeking tax exemption, trying to obtain the option to buy, and seeking to interest mission executives in being consultants and helping us with our task.

From time to time various ones on staff had felt inexplicably depressed. In that mood it was easy to assume with Elijah in I Kings 18:22 "I, even I only remain." Because we knew so certainly that God had called us to start the Center, we often asked ourselves why we felt so very discouraged.

It was bad enough when I felt depressed, but when I sensed that the few volunteers who had joined our staff also seemed unusually discouraged at the same time, I began to examine the situation.

"Is the outlook now more dark than it has been?" My answer was, "No."

"Is there suddenly more criticism or opposition from some source?" Again the answer was, "Not that I know of."

"Are we all fighting off the flu, perhaps?" And again everyone insisted they were well.

"What is it, then?" I asked Prudence. "Why do so many of us feel so *down*, all of a sudden?"

And a light of understanding sprang to her eyes! "So that's what it is!" she said.

"What?" I persisted.

"Several years ago, when I was the regional travelling representative for Campus Crusade, on several occasions I had experiences of this sort. The first time it happened I was confused, as you are, and then someone pointed out to me that it might be Satanic oppression, and urged me to follow the Biblical pattern of dealing with it. He said we have to remind Satan out loud that in dying on the cross Jesus has already won the victory, that we belong to Him and share in that victory. We must tell Satan that he has no authority at all over us, then in the name of Jesus, bind him and praise the Lord for our deliverance."

She called the staff together and explained what she felt was happening to us. We prayed together, then followed the pattern she outlined. Immediately it was as if a tremendous burden was lifted from our shoulders. We were full of joy and confidence in our Lord once more. And we thanked God for the valuable lesson we had learned.

But we still didn't associate this oppression with the presence of Summit International on our campus until one of the Christians in the community, who had been hired by the college to do work around the campus, informed us that Ralph's name was tacked onto the base of the large Buddha which had replaced the "old fashioned mourners bench" in the auditorium. Also prominently displayed, he said, was a notice that incantations should be chanted against us hourly. We were too naive, however, to understand just what all this meant.

One day in April, however, Erik Stadell showed Ralph a letter written by a young Christian who some years before had been a highly placed member of the cult now on our campus. We were fascinated by his letter since all we knew about the Church Universal and Triumphant came from long, friendly articles in the local newspaper

45

and bits and pieces picked up from Christian neighbors and friends.

Two days later, as Ralph and I were working on a chapter for a book soon to be published, Erik walked into the office, followed by a pleasant-looking, bearded young man in a light tan sports suit. His bright blue eyes were sparkling as he gripped Ralph's hand and said quietly, "I'm just praising the Lord. I'm so glad you're the ones here."

Stan Petrowski told us he had felt led of the Lord to come to Pasadena to see what Summit was up to. "I walked through the campus and then decided to see what the neighbors felt about them. So I knocked on a door down the street. The people there happen to be Lutherans and they told me that you people in the building on this side of the street are Christians, and that I should come to see you. So here I am."

This is the story he told us.

About eight years earlier Stan had been born again through contact with a few Christians who had helped him when his life was in a shambles. Almost immediately afterward, he had moved from the West Coast to Pennsylvania, where he knew no one. There he had set up a health food store as a way to support himself and also to attain the physical purity he sought. And there, alone, he tried to grow in his newly-found faith. But without Christian guidance of any kind, he was soon led astray.

People of all sorts came into his store looking for health food. Some came in to distribute "health literature." Among this literature was the *Aquarian New Testament,* which he was urged to read, and the Chinese book of divination called *I Ching.* Stan was not mature enough in the faith to recognize the additions to and misinterpretations of scripture included in the *Aquarian New Testament,* nor did anyone warn him of the dangers of becoming involved with *I Ching* and yoga. Over a period of time, while seeking to know God better, he was drawn into contact with various psychic and religious organizations.

Eventually, Stan found himself in a "monastery"—the Summit International headquarters located, at that time, in Colorado Springs, Colorado. There, the mixture of meditation, yoga, mantras, scripture and psychic practices coincided perfectly with his recent experiences. Unlike others he had known who were involved in such phenomena, these people seemed to be highly ethical, well dressed, and he was pleased to find that they stressed physical purity through abstinence from meat, alcohol, tobacco and drugs. The only thing that troubled him at first was their emphasis on wealth and their obvious materialism.

Summit leaders told him that the Bible was inaccurate, that ancient copyists had left out many things that were in the original documents of the early centuries. These left-out portions, they said, were being dictated to the leader of their movement, who was then Mark Prophet, by people now "ascended." His confidence in the Bible destroyed, Stan delved deeper and deeper into the "ancient wisdom" of which Summit leadership spoke.

Over the following years Stan rose in the Summit International movement until he was one of their top staff. He told us that at that point he had the ability to read other people's minds and, to a certain extent, even control their thought processes. This was all done through spirit power —an unholy spirit power, he added. Later he was sent to India and Nepal to visit a number of monasteries in order to incorporate into the cult's teaching the "truths" from Buddhism and Hinduism. Yet deep within he was hungry for the true and living God.

After four years, Stan left the organization and returned on his own to Nepal, searching for his "personal guru" who, he said, had contacted him psychically. He walked barefoot in the snow for 200 miles, visiting monastery after monastery, only to realize that what (or whom) he sought was not there. One day, trekking across a high mountain pass in the Himalayas, stumbling in the snow toward yet another Buddhist monastery, he fell on his knees and cried out, "Oh, God, what is true?"

Prostrate in the snow, in tears, he felt a Presence he had not known before, and heard Someone say to him, "I, Jesus, am the way. I am the truth. I am the life. No man comes to the Father but by Me." He was stunned! At the Summit monastery he had often chanted the first part of that phrase, but the last part had not been there. There, the "I AM" had referred to some god-presence which he himself was supposedly becoming. Now, Jesus was saying that He was the only way, the truth and the life. Moreover, *there was no other way to the Father but by Him.*

In a flash Stan remembered his experience long years before on the West Coast. That, then, had been the true way, and he had wandered so far, so needlessly.

Three days later he arrived at the monastery, but knew in his heart that the One who had spoken to him on the way was the One he had so long sought. After waiting out a small snow storm, he left abruptly and returned to the States. There, after days of prayer and fasting, he was led to a group of Christians who laid hands on him and prayed. For the first time in years he felt released from the spirit of oppression which only later he realized had been demonic. In his own words: "I went through a process of systematically renouncing every false religion that I had ever been involved in, in the name of Jesus Christ." It took long months of Bible study and many, many hours of communion with God before he learned to distinguish between spirits. But now he is a burning witness to God's power to rescue His own from the clutches of the "false prophets."

Today Stan spends his time on the road, warning Christians about false prophets and witnessing to young people caught up in the cults.

That day in April, 1977 was an eye opener for us. As

we listened to Stan, we were both fascinated and appalled. The world he spoke of was one we didn't know and couldn't understand.

He took more than an hour, talking about chants that have an unholy spiritual power, of "balancing kharma," of communication with people now dead and with powers in the spirit world, of incantations, mantras.

We were quiet, too shocked to know what to say, and perhaps a bit unbelieving. All we had set out to do was to buy this campus and to set in motion a new wave of mission interest that would complete the task of world evangelization. It seemed that, inadvertently, we also had stumbled into a confrontation with the occult. And we felt inadequate for what might lie ahead.

"What can we do?" I blurted out when Stan had finished.

"You just claim Christ's victory. And you pray. This situation is going to take a lot of prayer power." And Stan touched his knees as he looked straight into our eyes.

"You'll pray for us, too, won't you?" we begged.

"Listen, I'll pray for you every day. I know what you're going through. I could tell when I walked in that the devil's been giving you a rough time. But God's on the throne. Don't forget that. And Christ has already won the victory."

We prayed briefly together and then Stan was gone, to reappear again, unannounced, at the very end of June, the day before the cult's largest conference of the year was to begin.

11

"MY GOD WILL SUPPLY ALL YOUR NEEDS . . . "

(Philippians 4:19)

It hit us all like a ton of bricks. We had been working and praying so hard, trying to get the legal option to buy, that we almost forgot the next step. Now it hit us: "We have less than six months to raise $850,000, the first part of the $1.5 million needed for the down payment. What shall we do?"

There were pitifully few of us on staff, and most were part-time volunteers. None of us had any experience in raising large amounts of money. And, as Ralph cautioned us, we knew we couldn't start appealing for funds without first getting public backing from well-known people. That would involve Ralph in endless phone calls, hundreds of letters, and all of us in much, much prayer. How could we possibly get in $850,000 by October?

It took all of May and into June to line up consultants,[1] people whom others trusted, who would vouch for us when asked about our project. Every Sunday at church friends would question, "How is it going? How much money have you raised?" At first, I appreciated their concern, but as the weeks went by and we were still spending most of our time lining up consultants, I wanted to avoid them. The time was getting short; how we knew

50

that! How could I answer that we had not even started raising funds? Yet whenever I expressed my anxiety to Ralph, he only answered, "We have to get our consultants first. We don't dare move ahead without their backing."

I don't know what we would have done without Ralph's secretary, Prudence. She had come to Ralph's office at the seminary the year before, admitting somewhat apologetically that she wasn't a great typist. But she had been told that Ralph was looking for someone to organize him. She thought she could do that. Prudence was truly God's gift to us. She was office manager, public relations director, personnel manager, social hostess, chaplain—all at the same time. If we needed something, she "just happened" to know someone or something about it. Best of all, she was a person of faith, unafraid to tackle hard things.

But she was also human. Just how much can one person carry? I was working every day alongside Ralph and Prudence, but the job was just too great, even with those wonderful volunteers who came for a few weeks or months at a time.

One Saturday in early June, Ralph was working alone in his office while I tackled the accumulated undone tasks at home. The office phone rang and Jack McAllister, one of his newly-named consultants and a well-known mission executive, called him with a host of suggestions, all good. About halfway down the list, Ralph stopped him, cold.

"Those are great ideas, but how can we implement them?" he asked.

"What do you mean?" Jack replied. "Haven't I just told you?"

"One thing you forgot. I have no staff. I've just finished typing a letter to our consultants. While I'm talking to you, I'm stuffing envelopes and licking stamps. And then I'll drive this mailing to the Post Office. I agree that I should do all you suggest, but I just can't!"

There was a shocked silence on the other end of the

line, then, "Listen, brother, I'll put in the mail right now a check for $3,000. That will pay for a secretary for you for awhile. And when that is gone, I'll send some more. Now, can you find a good secretary?"

That was how Jane came to us. As May progressed, our winter part-time volunteers left for summer jobs or summer studies, and the Lord filled their places, usually with seminarians or college students, often from far away. We had never heard of most of them, and we wondered how they knew of us. Gwen came from Minneapolis after learning of us through a mutual friend. Our daughter in Boston and her husband in seminary at Gordon Conwell saw "Star Wars" one night and said, "What are we doing here when there's a great battle in progress in Pasadena?" They brought with them Hal and Liz Leaman and Dave and Debbie Bliss. After Ralph spoke at a conference in the Midwest, a young businessman in the audience dropped all to come and help out for "two weeks". . . and stayed three months! Ralph spoke at a church in San Diego; Jeff, on a visit there to his grandmother, responded to the challenge to come.

Most of these new staff were short-term helpers: we called them our "90-day wonders." And they were wonders! They helped in all sorts of spots and in all sorts of ways. Young people who had never written anything more important than a term paper were busily at work on publicity brochures, newspaper releases, pamphlets and seminar programs.

It was a time of stretching for all of us. At times, Prudence, Ralph and I felt like Moses with his motley crew. We had people from everywhere, from all sorts of churches, working at tasks they had never attempted, under the direction of people who had never managed others. Could God bring anything out of such chaos?

You'd better believe it!

———

1. Some of the early ones to agree to be consultants were Jack Frizen, Executive Director of the Interdenominational Foreign

Mission Association; Harold Lindsell, then editor of *Christianity Today;* David Howard, the organizer of the famous Urbana Student Missionary Conferences and now Executive Director of World Evangelical Fellowship; Donald McGavran, founder and Dean Emeritus of the School of World Mission at Fuller Seminary; George Peters, Professor of Missions at Dallas Seminary; Waldron Scott, then Executive Director of the World Evangelical Fellowship; J. Christy Wilson, Professor of Missions at Gordon Conwell Seminary and formerly pastor of the only Christian church in Afghanistan; Donald Hoke, Director of the newly established Billy Graham Center and organizer of the Lausanne Congress on World Evangelization; and Leighton Ford, now head of the Lausanne Committee but then a member of the Billy Graham team.

12

BETHLEHEM'S STAR

Summer had come! Already! It seemed like only days since we had received the option. For months we had been hard at work preparing promotional materials and contacting prospective consultants. It was distressing to see how few days there were remaining before our first major payment was due. In all those months of uncertainty, there was one little flickering star in the north which had cheered us.

Back in December, at Inter Varsity's Student Missionary Conference in Urbana, Illinois, Ralph and I had met a persistent, mission-minded veterinarian from Portland. Dr. Gene Davis had insisted on our coming the following April to speak at his church, Bethlehem Baptist in Lake Oswego, Oregon. The time there had been refreshing for us and, I think, a shock for the church.

In his sermon Ralph had suggested that this small but rapidly growing church of only 100 giving units become an example to other churches by pledging $100,000 to the founding budget of the Center. I gasped when I heard him. These people didn't really know us. And most of them, we had been told, were young Christians, basically unacquainted with the world of missions. Dr. Gene Davis was the unusual ingredient, however.

Toward the middle of June, while we were racing to

54

design a publicity brochure, send out letters, get our non-profit status from the government, and do everything we could to attract public attention, Gene called up and said, "I'm coming down with our pastor and three other men. We want to see the campus and decide about giving the $100,000 you asked for."

Ralph swallowed fast, then said, "That's really wonderful! We'll be ready."

They came, looked all around, talked long hours with us and left the next morning. Before going, Fred Lawrence, the pastor, said, "Brothers, we must pray about this. What Ralph is asking is far more than we can humanly do. But we have a big God. It is not too big for Him. Let us pray now, and then go on our way, and trust the Lord to show us what He wants us to do."

It was a precious time of prayer, ending with a pledge from all present to pray for fifteen minutes a day that the Lord would give us this campus.

Several days later we heard from Gene again. "All the way home," he said, "we talked about that $100,000. We've prayed a lot about it and have decided the Lord wants us to raise it, even if we have to mortgage our church property. The Lord will make this a blessing to us, we feel sure."

Our staff was walking on air when we heard the news. It was almost July, and all together we had only $25,000 toward the $850,000 due the first of October. That pledge was only a pledge, but as far as we were concerned, it was a bright ray of light in a very dark sky.

We had little time, even to rejoice. There was simply too much to do. And in a few days our campus would be inundated with people who had come to a conference we didn't want to see, to worship a god we didn't know.

13

THE CHURCH UNIVERSAL
AND TRIUMPHANT

With the coming of July, our campus was very suddenly full of people.

Uppermost in our hearts and minds, however, was the fact that in a few weeks the first part of our down payment was due. Barely three weeks before, we had begun, at last, to appeal to the evangelical public for financial backing. Fortunately, with summer had come an influx of volunteers, a few sent by some of the evangelical leaders who had consented to be our consultants. At last we had the staff necessary to begin to do all that we had to do. We began to send out letters, write news releases, contact churches, set up promotional luncheons, and process gifts. With so little time, we were extremely busy!

Since the visit in March of Stan Petrowski, we were careful to warn all newcomers to staff that we were involved in a strange, spiritual warfare. And we taught them how to claim victory in the name of Jesus by virtue of His blood that had been shed for us on Calvary.

Out of curiosity, from time to time, some of our new staff, who were still unrecognizable to cult leadership, crossed the street to Summit's bookstore and bought various pieces of their literature. Several of us studied these carefully to try to understand a bit more of their

56

teaching. Their literature was a confusing mixture of Hindu philosophy and terminology mixed up with quotations and names from the Bible. Jesus was often mentioned, but in a manner extremely foreign to historical and biblical Christianity. The booklets spoke of Elizabeth Claire Prophet as "the Divine Mother" and "the Mother of the Flame," reminding us of the ever-present bumper stickers: "Souls of great light are waiting to be born. Have one. (Signed) Mother" and "Abortion is first degree murder of God."

Quite often the literature spoke of communications from a certain St. Germain, whose picture was always prominently displayed. This person, who evidently lived in the Middle Ages, seemed to be their guiding light.

In the articles she wrote, Mrs. Prophet spoke of receiving messages from the archangel Michael, from Buddha, from Jesus, and other so-called "ascended masters," including her dead husband, Mark Prophet or "Lanello" (as he was called) who had started the Church Universal and Triumphant (Summit). Also, it seemed that the decisions of Summit leaders were sometimes submitted to what they spoke of as "the Darjeeling Council," and their members were encouraged to write to "chelas" around the world, a term we later found in Hindu literature.

The more we read, the more we understood how inquirers could be confused. Bible quotations were common, but often they were incorrect and always grossly misinterpreted. We wondered how Americans, who have so many opportunities to come to know the truth, get involved in such philosophical nonsense.

One afternoon two well-dressed strangers walked into our main office. "We're having a conference starting next week, and we're inviting the neighborhood to attend on Friday night. Can you come?"

Their warm invitation was startling. On all previous contact, cult members had been very cool to us. We wondered if they had not been warned to avoid conversation with any of us. Many of our younger staff had felt very frustrated at their inability to witness to these people, and thus counted this invitation as an opportunity which was too good to miss.

That morning Don Hamilton of the Association of Church Mission Committees had called Ralph with a strange request. Someone had broken into their offices a couple of miles away and stolen their typewriter. "May we send someone over to use a typewriter for a few hours?" he had asked.

Unknown to us, the one who came had previously done a research paper on the cult that was on our campus, and for months had been praying for an opportunity to witness to one of its members. He was there when our visitors arrived, and immediately jumped to his feet and engaged one of the two in conversation. Dave Cashin on our staff, now a missionary in Bangladesh, started talking with the other on the opposite side of the room. Prudence's desk was in the middle, and she heard most of each discussion.

"It was incredible," she told the two fellows after the Summit members had left. "You were saying exactly the same things, quoting the same Bible verses, making the same points almost in the same words. Obviously the Holy Spirit was speaking through both of you."

But Satan had his innings too. After the two cult members had left, Dave sat down to his typewriter, then rose to join hands in prayer for the two who had just left. As he stood up, his knee slightly brushed the bottom of his typing table. Immediately the table flipped over, almost as if lifted by an unseen hand. The typewriter, an IBM Selectric and one of only two that we had at that point, landed upside down, so damaged that it wouldn't work. But God knew how much we needed that typewriter in those critical days and took care of us. In a manner still new to us, we laid our hands on it and prayed, then sent it out for repairs. It was back in just two days with a bill of only $30.

The question we now faced, however, was what to do about that unexpected invitation. Should we go? Which ones? Together, or separately? Now that we were aware that we were the focus of an unusual spiritual battle, we didn't want to expose ourselves unnecessarily to unholy spiritual forces. On the other hand, if ever we were to witness to them, we needed to know more about them.

We spent several days discussing and praying about what we should do, and finally decided that several of our staff should accept the invitation. The rest of us felt strongly impressed to stay behind and pray.

14

"YOU FIGHT . . . AGAINST SPIRITUAL DARKNESS"

(Ephesians 6:12)

Holy Cosmos' violet ray (3x)
Work thy power through me, I pray (3x)
Holy Cosmos' yellow ray (3x)
Touch and heal, and light my way (3x)
Holy Cosmos' celestial ray (3x)
Fill me with thy love today (3x)[1]

The chanting grew almost deafening. Brad, sitting with Beth, found himself automatically tapping his foot to the rhythm. Jud and Walter were sitting together, as were Hal and Liz, Bruce and Christy, Stan and Sandee. They had gone to the meeting two by two, each couple sitting at a distance from the others. As they looked around, each one prayed that Christ would protect them all from any power the spirits would try to exercise over them.

They were not surprised at some things they saw. We already knew about the large Buddha, centrally placed, just in front of where the altar rail used to stand. But we were all very curious about what else they would find. What, for example, would the cult's public meeting be like? Would it be so "Eastern" that the average American would have culture shock? Or would it be rather similar

60

to the average Protestant church service?

Ralph was once again out of town, due to return the next morning. I felt convinced that God did not want me to go to that Summit meeting. I didn't know whether as Ralph's wife, Satan might especially attack me, or whether there was some other reason why God wanted me to stay away. I only knew I was *not* to go.

Becky, our second daughter, also knew she shouldn't go. For a long time she had not been really well. Only two weeks earlier she had graduated, exhausted, from the California Institute of Technology, and consequently felt physically unprepared for a battle with spiritual forces.

Bob intended to go, but at the last minute decided to dress up and had gone home to change into a suit. He therefore missed the pairing off, two by two, which Prudence had advised for those who would attend. Just after the rest left, he appeared, wanting to go, but having no partner.

I was especially concerned that Bob should not go by himself. A few years earlier, while a student at Caltech, he had come into a deeper experience with Christ. But being scientifically trained, he tended at that point to be a bit skeptical about the reality of "principalities and powers in high places" that war against our spirits. The whole idea seemed somehow too superstitious, too medieval. "Oh well, there's no one to go with me," he told me. "What can happen, anyway? I'll be okay." And he went alone.

"As we entered," Christy wrote later, "there were two guys and a girl up front with a guitar, singing 'mantras' —very Eastern-sounding. They would start out slowly, and as the short phrases were repeated again and again, they gained momentum, until the words seemed firmly implanted in one's mind and the atmosphere became intoxicating. Everyone seemed to be effectively drawn into a mood of receptivity. There was a feeling of anticipation in the crowd."

61

Later on, to the amazement of our group, the choir sang a song about Jesus, one which could easily have been sung in any evangelical Sunday service except where key words about the atonement had been altered.

Then Elizabeth Claire Prophet rose and began to chant, instructing newcomers and visitors how to participate. It began low at first, and the words were distinct and clear. Over and over again the same phrases were repeated. Voices became louder, words more blurred, the chanting more rapid.

Bob, seated alone, felt the mesmerizing effect of the chanting and began to pray, quietly at first and then aloud. It flashed through his mind that the devil was using rhythm to work a spell on all these people, so that they could be deceived more easily, and he determined to break that rhythm. All around him people were shouting, louder and louder:

Ho-ly Cos-mos' vi-olet ray
Work thy pow'r through me, I pray.

Bob started to pray louder and louder in non-rhythmic pattern, using different words and thus totally out of beat with the rest of the audience. The lady beside him became quite agitated.

"No!" she said as she leaned toward him. "No! That's not the way! Here! Here are the words! Say them with us!"

Bob ignored her and continued praying.

"Listen!" she insisted more loudly. "You won't feel the vibrations if you don't do it right!"

Suddenly, the chanting was at an end and the audience was dismissed for a fifteen minute break before "the Mother" would give a dictation from Lanello, her dead husband, now an "ascended master."

Bob almost ran from the building, praising God for what he felt to be a deliverance from Satanic power.

Beth came back across the street and started repeating

the chant. "Beth, how could you?" Brad asked in shock. "What did you memorize that for?!"

"I didn't mean to! I didn't chant. But those words and that rhythm just stick in your mind. I can see how people get sucked in, thinking it's innocent when it's really calling to something other than God. Never again will I think that chanting is just a simple religious game!"

---

1. Because all chants used by the cult are copyrighted, this is not an actual quote, but is similar in sense and meter to several actually used.

15

JULY 3, 1977

A POWER ENCOUNTER

That weekend was both physically draining and spiritually exciting. Several weeks previous the college had informed us that some of those attending the Summit conference would be staying in the dormitory where our offices were located. By Friday our building was full.

We had placed several booklets in our front entry through which they had to pass, and noticed that the one entitled "Buddha, Zoroaster or Christ?" from Inter Varsity was the one most often picked up.

After office hours on Friday and Monday, and most of Saturday and Sunday, many of our staff sat on the courtyard lawn, singing and praying. We noticed that a number of those attending the conference stopped just inside their doorways to listen. Only one ventured to join us, and she invited us to come to hear their "dictation from Jesus" which Elizabeth Claire Prophet was to receive that coming Sunday.

On Friday, Stan Petrowski and his wife, Sandee, returned to the campus. Because most of our staff were newly arrived, Ralph asked Stan to explain to us the Summit teachings so that we would know how to respond to questions anyone attending the conference might ask us. We were impressed once more by how far from the Bible those teachings were.

Early Saturday morning Stan took his place across the street, on the corner to the west of our building. He didn't want Summit to blame the U.S. Center for World Mission for his witness, and he rarely came near our building that entire weekend. In one hand he supported a large sign which read, "Who are the gods?"

"What do you mean by your sign?" asked a blond-haired girl wearing a conference badge, and he started to explain the gospel to her. "Oh, I'm a Christian. I've been filled with the Spirit," she assured Stan.

"Then what are you doing here?" Stan asked. And he started to explain to her the different teachings of Summit and to compare them with scripture. Almost immediately, twenty to thirty people gathered around them, listening. Some were Summit staff. We came to call them "guards" because they repeatedly tried to silence Stan or to get those listening to him to leave. Stan later told us that from that hour until the end of the conference these guards maintained a close watch over him. Two followed him everywhere he went, and two constantly sat, palms up, on the campus lawn across the street from where he stood, chanting decrees against him.

"Elizabeth (Prophet) would never let them talk to me," he told us. "But just think! Because they have to guard me, they hear everything I say to everyone. I get to preach the gospel to them over and over. Isn't that wonderful?"

At one point a police car drove up, stopped and checked out the situation, but apparently found that Stan was doing nothing illegal.

Ever since the beginning of Summit's conference, we had been singing and praying constantly, it seemed. By Sunday, some of our younger staff members were becoming restless, anxious to bear a more definite witness. But the moment they crossed the street, Bibles in hand, they were ushered off and threatened with a call to the police.

"I hope other Christians are able to witness to them," Beth sighed. "It seems we can't get near. Even those staying in our building rush past us, in and out, almost as if they're afraid of us."

"God can do more things through prayer than we have any idea of," I reminded her. "And they can't keep us from praying."

Monday was the last day of the conference, and by nightfall Bruce had decided that he wanted to try something else. He sought Stan out and talked to him about his idea.

"Stan, you know that one of our organizations rents the upper floor of the science building on the main campus. That's just outside the entrance to the auditorium where the conference is being held. What do you think about some of us going over there to pray? We won't sing or pray out loud. We won't disturb their meeting. We'll just go there and pray quietly. What do you think?"

"That's a marvelous idea!" Stan answered. "You know, it's important to them to be able to control the air waves, the so-called 'energies' and the force field surrounding the auditorium. That's the only way they can hear from their 'ascended masters'--Buddha, Jesus, Sanat Kumara, Magda, St. Germain, and so on. There's a host of them. Only then can Elizabeth Claire Prophet receive her dictations from the spirit world. But if you fill the air with prayers, those dictations won't be able to reach her; those spirits can't get through to her with their messages."

So Bruce asked Ray Carlson of International Films for permission to pray in their offices.

At 6 p.m. we met as usual on the lawn in our courtyard and began to pray and sing as we had been doing for a week. To all outward appearances, we had accomplished very little by all those extra hours of singing and praying. But we reminded ourselves that when Paul and Silas sang and prayed in prison, marvelous things happened. We had no other weapon to defeat Satan. Perhaps God would use our songs and our prayers in this battle. At least we hoped the enemy would be defeated in his attempt to deceive Summit guests, many of whom, we found out, were members of Christian churches.

Neither Ralph nor I knew what else our young staff planned to do that evening. Ralph, just back from a long trip, was busy in his office, and I was very weary. It had been a long week. After working eight hours every day, I had eaten a quick sandwich, then stayed to sing and pray with the fifteen others. All day Saturday and Sunday we had been at our vigil, covering our part of the campus with prayer and praise. By the end of the week I was very tired.

Although Stan was the only one we knew who was overtly involved in discussions of any length with Summit guests, none of us doubted for a moment that we also were involved in this very real, spiritual struggle. Throughout the previous months we had become acutely aware that when involved in spiritual warfare, it is very important to pray in the *name* of Jesus. Jesus told his disciples, "Ask anything *in my name*." I had always thought of that verse as a wonderful promise. Since childhood I had always closed my prayers with the words "in Jesus' name." That weekend when we battled as never before with unseen spiritual forces, we became conscious that because of Who He is, the name of Jesus spoken in prayer carries real spiritual power.

The meeting in the auditorium started early that last night of the conference. Every other evening, beginning around 9 p.m.., loud chanting could be heard for blocks: "I AM the way; I AM the truth; I AM the life; I AM the resurrection; I AM in me, my very own beloved Christ self." Whatever the chant chosen for that particular night, it always seemed to end with a thrice repeated, mesmerizing refrain such as "I AM the Word of God, I AM the Word of God, I AM the Word of God incarnate." I never failed to cringe at the blasphemy.

That night, the last one of their conference, there was no chanting. All was strangely silent. After singing and praying for some time, our young staff stopped, looked at each other and then rose from the lawn. It was still two hours before we usually finished praying, and I asked, "Where are you going?"

"We just thought we'd go across the street to the Science building and pray there," Bruce answered. "I checked it out with Ray Carlson, and he says it's okay. And Stan thinks it might be just the thing to do."

"But you know they'll run you off," I warned. "And we really don't want to antagonize them. After all, we have to live with them another year!"

Just at that moment, the door from the front lobby to the patio opened, and three of the top Summit staff walked briskly up the sidewalk by which we stood. I looked at them in amazement, wondering where on earth they were going. As they passed me, our young people moved in the opposite direction, down into the lobby, out the front door and across the street from which the other group had come.

I was both stunned and amused. The two groups seemed almost oblivious of each other as they both went their purposeful ways. I saw the Summit three stop before Ralph's office and knock. And I wondered, idly, why he didn't answer.

By then the young people were already across the street, and I wondered what I should do. Should I stop them, or should I talk to the Summit leaders? Where was Ralph, anyway? (Unknown to me, he had gone to another office to type a letter). "Lord, you'll have to show me what to do," I prayed. "I just don't have the wisdom for this situation."

A number of times we had been accused of trespassing on their property. In reality, a number of Christians in the neighborhood from time to time invaded the campus, witnessing to everyone who would listen. Usually we did not even know these Christians; nevertheless, invariably we were blamed for everything they did or said. Usually

68

we had not known what they had done until we were accused of trespassing. Once anyone on our staff was recognized by Summit members, we couldn't step even a foot on their property. But we were glad that someone else was trying to get through to them, just in case someone was truly searching for God.

So I sat there and prayed, looking first one way and then the other, wondering what to do. But the situation was out of my hands and Ralph's.

Several hours later our young people reported, "We had barely reached the steps of the Science Building when the men who had walked into our building came back across and saw us there."

"What are you doing here?" one of them asked.

"We're praying."

"Praying? What for?"

"We're praying for the meeting in the auditorium."

"What are you praying for that for?"

"We're praying that the people will come to know Jesus Christ as the only One who can forgive their sins."

One Summit leader, rather disturbed, asked, "Are you willing to submit your prayers to the will of God?"

"Certainly," Bruce answered, not really understanding what he meant by his question .

By this time, six other pastel-clad guards had joined the three, and attempted to engage the young people in theological argument. But Bruce interposed, "We didn't come over here to argue. We only want to pray. We will do it silently. We won't bother you."

"No, you must get off this campus or we'll call the police."

"No," Bruce answered. "The offices upstairs belong to one of our organizations, and we have been invited by them to come here to pray."

The guards moved away and conferred together. Then they returned, and one shook his finger at them and shouted, "In the name of the eternal Christ-self, I order

69

you to cease praying and to leave this campus!"

The young Christians would have been amazed at the oddity of using Christ's name to stop someone from praying had they not been so intent in their own prayers while Bruce talked. Nobody moved. It was a deadlock.

The guards moved away again to confer among themselves, and when they returned Bruce said, "Look, we don't want to make you angry. We'll just go upstairs and have our prayer meeting there."

And they did, joined about that time by one of our board members. They prayed and sang quietly for an hour or more, binding Satan in his efforts to deceive the people so near them and yet so far from the truth of the Bible. They rejoiced in the sense of the presence of the Lord there with them in that "upper room."

It was nearing 11 p.m. and still there had been no chanting that evening. Suddenly, there was a knock on the door. It was locked, as was the door on the ground floor entrance, but when Bruce opened it, three cult leaders entered. "We just thought we would stop by and say hello," the only woman said.

"Hmm! I wonder if this is an opportunity to witness sent by God, or is it a ploy to distract us from praying so that their medium can receive another 'dictation' from the spirit world?" Bruce thought. And before turning to talk with those who had entered, he urged some of the others to continue in prayer.

Valerie, the woman, asked why they were praying. "After all, we're Christians just like you."

"If you are, then you also believe that Jesus is the *only* begotten Son of God, the only One who can take away our sins," Judd, a Christian from the neighborhood, answered. He read John 3:16 from his Bible . "Do you believe that?"

"We believe that Jesus is God. But the Bible says, 'Ye are all gods,'"one answered, but he couldn't remember the biblical reference.

70

This theological debate, for such it was, lasted for some time while three of our group continued praying off in one corner. Our people talked about the Garden of Eden, about Satan's attempt to be "like God," about his tempting Eve with the words, "God knows that the instant you eat the fruit, you will become like Him" (Genesis 3:4). They were amazed at how the Holy Spirit brought the right Bible references to their minds at the right time. They felt the Holy Spirit was truly speaking through them.

The Summit people seemed to recognize that the only authority our young people would accept was the Bible, and they tried to quote from it several times. But they obviously didn't know it very well. One said at one point, "Like the Bible says, 'God helps those who help themselves.' "

Nobody even smiled when Bruce pointed out that this quote wasn't from the Bible, but later, when our young people recounted it to us, they all burst into laughter.

It was also clear that the Summit people were trying to find out who was behind the U.S. Center for World Mission. They questioned each of our group, one by one, as to their church connections, and could hardly believe that almost every one came from a different church. They were even more incredulous when they learned that people of many different denominations all over the nation were praying for us and shared completely a single biblical faith.

The discussion lasted for more than an hour. Almost as if she were watching a clock, Valerie suddenly said, "I think we can leave now."

"Let us pray with you first. May we?" Bob asked.

They seemed ill at ease, momentarily at a loss as to how to respond, but assented. Each Christian prayed a few sentences, asking the Lord to make himself real to these people. They wanted them to meet the real Jesus, not the "angel of light" who called himself by that name and led them astray.

Alex, one of the cult leaders, prayed too, but he acted

71

as if he felt very ill at ease. His prayer was part chant, part prayer—eyes wide open and afraid. Then they left.

The young people felt that it had been a great victory, and they praised the Lord. They thanked the Lord for giving them words that were effective and without argument. And they thanked Him for the sense of love they each felt in their hearts for these poor deluded people.

The chants that evening were either subdued or non-existent. Across the street I listened for them, but did not hear them. And once again I wondered if our prayers were responsible.

It had been a long and arduous weekend—both for us and the cult. We appreciated the experience of Elijah on Mt. Carmel as we never had before. We felt that we understood now what missionaries meant when they spoke of a "power encounter." We had been through one—not with human beings, but with forces opposed to the God of the Bible. And God had won!

Yet we still felt inadequate to meet the spiritual needs of those across the street, and prayed that all those leaving the campus we shared, going back across the country, would at least this once have to recognize that there is a God in heaven (Daniel 2:28), that no other god can do what this One does (Daniel 3:29), and that He alone is the God of all the kingdoms of the earth (2 Kings 19:15).

16

BARRELS OF WATER

(I Kings 18:33)

We had known from the beginning that God had placed us on this campus along with the spiritist cult in order to show forth His glory. Dr. Alan Tippett, a missionary friend and fellow professor at Fuller, often spoke of the tremendous witness that can result from a "power encounter" such as Elijah faced on Mt. Carmel (I Kings 18). There was not the least question in our minds that in our confrontation with the cult, they were testing the power of our God with theirs—a true "power encounter."

Along about June, another aspect of the story of Elijah began to impress itself upon some of our minds. That was the barrels of water. There were four of them, then four more, and again another four: twelve in all that were poured over the sacrifice. Elijah wanted no question at all that there had been any trickery. God's power alone would have to light that sacrifice. The wood was not only thoroughly wet, but the trench around the altar was filled to the brim. In no way could an accidental spark have ignited the wood.

For ten years we had lived and worked among Mayan Indians in Western Guatemala. At 8,800 feet, it was cold. I did every bit of work I could possibly do seated in our living room in front of the only source of heat, a wood-

73

burning fireplace. There was rarely an evening throughout the year when I didn't have a fire burning.

I loved the wood fireplace except when we returned to Guatemala from our furlough in the States. Then, naturally, there was no pile of previously dried wood, and the spark just wouldn't catch. I could buy wood fairly easily and cheaply, but it was always newly cut. It took months, literally, to dry it out so that it would burn, especially during the six months of the year when it rained every day. What a frustrating experience to try to light a fire in the fireplace when the wood was "wet"!

But there was Elijah, soaking that wood with barrel after barrel of water!

During those months after we got our option to buy the campus, we also had our barrels of water which God poured over our sacrifice. We also had to come to the place that, humanly speaking, there was absolutely no way we could meet the October 1st payment deadline.

For two years I had had a large lump about the size of an egg on my right arm. Two doctors had said it was probably okay, "just don't bother with it unless it starts to grow."

"Roberta," Ralph said one day in March, "I think your lump is getting bigger."

"Oh, surely not," I answered. But for the thousandth time I measured it with my left hand, and looked at it in the mirror and wondered: "What if . . .? Oh, Lord, not now . . . please, not now. If it is cancerous, what will Ralph do without me? Can he bear the agony plus fulfill your call? And where will we get the money for surgery?"

And again for the thousandth time I committed it to the Lord and went on about my business.

In March, Ralph and I were asked to take part in a student missionary conference at Westmont College in Santa Barbara, the first they had had in five years. We were to stay in the president's home. Dave, Ralph's brother, had been the president for only one year, and his children greeted us warmly as we rang the doorbell of their beautiful home.

But Dave and Diane were gone to a meeting of Christian college presidents, and Diane's mother had come to be with the children.

"Oh, dear," I thought. We had lived overseas most of the time since Dave had married, and after returning to the States had seen them only occasionally when they visited from Michigan or Spokane, Washington. I knew Diane's mother casually, but certainly not well enough to drop in on her, already burdened with three youngsters.

I think she was as unenthusiastic about the arrangements as we were, but she graciously showed us to our rooms.

Several days before, my sister had loaned me two books by Merlin Carothers, *Prison to Praise* and *Power in Praise*, and I took them with me to Santa Barbara. At first I found Carothers' thesis incredible. "Are we really supposed to thank God that we have a terrible habit of smoking, or are an alcoholic, or have been abandoned by our mates?"

But as I began to understand what he was saying, I began to praise God for the things we had found hard— the fact that good friends avoided us because they did not want to be associated with something that might fail and look silly; or that others accused us of wanting to make a name for ourselves; and for our old cars that were constantly breaking down; and for the tremendous financial need we were facing; and even for that lump on my arm.

Mrs. Fischer, Diane's mother, saw the book tucked in my knitting bag and said, "Oh, you're reading Carothers. Isn't he great?"

And I showed her my lump.

Right there in the front hallway she put her arm around me and said, "Let's pray for that lump, right now."

Afterward, she told me about her oldest son who had had a lump on his chest some years previously. It was removed several times before God finally healed him. Then she urged me to see Dr. Byron.

At that time, Dr. Byron was the chief surgeon at the City of Hope, a cancer research center in the Los Angeles area. Only those cancer patients with a good chance of being cured are accepted at the hospital. Once accepted, however, whatever is not covered by a patient's health insurance is covered by the hospital. What's more, having been once accepted as a patient, a person is eligible for care at the City of Hope no matter what medical problem he might have.

I knew that getting into the City of Hope was somewhat like the Bible verse which says, "Many are called, but few are chosen," and I wondered how I could even get to see Dr. Byron.

I had wonderful fellowship with Mrs. Fischer that weekend and really came to love her. And at her insistence I called Dr. Byron, who examined me, did a number of tests, and admitted me to the hospital. Unlike most doctors, he prayed with me that the Lord would heal me, using him however He would. Friends at the Center also prayed, but the lump remained, and I had surgery.

The doctor told me later that tumors on the arm are fairly common, but are usually above the muscle. What had concerned him about mine was that it was below the muscle and seemingly attached to it. It could have been cancerous. Praise the Lord, it was not!

It was a time of recommitment for me, and a time when Ralph, also, learned to recommit me to the Lord. Our minds and bodies were totally immersed in the urgency at the U. S. Center for World Mission, and our hearts were very much exposed to the mercies of the Lord. But we found them to be, oh, so tender.

The stress of all this, however, was the first barrel of water over the sacrifice.

Time was passing fast. Ralph had been working night

and day from April to June to line up consultants and a board of reference. Almost every day, top men in the field of missions responded: "I'll be honored to be a consultant. I think it is a great work you're doing there. Please keep me informed." By May 13 we had 16, a few weeks later 20, then 30 and 40—all well-known Christian leaders. The list was growing so rapidly that we had to reprint our letterhead stationery almost every week.

The consultants asked hard questions, which Ralph circulated with his answers in a VIP letter which he sent out every week. Each letter mailed, however, reminded us that we had one less week to get the down payment we needed.

For weeks Ralph had been trying to reach Bob Schuller of the Garden Grove Community Church. "He's interested in missions. He has a television program where he can appeal to Christians. Maybe, just maybe, he will help us."

But we couldn't even get to him. He was out of the country. That was our second barrel of water.

Then Ralph tried to contact Channel 40, a Christian television station.[1] The brother-in-law of one of our interested college students was high up in the staff there. He suggested that maybe they would help.

But again, no response. Another barrel.

We heard that several people had recommended us to the 700 Club in Virginia—a program on another Christian television station.[1] And a month or so later we again heard that we had been recommended. We received a questionnaire to fill out—then silence.

"Have we heard from the 700 Club?" Bob asked one day as we passed in the corridor.

"No. I guess that must be another barrel. God just isn't letting us rely on any human help, it seems."

I thought about the cattle on a thousand hills, and all the silver and gold and oil that belong to the Lord, but I couldn't imagine how some of that would land in our bank account at the Center.

We were working like mad on a color brochure. All the experts from other mission agencies insisted that the first thing we needed was a nice brochure, and our volunteer help wrote and rewrote, sketched and resketched, planned and replanned. The graphics department was about to go crazy with the constant redoing.

Ralph wanted a famous personality for the front cover. He is, himself, fairly well-known in mission circles, but not far beyond that. We didn't have the nerve to ask Billy Graham. Maybe Corrie Ten Boom would be willing?

She probably would have been, but her board wouldn't let her even see our letter. "She is already far over-extended," they explained. "She's such a soft touch; she wants to help in every Christian endeavor."

About that time the sacrifice seemed really drenched—at least to us. But God said, "No! Pour on more water."

"Maybe now it's time we try some professional fund raisers," some of our staff suggested along in July. "Here we are, only ten weeks away from our due date, and we have barely raised any money at all. It's too bad to have to give fund raisers a third of what we raise, but they really know what they're doing and we'll come out ahead. Anyway, it's the only chance we have."

Ralph didn't want to seem stupid, or obstinate, or know-it-all, so he agreed to talk to some. One man who was highly recommended to us had raised millions of dollars for a Christian project in the Northwest. He was interested in what we wanted to do, but, "No thanks!" He had too many jobs already. As he put it, "You don't even have a mailing list."

Then we talked to someone recommended by a Christian organization, and another recommended as having raised millions for a project in the Midwest. And then another. The answer was always the same: "There just isn't enough time to raise that kind of money." One man came to see us on his own initiative and promised the sky. We thought, "Maybe this is God's answer." But things didn't fit together, and again, God shut the door, hard! Another barrel!

We were stirring up a lot of dust, but it didn't look like we were accomplishing much. Our volunteers were working day and night, setting up businessmen's luncheons, calling churches to set up presentations, completing the brochure. But having no mailing list to speak of, we were starting from scratch.

"How about a promotional movie?" someone suggested. So Ray Carlson of International Films, one of our member organizations, made one in one week flat.

How about asking the other now-well-off Christian organizations to help us? Or how about contacting foundations? Or maybe some godly millionaire would want a building named for his mother? Or how about . . .?

Our heads spun with the possibilities, and our hearts danced in joyful faith that God would work his miracle that way!

But it was not to be. And that was another barrel of water. And another. And another.

Mr. A was out of the country. Mr. B had already committed all of his money. Mr. C didn't believe in giving money to buildings. Foundation X had lost a lot of money through an unfortunate, unavoidable circumstance. Y Foundation might help us next year, but not now. Foundation Z wouldn't even listen to our cry for help.

Everywhere we turned, trying to "hook a big one," we caught nothing. Absolutely nothing!

"God, what are you doing?"

It was near the end of July. We had on hand roughly $25,000, a promise of $100,000 from that small church in Lake Oswego, Oregon and a few $1,000 pledges from several struggling college students! That was all! Our down payment was $1 1/2 million, and as a minimum we

79

had to have $850,000 to enter escrow on October 1st. We had been warned that if we could not complete the down payment in six months (another $650,000), we would lose a great deal of the amount we had already paid. It therefore seemed foolish, humanly speaking, to pay the first $850,000 if we could not be sure of getting the rest. As the days and weeks passed, we prayed for wisdom, and also prayed earnestly that God would give us the whole amount right away.

But God said, "No."

About that same time there fell what seemed to me to be the final blow. "Mommie, the doctor thinks I have tuberculosis!"

It was like a thunderclap. Linda had been working at the Center all summer, and part-time during the previous year. She was now transfering to a state university for her last two years and had gone that day to complete the entrance requirements.

"How on earth could you have gotten tuberculosis?" I asked. "Do you have a bad cough?" I hadn't noticed anything unusual. "Are you running a temperature of any sort? Do you perspire at night?" I went through all the symptoms I could remember in my frantic state. "Why does he think you have tuberculosis?"

"I had to have X rays, and he says . . . he says . . . there's a spot on my left lung." Her voice broke.

We were talking over the phone, and I could visualize her in tears. They started running down my face as well. "Oh, Linda, surely not!"

I felt so alone in this crisis. Ralph was in India speaking at a conference and helping to set up the South India Center for World Mission. It was always hard for me when he was gone. Though I had no line authority, I still felt responsible that all would be done as he wished, and on time. But now this!

"Oh Lord, haven't we had enough?" I breathed.

"This also is in My hands," I sensed Him say, and my

spirit quieted.

"Okay, Lord, if it is in Your hands, then You will take care of it. Just make us able for the test."

Was this another trick of Satan to stop us? He wasn't giving up easily, there was no question about that. I reminded Satan again that Christ had once and for all gained the victory, that he had no power over us at all except as Christ allowed it, and that we belonged to Christ.

Linda went on, "Mommie, I have to go back for a lot more tests tomorrow." Again her voice broke.

"That's okay, honey," I said. "I'll go with you." As we prayed together over the phone, I committed her once more to God.

It was a rather restless night for both of us, constantly awakening, constantly pleading with God, constantly recommitting.

Linda was born in Costa Rica and, at five months, had moved with us to Guatemala. In the Indian tribe where we worked there was a great deal of tuberculosis, so we had the whole family innoculated with BCG, even though doctors felt it to be of little value. As an infant, Linda was carried on the back of the girl who helped me in the kitchen, but that girl had been very clean and healthy, and I couldn't understand how Linda could have gotten tuberculosis from her.

But then I remembered how, repeatedly, when she was playing with the Indian children at age three or four, I would catch them eating off the same apple or sharing the same stick of gum, as children do. She might have contracted it then.

Or, I asked myself, "Did she work too hard her first year in college, when she would arise at 4:30 in the morning and walk through the snow at Wheaton to work in the dining hall? Or perhaps she had contracted it this past year? She had worked hard to get money for college even while carrying a full load. I remembered the twinge I felt when she was the first college student to donate a thousand dollars to our payment. I knew what it cost her!

The next day I waited somewhat impatiently at the university medical center while the doctor did further tests. He must have taken twenty X rays, and I worried a bit about the amount of radiation she was getting. Would it cause cancer later on? When the nurse placed four of the X-ray films on the lighted screen for the specialist to examine, I went over to look more closely. There was absolutely no doubt about it. She had a spot about the size of the end of my little finger in her upper left lung.

It seemed right then that even the trench around our sacrifice was full of water.

"Oh, Lord. Help! If I could only talk to Ralph it would help, but I can't! Lord, in his absence, You'll have to take care of us!" And once again I felt that strange peace.

"Mother, he says it's all sealed off. I must have had TB when I was a child, and you didn't know it. But it's okay now. I have to take care of myself, and not be around anyone with the disease, but I can go on to school."

Again the Lord had answered prayer, even before we knew enough to ask. How I praised Him!

Barrels of water! Of what value were they to us? Satan meant them for our harm, but the Lord used them to strengthen our faith, to let us know that we could depend on Him and on Him alone. He was sufficient.

And then the fire started to fall.

---

1. In the intervening years to 1986, we have appeared on both of these television stations several times as well on others which are either nationwide or regional. They have given exposure to the vision, but, so far as we know, have not been of significant financial assistance.

17

AUGUST 1977

"NOT MANY MIGHTY"

(I Corinthians 1:26)

"Would $50,000 help?"

Hal Leaman gasped, then said, "It certainly would. Who is this calling, please?"

"Howard Ahmanson."

Two weeks before, on Friday night, Beth and Brad had gone to a seminar in Newport Beach led by Chuck Miller. Chuck had married them a year and a half before, and both of them had tremendous respect for his leadership in discipling.

At the seminar they were separated into small groups, each group studying the Bible in Chuck's unique, fresh way. As the weekend progressed, they became well acquainted with the others in their small groups. Beth was in Howard Ahmanson's.

"Ahmanson, Ahmanson . . ." she said to herself when first introduced. "Where have I heard that name before?" But she just didn't connect this young man in a Bible study setting with the Ahmanson Music Center in downtown Los Angeles, nor with Home Savings and Loan.

Howard had become a Christian the year his father died and he became one of the trustees of the Ahmanson Foundation. It was a heavy burden for a young person still in college to carry, and he struggled under the load.

Somehow, during that time he had become acquainted with young people involved with Chuck Miller and had been invited to come to his Bible study seminar.

In the course of that Friday evening someone in her small group asked Beth what she was doing, and a brief summary of the story of the U.S. Center for World Mission spilled out—all about the 2.4 billion people beyond the range of current mission efforts, the spiritual struggle with Summit, the desperate need for money, and the great challenge if we should succeed.

In the larger meeting later, Chuck echoed some of her words, speaking about the Center's tremendous need and the fantastic opportunities, should God grant us success.

Howard called us on a Monday. He could promise $50,000, he said, and could hope for $100,000 more. He didn't know it, but his gift was the beginning of a great groundswell of interest and response on the part of all sorts of people, none trustees of foundations, but many matching him in excitement about God's concerns. And his gift buoyed up our faith when we most needed it.

It also turned my hopes to foundations.

I was really counting on foundations. Over and over we had been told that it was impossible to raise big money in a short time without receiving a number of very large gifts from foundations or wealthy people. "All the Christian nonprofit organizations depend on these foundations," those who knew told us.

It was hard enough, being novices, to find out which ones to approach. It was harder yet to approach them. A Wycliffe executive told us, "The proposal you write to present to foundations has to be good. Proposal writing is a specialized job that requires a lot of skill and usually costs several hundreds of dollars. But we believe in you. We will arrange for one of our proposal writers to do one for you."

The resulting proposal was good. It was professional. We were proud of it, and very grateful. Ralph took it with him, along with a notebook full of background data, when he went to visit some foundations in the Southeast.. The directors only glanced at the material, and started firing questions. That didn't bother Ralph. What would have troubled him is if they hadn't bothered to ask any questions at all. Some, he noticed, seemed genuinely interested.

Back home we prayed, "Surely, Lord, this is the way You will answer our need. These people have money to give to Your cause. We need that money which belongs to You, and *we need it in two weeks' time* or we will lose the campus to those who will lead people away from You. What are You going to do about it?"

The foundations didn't turn us down—not exactly. They just didn't pick us up.

Maybe it was because we didn't give them enough lead time. Maybe it was the time of year. Certainly it was not God's plan for that first payment, because the money didn't come—not that way! The only Christian foundation that helped us was the one related to Billy Graham. One Christian foundation told us, "If Billy Graham's foundation gives, we will too." Billy Graham did; the other did not!

"Evidently," we consoled ourselves, "God doesn't want this campus to be bought with the money of a few wealthy individuals. Perhaps He gets more glory out of the sacrificial giving of college students, missionaries, unsalaried people, and ordinary laymen from all sorts of backgrounds and from all kinds of churches."

I was often reminded of the verse which says, "Not many wise, not many mighty . . ." Some who easily could have given $1,000 gave only $15. Others, hard pressed, were embarrassingly generous. Students, working part time to pay their way through college, sent in $1,000 apiece. A girl who was to be a bride in a few weeks gave her wedding money. Missionaries gave their entire savings accounts. One girl sold her car, and then traveled to work by bus. People from very modest homes in the neighborhood around us walked into the office with $100, $200, and $500 checks.

What was really the hardest thing for me to accept was when our staff, who worked for us all summer without pay, gave what little they had in their savings accounts, saying, "The Lord has provided for us thus far in a miraculous way. Surely we can trust Him to continue."

We presented programs in local churches, and were grateful for their gifts. Two, both in Portland, Oregon, matched those students in their unusual and amazing generosity. One was Bethlehem, Gene Davis's church. The other was Aloha.

Aloha, also a Baptist church, was like a sister congregation to Bethlehem. Some of its members had heard Ralph speak at a banquet sponsored by the Bethlehem church. They wanted their church to get in on the blessing of proving what God can do for those who truly trust Him and asked Ralph to speak at their church on a Sunday morning near the end of August. They hoped to match Bethlehem in its large gift.

"We don't know how to tell you this," they greeted Ralph when he arrived at the Portland airport several months later.

"Yes?"

"Well, our church burned down last night. Someone set fire to it, and the main sanctuary burned completely down. We have a suspicion that it may be somehow connected to the public stance the church has taken against allowing homosexuals to teach in our schools. This is the sixth church in the area to have had a mysterious fire in the last few months, and almost all of these were active in that vote."

"What should I say in a situation like this?" Ralph thought. "I can still talk about missions and about the 2.4 billion who need to hear, but how can I ask these people for money to help us get that campus so we can reach the unreached? They are going to have to rebuild. They won't be building to have greater or nicer facilities. They have to build in order to have a roof over their heads. What can I say?"

He spoke at both services the next morning, held in a large room in the education building. After the service, the pastor and elders met to discuss what the church should do about its building—and about the challenge Ralph had presented to them.

That evening Ralph heard an amazing report:

"We believe the Lord wants us to tithe our insurance adjustment on the fire," they told him. "We hope that will bring you about $50,000, but it may not come in all at once. Then maybe we can bring it up to $100,000 like the Bethlehem Church. We will do our best."

18

MAIL TIME

Every day now the stack of mail was getting larger. And every day, almost every letter that came carried a check. Some days, the total was $1,000, or $5,000, $10,000, or even $20,000. Two missionary families gave $10,000 apiece. The Lord was answering prayer. But would we have enough soon enough?

Ralph couldn't follow in detail the amount of money that came in, nor the types of people who were giving. But he was greatly encouraged that instead of a few very large gifts, we were getting hundreds of $50 and $100 gifts from people of modest means. To him, this meant that Christians at the grass roots were with us.

And they were. We had gifts from Nazarenes, Baptists, Presbyterians, Episcopalians, Methodists, Pentecostals, Lutherans, independent church people, people in the Midwest, in the Northeast, in the South, in the Northwest, in the Southwest . . we still do not know from how many different places. The only explanation is that God prepared the hearts of His people all over the country, in all walks of life and from all churches to reach out in answer to His concern for those we were trying to reach.

Some people read about us in newspapers, in articles that were slanted against us, and sent in money because they recognized the spiritual battle we were facing. A man

88

3,000 miles away, not a Christian, wrote to us because of unpleasant contact he had had with Summit.

Our receptionist had one of the most exciting jobs. She was the one who opened and sorted the letters and answered the concerned enquiries by phone. So many calls came in that we had to install five additional lines. Our staff staggered their work hours so that the phones would be covered from 6 a.m. until 10 p.m. daily. Even Saturdays and Sundays during the last few weeks we had someone take calls so that people praying for us could find out how things were going.

Even so, the money coming in was not nearly enough, and time was running short!

19

"HE DOES EVERYTHING WELL"

(Mark 7:23)

"Roberta," Mercedes said to me one Monday noon in early August. "What do you think of putting on a benefit concert?"

Mercedes Gribble was the founder of Providence Mission Homes, an organization working closely with us which found housing for furloughed missionaries. She was a woman of great faith and persistence. And she was 100 percent for us. But her idea was a new one for me.

"I know absolutely nothing about such things, but why not? Who would do it?" I asked.

Norma Zimmer, her first choice, couldn't come. By the time Mercedes got her answer, she had already booked the civic auditorium for one of the only two nights it was available in September. What a shame to have to cancel!

"I have a good friend who knows Pat Boone very well," Ralph suggested. "He says he's a great, Spirit-filled Christian, really interested in missions. He is even on several mission boards!"

The idea of asking Pat Boone seemed ridiculous. He was far better known than Norma, and if she couldn't come, would he?

But Ralph called his friend, who called back to

Mercedes. "You realize that Pat's schedule is usually very full, and that he gets $20,000 per performance. A benefit performance, of course, would be free. I'll ask him. You never know, he just might do it for you!"

Amazingly, the only night Pat Boone had free was the only other date available at the civic auditorium. His secretary, a wonderful Christian girl and a minister's daughter, had read about us in *Christianity Today* and was warmly sympathetic to our cause. "There is just one question Mr. Boone has," she said over the phone. "Is this project likely to succeed?" Mercedes took a deep breath and answered, "Yes." And that was that!

The next three weeks were a flurry of activity. David Bliss, volunteering from Boston and en route to South Africa as a missionary, just *happened* to have had experience organizing a Leighton Ford crusade on Cape Cod. The day he started to work organizing our concert, Mildred Reilander just *happened* to walk into our offices and volunteer her services. For years the extremely capable and efficient owner of a secretarial pool, she seemed to know just whom to call for whatever we needed. Moreover, because they knew her personally, almost without fail they donated their services.

Pat Boone's office had suggested we have a second performer who could spell him off for a breather from time to time. Mercedes remembered Nancy DeMoss, a talented young musician and head of the primary children's ministries at Lake Avenue Congregational Church, though she was only nineteen. For years she had been very interested in missions, she said, and added that she knew Pat well; she had been in his home and he in hers. Of course she would help.

"We need some testimonials about the Center from well-known Christian leaders," David told Ralph, and they called Dr. Harold Ockenga at Gordon Conwell Seminary and Dr. Billy Graham. (It was quite exciting for our receptionist when Billy called back and told her who he was!) Both men were glad to help. David planned that we would call Ockenga from the concert and amplify the conversation so that the audience could hear. But Billy Graham's comments over the phone would have to be taped since he would be out of the country at the time of the concert.

David shook his head about that one. Where could we find decent recording equipment? That evening at the Prayer Council he had set up, he asked for prayer about it, and the vice president of a chain of radio stations just *happened* to be there and volunteered his equipment.

It was that way all along—providence after providence, God providing all the way. The concert could have cost us thousands. Except for the rental of the auditorium and the cost of printing materials, everything was free, from radio spots to graphic design to bouquets of flowers. Wonderful Christians in all sorts of businesses pitched in to help, even though they really didn't know us. How wonderful to belong to the kingdom of God and to have such beautiful brothers and sisters!

We had only three weeks to get ready—not nearly enough time. So many things could have gone wrong, but didn't, in spite of our inexperience and frenzied preparations. And before we knew it, the night had come.

Seated several rows back out in front of the curtain, I froze when my sister tapped me on the shoulder and asked, "What are those tracts being passed out, out in front?"

"Oh, no!" I thought to myself, and went to look. There were two kinds, one put out by a semi-Christian cult (not Summit), and the other by its detractors. The people passing them out were on public sidewalks, so there was nothing we could do. Going back inside, I glanced to my left and again froze when I saw an entire row of people dressed in light blue—all Summit top staff.

"Lord, it's in your hands," I prayed. "You have taken care of everything so far; now don't let Satan spoil it for us now!" We didn't know until later how perfectly God answered that prayer.

Bob, inserting the slides for the multi-media into the carousel, realized that he had left one complete set in the studio several miles away. It was rush hour traffic, and his car was ancient, but he got there and back just as Pat Boone walked in the door.

Because of the difference in time zones between the east and west coasts, Dave had scheduled the amplified phone call to Dr. Ockenga for early in the program. All the details had been carefully worked out ahead of time and Dr. Ockenga said he would be ready. Ted Engstrom of World Vision, our master of ceremonies, three times dialed the number Dr. Ockenga had given. But each time the operator responded, "I'm sorry. You have reached a disconnected number."

"Dial 1," someone in the audience called, and we all laughed.

Then Dr. Ockenga was on. "Dr. Ockenga, I have Pat Boone here beside me," Ted Engstrom began.

"Pat who?" In Southern California, that question brought down the house.

Pat was smooth in his performance, and warmly spiritual in his approach. Ralph told me later he had tears in his eyes when Pat sang "Jesus Loves the Little Children of the World."

Nancy also was very good, especially with the mission medley which she had worked out. And we were having fun, wonderful Christian fun, happy in the Lord and in His care for us.

High up on one of the multi-media platforms behind the curtain, Bob was trying to catch his breath. He had been working all night and all day on the slide show, and then had that mad dash to the studio and back. But now at last his slides were ready. "How I wish we could have gone through this thing just once, " he thought to himself. "But Lord, you know we haven't had time. We've done

93

our best. Now please make it right."

I was pleased at how well organized everything seemed. Just the right pictures. Just the right words. The slides faded into the motion picture portion, then back again, only one slide slipping slightly at one point.

Out in front we didn't know the half of what was going on behind stage. The movie projector had started to smoke, and Bob was blowing on it furiously to keep the film from burning. By the time the slide projector clicked in again, its light burning into Bob's eyes, he had become quite faint from hyperventilation, and losing his balance, almost fell the twenty feet from the high platform where he sat. Out in front, we saw only the slipped slide.

That was the way the entire evening went. To those of us out in front, it was a beautiful, polished performance. Backstage, only God held it together. Not one of us could doubt that this was another of His miracles.

20

THE JERICHO MARCHES

There were three loud blasts of the trumpets, followed immediately by "Hallelujah! Praise the Lord!" shouted by the hundred or so marchers who followed the trumpeters. Farther back, a second group took up the refrain: "For He has done great and mighty things!" Back and around the corner, a third group of one hundred echoed, "We will praise His name for ever and ever!" And the first of two interspersed choirs began to sing.

It was the seventh and last of our Jericho marches. Six Sundays before, we had been a band of about 50 who gathered to pray in silence as we marched the 1 1/8th miles around the campus we were claiming for God. Today we numbered 350, including three trumpeters, two banner-bearers, ten ministers, two choirs, and the three praise groups of over 100 each. Because we had to march two-by-two on the sidewalk, the group stretched for blocks, never in a straight line, as it wound its way around the campus.

The six previous Sundays had been without incident. We marched in silent prayer, and only a few people noticed us. In cosmopolitan Southern California, those few had not bothered to find out what was going on.

When Ralph had first suggested that we march around the campus, there was almost no one on the staff who

95

wanted to do it with him. It was too bizarre.

"This isn't Jericho, and God hasn't commanded us to do it," they said.

Some were adamant. "Do we really want to seem like kooks? Is that the message we want to give the community?"

It was true, God had not commanded us, and Ralph didn't really know why we should do it. He just felt that by this means we should announce to the world that we were claiming this campus for God and for His cause.

"There is something about a public witness that is good for us as well as for the community," he said to me.

Even I had qualms at first. But not for long. On that first march in August, I prayed as I walked, and as I prayed, I wondered if the Children of Israel hadn't felt foolish just walking around the city and not fighting as they were prepared to do. The people of Jericho must have leaned over the walls and sneered at them. "Do you think you can capture our city that way?" they must have said. "How stupid can you be!" And it must have taken courage to be willing to seem stupid.

Shortly after we first discussed doing Jericho marches, a newly-arrived member of our staff, out of curiosity, visited the Summit campus bookstore and bought a tape made by Elizabeth Claire Prophet, the cult's leader. On this tape, in the middle of the decrees and chants which she led, Mrs. Prophet had spoken about Joshua and the city of Jericho. She commented about how ridiculous it would seem if anyone were to do that type of thing today.

"I really believe we should do it," Ralph insisted when he heard this. "Those who really don't want to go don't have to; but those who want to, come with me in confidence and faith."

So we did.

Actually, though, Ralph was out of the country for the first three marches, and so Hal Leaman, as Associate General Director, led us. Bob Pierce, the founder of

96

World Vision, joined Hal on the first march. We will probably never know how hard it was for him to do that. The doctor had told him he was slowly dying of leukemia. He had been in bed off and on for extended periods of time, but refused to stay there. Instead, he visited mission stations around the world, and raised money to help with the needs he saw.

"Ralph, I'll be glad to march with you. I am leaving Sunday evening for the East and then on to Irian Jaya, but I don't want to miss this," Bob told Ralph.

So there he was, in the hot sun of August, walking that 1 1/8th mile with us. He was flushed when we got back, and I worried that we had asked too much of him.

"I came to this campus as a 12-year-old boy and stayed here until I was 20," he commented. "As we walked around the campus, I recognized house after house as having belonged to one or another of my professors at the college. Almost daily I would walk home with Uncle Buddy Robinson, a real saint of the Nazarene Church. And there by that fountain in front of the school, I used to talk with Dr. Wiley, the president for so many years.

"This campus has belonged to the Lord since just after the turn of the century," he continued. "We can't allow the devil to claim it now.

He glanced at us. We were so few to claim such a large campus. And he remembered the early days of World Vision, which he founded.

"Do not despise the day of small beginnings," Bob quoted from Zechariah. "All great things have started small, and if God is in it—as I believe with all my heart He is—it will succeed."

The next-to-the-last Sunday of Jericho marches was a glorious day. Pastor Ortlund from Lake Avenue Congregational Church joined us with a number of his parishioners, so we had almost 200. Some from Center staff smiled at his slight hesitation when, that morning, he informed his congregation that he was going to march and invited others to join him. We remembered our own mixed feelings five weeks before.

But we weren't surprised when, that evening, he reported to his congregation: "I went on that 'Jericho march' this afternoon with the staff of the Center for World Mission. Wow! What a blessing! Did you ever miss God's moving if you weren't there! It wasn't just the 200 or so who marched. I could sense the presence of the Lord Himself with us. I felt almost like I was actually with those Children of Israel when they marched around Jericho!"

The week after that Sunday when so many had marched, the devil started talking to me. "This last Sunday you can probably count on 50," he told me. "Those are the old faithful. But after last Sunday you are really going to look like losers. Pastor Ortlund will be gone to a conference, and his people probably won't be back. You thought you could get a great group, but you'll never make it."

"It is Your Name at stake, Lord Jesus," I reminded Christ when I prayed. "We've been willing to seem foolish for Your sake. But now You'll have to bring the people we need to help us."

We wanted to follow the Biblical pattern as much as possible, so we decided to have trumpets, ministers (as our "priests") as well as the rest of us who would function as the ordinary "soldiers." As usual, Prudence was thrown the job of organizing it.

Every day those on staff who could sing met to practice. But we were very few. Prudence called everyone she could think of to locate several trumpets, but she ran into a blank wall until one day Mrs. Fischer, who had prayed for my tumor, called and said that her son played the trumpet, and wanted to help. Would we call him?

He was not only willing to come and play his trumpet, but he brought two other trumpeters, a banner, and an entire church choir. With them, our old faithfuls, and others who came after hearing of the marches at the Pat Boone Concert the night before, we had seven times the number of people who had come with us seven Sundays before.

How could we get more biblical than seven times the original number on the seventh march?

In keeping with the biblical pattern, on this last march, we decided to circle the campus seven times. Not everyone would be able to go the entire way: altogether it would be almost eight miles!

We had planned that this would be a victory march. It was scheduled for September 25, only six days before our payment was due. "Surely, if God is going to answer our prayers, He will do it by then!" we had told ourselves two months before.

Instead, this march was a march of faith. On that day, instead of $850,000 we had a total of $157,000 in the bank and an additional $222,000 in pledges! We were not even halfway to the goal!

As fifty of us silently circled the campus six times before the final triumphant march of faith, we remembered God's words, "Not by might, nor by power, but by my Spirit, says the Lord" (Zech. 4:6). Humanly speaking we had failed. We had done our best, but we were too weak. We had failed!

But doesn't the apostle Paul tell us that God loves to use the weak to confound the mighty? Doesn't he insist that all God needs is people who will let Him use them? (See I Cor. 1:26-30.) We abundantly fulfilled that requirement. So we marched in prayer and in faith.

The first, second, and third marches on that last Sunday were uneventful, except that, for the sake of time, we had to move fast. Ralph's 82-year old father had marched with us each Sunday, and wanted to go the entire way, but we went so fast he had to drop out. After the first few rounds, several others, much younger, developed blisters and had to drop out, only to be replaced by others.

As mile after mile was traversed in silence and prayer, we found our hearts anticipating a great victory. We didn't know how God was going to work, but we believed with all our hearts that He was going to do something very special.

All the previous Sundays the Summit people had completely ignored our marches except for broadcasting classical or Christmas music (in August!) on the loudspeaker as we approached the front of the campus. This Sunday, by the time we were completing the fourth march, some of them had gathered on the lawn in front to watch us. We wondered what they were thinking. And we prayed for them as we passed by.

A couple of marchers were splattered with raw eggs from a window of the dormitory occupied by Summit members. Mostly, however, it was a silent, inexorable march to the final and last triumph. As we rounded the back of our building after each circuit, people gathering for the final march would questioningly hold up fingers, asking, "Which round is this? How many more times to go?" Summit personnel also wanted to know. As we approached the campus from the front, one of them asked, "How many times have you gone around now?" And he breathed a sigh of relief when the person at the end of the line held up six fingers.

Finally, a couple of hours after the six silent marches had begun, those participating strode somewhat wearily, yet expectantly, into our courtyard. They smiled broadly when they saw the crowd that had gathered for the final circuit. And the crowd burst into applause for them.

Prudence had spent days planning the sequence of that last march. Unlike the Children of Israel, we had no "fighting men." Our soldiers were the "praise troops." But, like them, we were led by trumpets. Next came the banner and the ten ministers (like Joshua's priests), followed by Praise Troop I, Choir I, Praise Troop II, Choir II, and Praise Troop III.

Only the choirs were supposed to sing lest we get out of tune and meter with each other, strung out, as we were, along the 1 1/10th mile loop. But as the trumpets and ministers rounded the last corner on the last march, observed by Summit members from every window and along the lawns, all of a sudden Choir I began to sing "Jesus, Jesus, Jesus, there's just something about that Name!" Like a wave that will not be stilled, the entire line of march, blocks long, spontaneously burst into song.

To the Summit people, Jesus was only one of a number of ascended masters. To us, He was Lord of Lords, and King of Kings—the One at whose Name one day every knee shall bow and every tongue confess that He is God, the only One worthy to receive the power, the riches, the wisdom, the strength, the honor, the glory, and the blessing (Rev. 5:12).

21

OCTOBER 1, 1977

D-DAY

Jamie, the receptionist, usually rather quiet, picked up the stack of mail she had just opened and headed upstairs to the accounting office.

"Do you know how much came in today?" she exclaimed to Mary Fran as she passed her desk. "Twenty-seven thousand dollars! Just look at this stack! Most of it is in checks of $100 or less! The Lord is really answering our prayers!"

Ralph had urged people to call us during this last week to find out how we were doing. Consequently, our lines were very busy. The Billy Graham Foundation called with a pledge of $10,000. World Vision called, and later hand-delivered $25,000. Gospel Light Press brought in $10,000. Providence Mission Homes gave the $26,000 earned from the Pat Boone concert.

But we still lacked almost $400,000. Had we misunderstood God when we went into this venture? Many friends were telling us we had. Yet He was working so many miracles and had constantly reassured us.

On the Thursday before October 1st, we had a wonderful idea. Hey! The 1st is on Saturday. Does that mean that the money can be paid on Monday morning because of the bank holiday?"

But the college lawyer said, "Read your contract again.

102

It says 'before the six months is out,' and that's tomorrow. We'll be over in the morning."

"Can't they even give us until 5 o'clock?" I thought rebelliously. But we went to prayer again and cried out to the Lord.

Meanwhile, our governing board went into session—and also to prayer. Some weeks before, three different Christian sources had offered to advance us $100,000 each if we found we needed it at the last minute. Even with those loans we would be short, but they would at least bring our total into a reasonable distance of the required amount.

We had not asked for those loans. Were they—could they be—God's provision for us?

The young people on our staff said, "No way! We asked God to *give* us the money. Now we've got to trust Him to *give* it to us, not to loan it."

But the board, all mature men of prayer, were not so sure. After agonized prayer, they finally decided that we should accept these loans. Those offering the money were all godly men. God had placed it upon their hearts to offer these loans. We simply could not disregard their faith. Even though this was not the way we would have wanted God to answer, it was nevertheless God's provision, and we should accept it with thanksgiving.

It had been a real crisis of faith and of trust in our leadership. One board member, Jim Montgomery of Overseas Crusades, was reachable only by phone. The next day he wrote: "While our board-member phone conversation last night was somewhat somber and subdued, I found myself walking and leaping and praising God around the house after I hung up. I trust the narrowness of this victory will not rob us of the joy nor rob God of the glory of what has happened. Satan wanted to keep us from getting the property in the first place; now he will try and rob us of the joy of victory and God of the glory."

But we were still short! Some money that had been

pledged was sitting in branch banks and, it seemed, might not arrive on time. The $50,000 Ahmanson check, delivered by mail the week previous, sat in our files, waiting for the university's IRS non-profit status to come through.

Friday, the college lawyer and business manager came early. Our hearts were heavy because we were not ready. We had the promised loans, and we had some outstanding promised pledges, but we didn't have all the money in hand as they had required.

The staff watched soberly as Ralph, our lawyer, and a couple of others crossed the street to the library building where the negotiations would take place. We couldn't believe God had failed us after all He had brought us through. But we simply didn't have the money! All we had were empty stomachs from three days of fasting, extremely weary bodies, and a flickering faith.

Oh Lord, HELP!

So we went to prayer again. I felt much like the children of Israel must have felt as they faced the Red Sea: "Lord, why did you bring us to this difficult place?" We were praying around the circle, and when my time came I could only cry, "Lord, you promised!" Then my voice broke, and I fled from the room.

In the library across the street our staff were equally somber, not knowing what to expect. Ralph's nephew, Eric Winter, recently admitted to the California Bar Association, was our only legal counsel, and he was firm: "The Center received the option agreement two weeks late, and they did not feel they could start raising funds until they had it in hand."

"Yes," admitted the college representatives. "That's true. Okay, why not take another week?"

"Thank you, Lord!" our men breathed silently.

"Also," Eric persisted, "we feel some precise agreement must be reached about the off-campus housing and the Summit lease."

For two or three hours the discussions continued.

What a blessing to be dealing with men of such sterling Christian character!

The Lord must have been in that room, for the terms hammered out were in every respect better than we had dared to hope. We were given almost a year, until September, 1978, to pay the rest of the down payment ($650,000) and get out of escrow. By then, Summit would be off the campus, eliminating any problems we might have with them were we to take ownership before their lease had expired.

Then, knowing we had given all the money we had to make this payment, the college generously agreed to accept a mere $5,000, payable immediately, for the option agreement on the 83 off-campus houses, worth then $2.3 million. We, in turn, agreed to pay on October 1, 1978 the $285,000 down payment for the houses.

How we rejoiced when our men returned and announced the extension of time and the terms of agreement.

Yet we felt a bit like prisoners in the dock awaiting judgment. We were still short hundreds of thousands of dollars, and we had one week's reprieve. That was all!

22

OCTOBER 7, 1977

GOD DID A MIRACLE

All the next week seemed anticlimatic. The huge mail deliveries fell almost to zero. Money still trickled in: $100 on Monday, $50 on Tuesday, $30 on Wednesday, but the well was dry. Once in awhile friends would call to ask what was happening, and we would tell of our extension of time and our continuing need. And we would then ask them to pray.

Friday morning, October 7th, we were all at the office early. By the time the banks opened, David Kolb, our accountant, was already at the teller's window. He had carefully deposited all gifts for the property in a savings and loan association, hoping thereby to gain a few extra dollars of interest. Now he withdrew all but the dollar necessary to maintain the account and drove several blocks away to the bank where we had our checking account.

For two weeks we had been expecting the two checks from Portland. One was a loan for $100,000 from Mr. Ottomoeller, who had given us the $10,000 toward our option. The other, a check for $45,000 was the tithe from the insurance adjustment on the Aloha church fire. Almost daily, David had checked with our bank to see if that money had yet arrived. Each time, our bank informed him that, unfortunately, those funds were still tied up in the branch office in San Francisco.

106

But today was the day the money had to be paid, and David was desperate. "What would you suggest we do?" he asked the teller. He knew that our bank would not honor those funds until they were on their premises in Pasadena.

That was not our only banking frustration that day. Sheri, running back and forth between the office and the bank, reported a new crisis each trip.

"Dr. Winter told David to pass the money withdrawn from savings through the checking account so we would have a bank record that would cover all transactions. Now, just *after* David finished depositing that money, they informed him that there is a bank policy forbidding large withdrawals less than a week after a large deposit is made."

The next trip: "They can't find that $46,000 deposit I made yesterday at closing time." She was really in a panic over that one.

"Sheri, don't you have your deposit book, or a signed duplicate of the deposit slip, or something?" I asked her.

"Oh yes! Of course I do," she beamed, and dashed off to the bank again.

We had a property deed, given us by John Patterson of Bethlehem church, one of our most faithful helpers throughout the summer. It was worth about $11,500, but now we needed cash.

"The college authorities may not want to accept a deed," Hal worried. "But if they insist on cash, we'll have to take out a loan. But where will we get the money?"

"How are you coming? Is all the money in?" a man from the area called. Jamie, our receptionist, somewhat dejectedly told him about our problem with the deed.

"How much is the deed worth?" he asked.

"Eleven thousand, five hundred."

"Oh, is that all? Well, I can lend you that much for a few days. No problem." And he got in his car, went to the bank, and arrived at our office in time to catch Sheri on her next run to the bank.

All that morning we had been wondering what to do about the $50,000 Ahmanson check. The other large checks we had received had all come from organizations having their own tax-exempt status, and thus could be put directly into our accounting system. But the Ahmanson Foundation had donated this money to the university, and had requested a university tax deductible receipt.

Several months before, we had applied for non-profit, tax-exempt status for both the U.S. Center for World Mission and the William Carey International University. Everyone warned us that even if correctly filed, it would take anywhere from six months to two years for our papers to be processed. Most people assume that only lawyers can properly fill out the forms. But the IRS office in Washington D.C. admitted we could save the lawyer's fee and fill out the forms ourselves. They had even hinted that personally filed forms received preferential treatment.

There had been a minor crisis in our office, however, when Ralph decided to follow the suggestion of the IRS office in Washington instead of conventional wisdom. "If you broke a leg, would you try to fix it yourself?" one asked.

Bruce Graham, our young aeronautical engineer and a graduate of the Massachusetts Institute of Technology, worked diligently on the forms, calling the local IRS offices whenever he ran into a snag. Fortunately, the people there were very friendly. They knew of our crisis and promised to call us when our tax-deductible status had been granted.

Six weeks had now passed, and we still had heard nothing from the IRS.

The previous morning Ralph had left for Columbus, Ohio where he was to address the International Society of Christian Endeavor. He had accepted this engagement months before because the date was beyond our first deadline. Now, in spite of our crisis, it was too late to cancel.

"I'll just have to keep in touch by phone," he told me when I expressed dismay.

It seemed as if he called every hour, but our problems were so many, it still wasn't often enough. On one of his calls, Hal mentioned that we still didn't know what to do about the $50,000 Ahmanson check.

"Why not have Bruce call the IRS," Ralph suggested.

Why not, indeed! Such a simple solution!

"Oh, I'm so glad you called," the IRS secretary told him. "We've been trying to reach you. But I seemed to have misplaced your phone number. We're happy to tell you that you have your tax-exempt status—for both for the U.S. Center for World Mission and for the William Carey International University. Congratulations!"

We were walking on air when we heard the news. "Thank you, Lord! You've worked another miracle. Tomorrow would have been too late!"

And Sheri flew back to the bank with that $50,000. She found our accountant and the bank officials still in consultation.

"We know that $189,000 is caught in the bank in San Francisco. And we know the crisis you're in. Even though, technically, we're not supposed to honor that money until it arrives here, we'll make an exception.

"Now, about that other problem. There is a banking rule against withdrawing money you have just deposited, especially if it is a large sum. That's in order for the bank to know the deposit is good. But we know that you just took it out of savings and that the money is good. So go ahead and withdraw it, " the official said. And David visibly heaved a sigh of relief.

Altogether, scraping up every available penny, we still lacked almost exactly $100,000. Some weeks before Campus Crusade had offered us a loan of exactly that amount, "should you need it." Obviously we did, and called them to that effect.

"How can we get it to you?" their business manager

asked. "There's not much time left, is there?"

"We have to turn over the money at the office of Point Loma's lawyer. That's in Pomona, which is about half way. How about meeting us there?"

Time was running very short. Already it was after four in the afternoon. Though ordinarily it takes only thirty minutes or so to get from Pasadena to Pomona, during rush hour traffic, especially on Fridays, it can be very slow. And David was still at the bank.

"Look, I think we'd better send someone to pick up Campus Crusade's check and then hold the lawyer in his office until we get there. I'll go over to the bank and see what the delay is now," Hal said. And off he went.

"Their check writing machine can't write a check for $750,000," David told Hal when he arrived. "They're having to give us five checks. That's why it's taking longer."

The rest of the story was one of a mad dash by freeway during the worst hour of the week. Hal got there a few minutes late, but the lawyer was still there. Hal handed over the checks; the papers were signed, and within minutes our men were on their way home, having paid the impossible $850,000 in full.

The struggle had been great, yet in a very strange way we felt like mere instruments—puppets, almost—in the hands of a purposeful God. Things were obviously beyond our control. Not even by faith could we have foreseen how God could possibly answer our prayers. Yet He did!

In the eyes of our staff and the Christian community, God won great glory from this miracle. More importantly, perhaps, He was glorified in the eyes of the cult.

Two weeks before, a long article had appeared in the Pasadena newspaper about Summit. The newspaper correspondent, warmly admiring their leader, Elizabeth Claire Prophet, had quoted her as saying, "We want the will of God. If He wants them to get the campus, that's fine."

We had known for a long time that we were in a "power encounter," not so much with the cult as with the gods they served. It was a power encounter of the same sort when Elijah on Mt. Carmel challenged the priests of Baal to call down fire from heaven on their sacrifice. "If the Lord is God, *follow* Him!" he challenged the people. "But if Baal is God, then follow *him!*" (I Kings 18:21).

Instinctively we knew that our encounter was important. Cult members, deceived in a mind-bending philosophical system of high sounding words, needed to know that there is a God who is above all gods, who is not something we will ever *become*. He is the creator of the universe, and the only redeemer of our souls. They would never be convinced by our words. Only God Himself could demonstrate His power to them, and He would have to do it very visibly and against all sorts of odds.

Elizabeth Claire Prophet had seemed very democratic when she essentially said, "May the best man win." But she had referred to the *will of God* , and that has nothing at all to do with democracy. God is interested in truth!

For us, what a time of rejoicing! What a time for praise!

What a time, also, to remind ourselves why God had done this miracle. It was not because we were so good, or so holy, or so full of faith. It was because we were co-operating with His will, as Mrs. Prophet unwittingly implied. Long centuries ago God announced, "I am God, there is no other. I have sworn by Myself and I will never go back on My word, for it is true. Every knee in all the world shall bow to Me, and every tongue shall swear allegiance to My name" (Isa. 45:22-23).

And our hearts echo, "So be it, Lord. Amen!"

23

OCTOBER 1977

"YOUR YOUNG MEN SHALL SEE VISIONS""

(Joel 2:28)

D-day with its mighty miracle had come and gone! After so many months of uncertainty, the campus was ours. At least, that is, we had entered into escrow.

In many ways we felt like a diver who must surface to get his bearings before striking out across the lake. Now that our first major crisis was behind, we felt we had to take stock and try to ascertain God's direction for our future. We knew that long years of financial crises lay ahead. The down payment itself was, as yet, incomplete. In spite of God's wonderful grace, we could still fail and lose everything. Not until our final balloon payment would be made, years from then, could we know that the campus was securely ours.

We couldn't forget finances, and yet there were other battles to fight and other wars to win.

It was an abrupt transition for me that day, just a week after our victory, when Ralph called all of us together and asked, "What now?"

I wanted to press on in fund raising efforts and pay off the campus as soon as possible. But Ralph said, "No. We mustn't forget what the campus is for. We're not here

112

just to buy a campus. God may very well give it to us, but I don't think He will unless we show that His concerns come first. We must do all we can to help make missions a top priority again."

For two entire days we brainstormed as a staff. "What has to happen in order for all the unreached peoples in the world to be evangelized? And what is happening now? We know that there is a big gap between these two, and our problem is to find out what we can do about it. Let's start there," Ralph suggested.

Usually, only the top staff of an institution is invited to participate in this kind of no-holds-barred brainstorming. At that time our staff was still very small. Although they were mainly still in their twenties, all had been committed to the same vision for several years.

"Who knows, perhaps our young staff will be the most important ones to include in this brainstorming," Ralph commented. "More than a thousand years ago Benedict said that God often reveals his best ideas to young people. Let's all work on this together. Now, where shall we start?"

"First of all, let's discuss what we believe needs to happen in this country in order to make the cause of missions move forward. It seems to me that before Christians worldwide can finish the job Christ gave us, there must be a massive new movement with thousands of new recruits going overseas. What could we do, for example, to help start another student missions movement like they had 80 years ago? That one brought 20,000 more missionaries from America alone. What would it take today?"

"Well, for one thing, I think we need to push the SCOWE conferences more," Becky suggested. "No one is doing a methodical job of organizing them. Someone needs to do that."

The Student Conference on World Evangelization (SCOWE) was the dream of Bill Haines, one of Becky's classmates at Caltech. At her urging, Bill had attended the second Summer Institute of International Studies (SIIS) at Wheaton. When he returned to Caltech, he plunged into plans for a missions conference which would draw students from all over Southern California. Ralph and I gasped when Becky told us they had rented Caltech's prestigious Beckman Auditorium at $1000 a day, and that their conference was scheduled for the end of January, just five months away.

SCOWE from its very beginning was student sponsored, student organized, student run. We were thrilled when 650 showed up that first year.

In the years to follow, Bill graduated and went on to Stanford for graduate studies. In his absence, other "Techers" picked up the baton, but if the SCOWEs were to continue and expand into other cities, these students needed help!

Then, "What about the children?" Mary Fran wanted to know. Mary Frances Redding had been a Christian Education director for years, and was more aware than most of us how little about missions there is today in the Sunday School curriculum. "You know," she reminded us, "most missionaries got their vision as children.

"Perhaps we ought to set up an office to write Sunday School materials."

"I'd like to see more than just Sunday School materials," I said. "We need to write interesting mission stories that children will want to read on their own."

"And what about the adults? What can we do to motivate them?" Ralph asked. "There are Bible study groups all over the place, some of them huge. But who goes to missionary meetings anymore? Most churches don't even have an active Women's Missionary Society."

"For one thing, we've got to set up mission prayer groups." David Bliss insisted. I knew he was thinking of the impact on his life of the noon prayer group at Gordon Seminary which J. Christy Wilson, recently returned from Afghanistan, had organized. Fifty students met to pray for missions every noon, we were told.

"But how can you get people to come to something like that?" another asked.

"Do you know, when I was at UCLA, I was the only one out of 90 Christians in our dorm who was the least bit interested in missions," Beth commented. "I guess I really bugged that group about missions because one day the student leader told me he was praying that I would get off this 'missions kick' and get back to what God was most interested in—discipleship and evangelism here!"

She laughed and went on. "I challenged him to read just four books and to let me have ten minutes of each of our house meeting times to give a capsule report on some unreached people—like, where they are on the map, what the newspapers are saying about them . . .things like that."

"It was unbelievable, but in just a few months, ten of those students were so excited about missions that others started praying for *them* to get off the missions kick." She laughed again.

"What I'm saying is, somehow we have to get people—the churches—more personally acquainted with those who need reaching."

"And you think maps, newspaper articles, and research is the way to get started?"

"Why not?" Ralph agreed. "What we really need is a magazine of the quality of *National Geographic* exclusively dedicated to the evangelism of unreached peoples. It should be full of good pictures and articles and be paid for by subscription. We could send roving photojournalists around the world to write articles and take pictures for it as well as produce movies and video tapes for churches and student groups."

"It seems like to me that we also need a university, run by missionaries, that can help people get into 'closed' countries as Ph.D. students! They could do research papers on people groups that are unreached. And some of them could teach English to support themselves. Almost every country in the world wants English teachers." Ralph paused. "Such a university could train our students in all kinds of skills that would allow them to work in 'closed' countries: agriculture, water resource development, community health, literacy . . . There's almost no end to the needs that could be met."

"And how about an office that would help ordinary American Christians live at the same consumption level as, say, a missionary on furlough? Just think of the money they could give to missions! Even if only two Christian families in a hundred did that, we'd probably have another billion dollars a year for missions!"

"Wow," I thought, "some of these ideas are really wild! But wouldn't it be great if we could do them!

"Maybe, in God's providence and time!"

24

NOVEMBER 1977

"I'LL SHOW YOU WHICH ONES"

(Judges 7:4b)

One fact of which we became acutely aware during our brainstorming session was that, as a staff, we were almost back to where we had started the year before. By November the wonderful summer volunteers had all left. Now that we could begin to work on more than simply raising funds, we had almost no one to do the work!

It is true that 35 or 40 people worked at the Center every day. But more than half of these were the staff of other organizations on campus. All shared our concern for the unreached, but each organization was doing its own thing. The burden of buying the campus for the use of all rested on the shoulders of what we came to call our "central staff." But it was only *one* of our jobs. We also had to work on mobilizing thousands of churches, figure out how to mobilize and train thousands of students in missions (especially those studying in secular universities), and coordinate the research that was being done on our campus. Because central staff numbered only about fifteen at that point, we were truly in a crisis. Somehow we had to get more staff, staff that would come to stay.

It wasn't that people didn't *want* to join us. Every week we received interested inquiries. But when we told them that we followed the missionary pattern of support, many backed away. Except for those who had been missionaries, those who were older were unwilling to appeal to churches and friends to support them in this missionary venture. As a result, those who came tended to be younger. Usually they came with the attitude that they would give us two years, but then they planned to go overseas.

At first these young people came with very little support. Most mission boards, especially those whose principal work is in the U.S. (such as Inter Varsity and Campus Crusade for Christ), accept candidates only *after* they have found adequate support. But the Center would never have gotten off the ground if we had followed that policy. That first summer I often wondered how our young volunteers survived without salaries or any other source of income. However they did it, by the fall of 1977 their savings were gone. They had nothing left.

Ralph and I certainly couldn't pay salaries to those who decided to stay; we were dependent on churches and friends for our own support. And considering the huge sums of money the Center had to raise merely to buy the campus, it seemed unreasonable for the administration of the Center, meaning Ralph, to also try to raise funds for everyone's salary. The time-honored missionary policy was that churches and friends respond best when they have personal financial ties with their missionaries. From the beginning we decided to identify with the mission agencies, even in their pattern of support raising. Consequently, our staff would have to find their own support, and do so quickly!

Support raising is scary for the uninitiated. It was scary for even us. If our staff were joining long established missions or were going overseas, they would have had fewer problems. But they had come to work in a new, relatively unknown, U.S.-based operation. Would churches and friends give on a monthly basis to support them here?

118

Again we thanked the Lord for Prudence and her years of experience with Campus Crusade. She taught our staff all she knew about writing support letters, explaining our work to friends, and setting up special times to tell about the Center and its goals.

"It usually takes at least two to six months to raise your support," she told us. "We'd like to give all our staff members that much time, but we can't. There is no one to replace you while you are away. So we will each have at least a half a day a month to work on support letters and accounts. One at a time, we'll take off for more intensive support raising." So we began writing letters and talking to friends and church mission committees about our personal needs.

It seemed hard to believe that only a year before Ralph and I had gone through a similar experience. Because we were beginning to seek support at the very moment church mission budgets were being decided, Ralph wrote a number of his pastor friends special delivery letters, telling of our immediate need. I remember the elation we felt as some letters came back with sure promises of support. And also our dismay when we were told, "Sorry, you're too late." How I had wished back then that God would supply without all that frantic correspondence! I knew He could, but He didn't.

We came to find, however, that requiring staff to raise their own support was God's blessing in disguise. It helped us to know whom God had called to work with us.

Prudence carefully sorted out all who applied. Were they spiritually qualified? Were their hearts given to missions? Or were they just looking for a job? She always told them, "We'll help you as much as we can in raising your support. We'll give you guidelines, supervise your efforts, and perhaps even approach churches on your behalf. But in the final analysis, you are the one responsible. You will have to pray and work hard, but we believe that if the Lord wants you here, He will verify this by providing your support."

She then told them about Ralph's deepest concern: "You must enter into this in faith, not with your own needs uppermost in your heart. Remember that the Bible says, 'Give and it shall be given to you.' Instead of thinking about your own need, concentrate on giving your church and friends the thing that you have which is your most valuable possession—the conviction that God is moving in a new way in our world, clear out to the final frontiers, and that you and they can be part of His advance. Don't expect to receive financial help unless you truly minister in this way to those you approach."

With dismay, we watched some that seemed most desirable turn away. "You're not really serious!" they would say. "I can't imagine doing that kind of thing."

I could understand their reactions. We didn't say it would be easy.

The result was that many, initially interested in joining us, drifted away or sought well-paying jobs in Christian organizations elsewhere. As a result, we learned not to look at potential staffers with too much hope. They still had to pass all the tests before we could count on them.

The situation we were in reminded me of Gideon. When God first called him, he was just a young farmer, too scared of the Midianites to do his threshing out in the open. Yet, ironically, God called him a "mighty soldier." According to his own testimony, he was not thought of as a leader. In fact, he admitted that he was the least member of an insignificant family. But God was calling him to what seemed impossible, even for people more mature with greater prestige and ability. One thing only Gideon possessed: the knowledge that he could not do this alone. He would have to rely on God.

Gideon first tested God with his fleeces. Then God tested Gideon, first with arousing the wrath of the entire village, then sounding the call to arms. This young upstart!

The Bible states that when Gideon sounded the call to arms, the united armies of Midian, Amalek, and the other nations of the East were already mobilized in one vast army, "crowded across the valley like locusts—yes, like the sand upon the seashore—and there were too many camels even to count" (Judges 7:12-13).

How foolish it must have seemed to go against such a foe! Especially under Gideon! Amazingly, 32,000 responded to Gideon's call!

How Gideon must have praised God for those men! Perhaps, with God's help, they would win the battle. It would be tough. But maybe God would do a miracle. I'm sure he thought these thoughts.

But what did God say? "There are too many of you! I can't let all of you fight the Midianites, for then the people of Israel will boast to Me that they saved themselves by their own strength! Send home any of your men who are timid and frightened!" And 22,000 left.

Gideon must have sighed as he looked at the 10,000 who remained. "But the Lord said, 'There are still too many . . . Bring them down to the spring and I'll show you which ones shall go with you and which ones shall not'" (Judges 7:4).

Our staff had never been adequate to grapple with our assignment from God. Once that first payment was made, it seemed that even the few we had were leaving. And those who stayed, like Gideon's 10,000, still faced that unavoidable, crucial test of "support raising." If they were afraid to tell friends and churches of their need, if they really could not believe that God would bring in their support, then they also would have to leave.

The test given Gideon's troops was not illogical. Those who lapped the water like dogs were obviously not watching for the enemy. Our test, too, was quite logical: unless one can believe that God will supply his personal financial needs, how can he possibly have faith that God will supply $15 million to finish paying for a campus?

It took faith for Gideon to watch his recruits leave. It took faith for us too.

It also took faith to work with what was left. We eagerly welcomed the talented young people who asked to join us. But they were trained to be engineers, computer scientists, nurses, teachers, and pastors—not managers, professional fund raisers, graphic artists and business administrators!

Yet God used them, and gradually He began to bring in a few more mature people with overseas experience. We were a motley crew, but out of that material God began to mold a team to do His miracles, miracles we would desperately need before we were through.

25

NOV. 1977 – FEB. 1978

GOD'S ARITHMETIC

One month after our down payment deadline, we were still on the mountain top, rejoicing in God's miracle, confident that the road ahead would be smooth. God's miracle power on our behalf was reconfirmed when a $25,000 check came in from a church in Tennessee. We used it immediately to start paying back our loans.

Then, all of a sudden we descended into the valley, so to speak. In reality, it was a dry wilderness where nothing seemed to change.

It was hard even to remember that we were supposedly the campus owners—at least on our way to being so—because the main part of the campus was still off limits to us. Women in pastel colored robes and men in light blue suits still roamed the grounds or sat glassy-eyed on its lawns, palms up, as they chanted to a "sea of energy in the cosmos." Summit's lease, signed before we had begun negotiating for the property, gave them still another year. It would not expire until July 31st, 1978, just a month before the remainder of our down payment was due.

On our side of the street we occupied the same rooms; we didn't even have enough money to rent more office space. Everything was the same except the volume of mail!

Back in September we had received a huge stack of

letters and thousands of dollars every day. Now, two months later, only a trickle came in. We had millions yet to pay Point Loma besides the $300,000 in loans. But everyone, it seemed, assumed that our crisis was past, and the giving stopped. The well was dry. Confused and weary, most of us felt dry also. It helped to remember that Elijah felt the same way after his major victory on Mt. Carmel (1 Kings 19:4).

Then, too, it seemed as if Satan was attacking us on all fronts—using anything that would discourage, distress or divide us. Ralph's diary (and mine) recorded various struggles—over finances, management decisions, staff assignments. Sometimes the hardest things to bear were the cutting words of associates and friends. Ralph wrote in his diary, "Oh God, I feel more lonely in this project than ever!"

Over and over again, well wishers would send professional fund raisers to see us. One of them chided him: "You're crazy to try to start big. Everyone knows you have to start small." Ralph commented in his diary: "He told us, essentially, that we cannot do what we are doing. It was not very encouraging." And he added, "I wonder what Hudson Taylor felt like?"

Our project was a challenge to these fund raisers. They were not accustomed to raising millions of dollars for an organization that had essentially no mailing list. Worse still in their eyes, Ralph insisted that we had to do things in such a way that it would not put us in competition for funds with our chief "client"—the mission agencies. "Many feel there is only a certain size 'pie' of available money," he told them. "It is not surprising if they're afraid that more organizations will mean smaller pieces of pie for everyone. But we're determined not to raid their sources of income. Rather, we want to enlarge the 'pie' by increasing the number of people actively supporting mission agencies. We are here to help them, not hurt them."

"The main reason mission agencies have trouble getting the funds they need," he told our staff later, "is that the churches have basically lost interest in missions. Oh, they have a missions Sunday once a year, or maybe even a week of missions. But the missions committee is the only group really concerned, and all too often they spend their time figuring out how to spend their budget rather than praying and strategizing how to win the world for Christ."

"If we are ever to reach the two and a half billion unreached in our world, this has to change. The American church desperately needs a renewal of mission vision. At least a million of the forty million American evangelicals must catch this vision."

A million evangelicals!

A million square feet of property!

Fifteen million dollars!

I can't say it came as a flash of light, but the day we idly worked out the arithmetic, we were astounded. Could this be God's way for us?

We took months, literally, praying about limiting ourselves to asking each donor for only $15 apiece. To do so seemed suicidal when we needed millions. Everyone told us so. And yet it met all the criteria which we felt God had given us.

We remembered that a hundred years ago when he started the China Inland Mission, Hudson Taylor had felt that God didn't want him to ask for any money at all. Yet God had supplied his needs. On the other hand, there were far more examples of wonderful Christian leaders who asked for large sums of money, and God honored them too. What did God want *us* to do? That was the question.

The more we prayed about it, the more we became convinced that God did want us to honor the agencies by not competing with them, and to also honor Him by truly trusting Him to provide.

By following the small gift approach, we wouldn't be

a threat to the agencies. We would be forced to reach out to thousands and thousands of people, thereby spreading the vision of unreached peoples far and wide. By so doing we would help the agencies as well as, hopefully, survive as an institution.

But how do you reach out to a million people with a vision they don't necessarily want and don't think they need? If we were truly hearing God's voice in this decision, then He would have to lead, we told ourselves. But we found that our faith would be sorely tested again and again before we were through.

26

"SEEK YE FIRST THE KINGDOM OF GOD"

(Matthew 6:33)

May, already! In three months the second half of our down payment would be due—another $650,000—and we still owed $150,000 on the loans we had received the previous September. We had been very eager to pay off those loans quickly. But after October, 1977, the money came in trickles . . . or not at all.

Back in November, Ralph had asked us to take a step of faith that seemed a bit foolish under the circumstances. Many of us had assumed that we would pursue the wonderful visions the Lord had given us *after* we had secured the campus; we felt we were too busy to do so before. But Ralph was convinced we shouldn't wait.

"I believe God expects us to begin immediately with the work for which the campus is intended. Anyway, how can we ask people to give to us if we have nothing to show them but buildings?" he asked. "We have to prove why this place is essential to the cause of missions. We can't just raise funds to pay for the property.

"I know that trying to start new projects and raise funds at the same time is difficult, but I don't see that we have any other choice. Jesus promised that if we seek first

127

His kingdom, He will give us all we need. We'll just have to believe that!"

For two days we brainstormed, trying to figure out what we should do that would spread the vision of the unreached frontiers throughout the United States. After the amazing miracle of $850,000 we had just witnessed, we felt ready (in Willliam Carey's words) to "attempt great things for God and to expect great things from God."

In just a few months we had our first World Awareness Seminars ready to be presented in nearby churches. Ralph wrote several key articles which were published in key magazines. Our amateur staff produced brochures, charts and maps—anything we could think of that would help the church see the world yet to be reached.

Ralph was away speaking much of the time. He flew to Oregon, to North Carolina, to Boston. On speaking trips in Brazil, the Philippines and Hong Kong, he also worked to set up Sister Centers for Frontier Missions, of which there were soon four.

There were some really big projects that consumed our energy. Becky, our second daughter, recently graduated from Caltech, worked with Ralph to design and produce our first Hidden Peoples pie chart. I remember how shocked even Ralph and I were when she inserted the small symbols that represented the number of missionaries working in the different areas of the world. Some areas had so many missionaries that she had trouble fitting in all the little figures. In others—the Muslim world in particular— she had an ocean of space in which to place only half a figure.

I was busy at work with three projects of my own. It took me months to check my facts, search diaries and put on paper the thoughts which eventually became *Once More Around Jericho,* the earlier edition of this book.

Whenever my inspiration lagged, I worked to complete a 2' x 3' wall chart called "Two Thousand Years of Christian Expansion," with some help from Bruce and Ralph.

Because we had no graphic artists on staff, I spent weeks over the drafting board, pasting on hundreds of names of people who, down through history, took the gospel to cultures beyond their own.

I also helped to finalize our *Word Study Concordance* and *Word Study New Testament*. Every holiday for years, our daughters had worked with us on these tools, transferring the numbers in Strong's *Concordance* to the *Englishman's Greek Concordance*, and then adding, at the top of every entry, the page number where that Greek word was discussed in all the major reference works. With these, even a layman without any knowledge of Greek could go directly to the Greek words, allowing for a much richer and more accurate study of Scripture. The concordance still lacked an explanatory introduction and a final section comparing the Greek words in several of the early manuscripts. Ralph had no time to do these things, so I did, under his guidance.

Then, in February, Ralph asked us to take the hardest step of faith we had ever taken.

He was concerned that we not compete for funds with mission agencies, and felt that God was leading us to a small gift plan in which we would not *ask* for large sums of money but rather for a one-time $15.95 gift. We still had parts of the large loans to pay off as well as the $650,000 balance on the down payment due in September. If, by God's grace, we should complete that, starting the following December, every three months for years we would have large mortgage payments. Our only strategy to meet them, other than prayer, was to inspire 14,000 new people each quarter to give $15 apiece. But to reach that many people we needed a much larger staff.

I felt overwhelmed, as did most of the staff. With our payment coming ever closer, to be involved in *anything* other than fund raising seemed foolhardy, to say the least. But we were doing all sorts of other things as well. Ralph commented, "It's sort of like building a boat out in the water,". . . and one of the staff added, "Yeah, while trying to win a race!" But little by little we seemed to be gaining, and that gave us heart.

But along about May another responsibility was dropped in our laps, one which we could hardly refuse.

For some years, Ralph had been concerned about the need to give American college students in secular schools a more in-depth orientation to the missionary movement. Every three years he saw thousands of students go away from the Urbana Student Missionary Conventions ready to give their lives to missions. But without further inspiration, within a matter of months their zeal would wither away and eventually die.

After the Urbana meeting of December 1973, while he was still a full-time professor at the School for World Missions, Ralph had started the Summer Institute of International Studies. It met for several years on the campus of Wheaton College in Illinois, utilizing mission professors from around the country for one week each. In the first three years, more than 200 students were "turned on" to the cause of missions by what they learned there.

But Ralph was not satisfied. "That's barely 60 per year. Somehow we've got to get to larger numbers," he had insisted at the SIIS board meeting held the winter of 1976, before the U.S. Center for World Mission was founded.

Several of the board members disagreed with him. Some were even irritated. "Fifty students is just the right number to try out something new," insisted one, an expert on educational models.

"If we have any more, we'll lose the sense of community, the feeling of closeness," another added.

Rarely have I seen Ralph so frustrated. He was thinking in terms of a *movement,* they in terms of an organization. He wanted to inspire thousands of young people with a compelling new vision; they wanted to perfect an educational and community pattern. He had

130

started the program yet, as a seminary professor, he had many other responsibilities. Reluctantly, at the board's insistence, he turned the program over to others for them to run.

I remember how Ralph paced the floor as he made that decision. "It's such an important tool for mobilizing students," he said. "We can't let it die. But Jack Frizen (Executive Director of the Interdenominational Foreign Mission Association) and I seem to be the only ones who feel it must grow rapidly."

As the months passed his "grow or die" fears proved well-founded. From a high of 120 students the summer of 1975, enrollment dropped . . . to 75 in 1976, 50 in 1977, and then . . .

In early May, 1978, Ralph sat listening, the phone to his ear. I could tell something serious was being discussed. Something serious . . . and a bit painful!

"Ralph, we have only 30 students enrolled for SIIS this summer. To break even at the University of Colorado where we intended to hold it, we have to have at least 60. I feel just terrible, but we're going to have to cancel the program. And I thought I ought to let you know."

Ralph also felt terrible. It was May already, really too late to do anything now. Whatever had gone wrong?

Our daughter Beth and her husband, Brad Gill, had met at SIIS the second summer after it started. He had come from Boston with a group of 21 students from Park Street church led by Bruce and Christy Graham, also now working with us. Brad recognized that without those early SIIS students, we would have no staff at the Center. Almost all were SIIS alumni.

"Dad," he said when he heard the news, "we came out okay with the 25 students we had here in January. Don't you think we can run the SIIS here? Anyhow, a lot of the professors we use come from this area. If we hold it here, we won't have to pay their travel expenses."

"Who would organize and run it?" Ralph asked. "I

131

certainly don't have the time!"

The situation was far from ideal. Bruce and Christy, who had helped out in Wheaton in earlier years, had run our January course. But now they were in India, planning a follow-up program which would give IIS [1] alumni a brief overseas exposure.

"You know, Brad," Ralph cautioned, "the one in charge has to have taken the course himself. With Bruce and Christy gone, that doesn't give us much choice. With so little staff, the personnel work you and Beth are doing is very critical right now. Do you think maybe Beth could handle the personnel office by herself so you could run the SIIS?"

More work! Right when we faced a major financial crisis!

Worse, some of those who had registered for SIIS when it was scheduled for Colorado decided to drop out. We were left with only five. "You'll have to get at least 20 more before classes can start," Ralph warned.

Like the crew of a becalmed vessel caught in the doldrums of a motionless sea, we had watched helplessly as the days and weeks came and went, wondering how God could possibly deliver us from all our problems. But, paradoxically, the almost impossible challenge to rescue the SIIS course served as a wind to fill our sails. God had called us to serve, not to save ourselves. Our duty was to obey faithfully. The results were His responsibility.

Our young staff swung into motion, arriving at 6 a.m. to call SIIS alumni whom they knew all over the country. They asked them for names and phone numbers of other students who might be interested in taking the course, and then called those. Incredibly, within three weeks they had recruited another 25 students.

With the students came the need for a dormitory, a cafeteria, and a classroom—all in existence across the street, but inaccessible to us for three more months. In the meantime we had to make do and pray that, by fall, God would send us more students (or agencies) to help fill the campus which would be ours if, indeed, God did work another miracle.

I had always thought that when Jesus told us to "seek first the kingdom of God and His righteousness," He was speaking of our need to seek salvation. And I am sure that in one sense He was. Now, however, I believe this verse refers far more to our priorities as Christians. If we will put His concerns first—if we will seek to advance and spread His kingdom, even if it means possibly jeopardizing a work to which He has called us—He promises to give us "these other things" as well: food and clothing, and all the other things for which we need money.

The seminars, the book, the historical chart, the concordance, the IIS study program, the talks Ralph gave all over the world—all these were done to advance His kingdom. In the time of our greatest financial need we had very little time to raise money. Would God really provide the funds we needed?

It was His promise; thus He had pledged Himself. We would rest on that.

---

1. I have used the terms *SIIS* and *IIS* somewhat interchangeably. The original organization was the Summer Institute of International Studies (SIIS), which operated only in the summer. In January 1978, however, we began on our campus an "interterm" one-month program which eventually led into programs running all year round in extension centers throughout the U.S. as well as on our campus. When the SIIS, under other leadership, decided to shut down, we continued the program, dropping the word "summer." It is now (in 1986) better known by its main course, "Perspectives on the World Christian Movement," and operates in 64 extension centers throughout the world.

27

APRIL - JULY, 1978

TEMPTATION

We felt very vulnerable. Our staff was small, our finances unsure, and our fund raising task enormous. If we were to ask for only one-time, small gifts, then indeed we would have to inspire a million people with new vision about the frontiers. How could such a limited staff ever do that? And how, especially, could we hope for enough $15 gifts to pay the $650,000 balance of our down payment by September?

Satan was well aware of our predicament, and tempted us immediately. In March, 1978 we received a letter from the Summit leadership. Their request was very simple but, under the circumstances, must have seemed humiliating to them. They wanted to know if they could rent the campus for two more years—now from us—if we successfully completed our down payment in September. They would pay us $30,000 a month, they said.

Thirty thousand dollars a month! It had been a long time since we had seen that much money. And we surely needed it! We needed a miracle by September, and after that we would face massive mortgage payments every quarter for years to come.

But the facts about Summit hadn't changed. It was still an Eastern cult. In the big auditorium across the street the big Buddha still sat, garlanded with flowers and

134

worshipped day and night. Chants still floated across the campus. Cult leaders still seduced Christian young people with their talks about Jesus and their strangely-altered music borrowed from evangelical hymn books. But their Jesus did not die on the cross. He did not shed his blood for their sins. He was not *the* Son of God but only *a* son of God—even as they themselves were becoming.

We felt that to rent to them, therefore, would be dishonoring to God. In my mind the temptation was very similar to that faced by the Israelite kings in the Old Testament. Many of them seemed to want to follow God, but for political reasons allowed the high places of idol worship to remain. Rather than displease God, therefore, we decided to keep the buildings vacant. God simply would have to provide for us in a way that was right. And we would have to trust Him to complete what He had begun, no matter how desperate things might look!

There was one additional factor. By faith, we felt sure that we would need the entire campus long before those two years were up. As the months went by, more and more mission organizations joined us in the building where we had our offices. And we constantly received other requests for space.

The letter from the cult alerted us, however, to the fact that in spite of reports to the contrary, Summit still wanted this particular campus!

The year before, just after our major victory, Mrs. Prophet announced the purchase of a beautiful piece of property, which she called Camelot. It was near UCLA, but had only three buildings, obviously inadequate for their needs. We wondered then if that purchase had been mainly a face-saving move, or if they planned to build.

The summer of 1978 was very different from the previous year. The Church Universal and Triumphant (Summit) was still just across the street from us, watching and waiting to see if we would be able to complete our down payment. We sensed that they were keenly aware of our financial struggles, as well as of the opposition we faced, even, at times, from within our own ranks. By all reports, they were ready to take over immediately, should we miss that payment. Indeed, one report said that they already had the money to buy the campus outright.

The summer before, many people in the area had responded to our need partly because of the vocal opposition by Summit. Perhaps cult leaders realized this because, in the spring of 1978, they chose to be silent. Even during their conference at Easter, they didn't challenge or harrass us. They stayed on their side of the street, and we stayed on ours.

It is true we still prayed daily for their salvation. And since they wouldn't allow us near them, as the weather allowed, we sought to witness by keeping our windows wide open while we sang songs about the blood of Jesus during our staff prayer times each morning. But we wondered at the unprecedented peace.

During this time I was working steadily on the first edition of this book. Toward the first of July the blueline arrived from the printer for me to check before the presses would roll. I sat in the downstairs lobby working on it and at the same time acting as receptionist.

The activity across the street, as well as what I read, reminded me of all the Lord had brought us through. It was once again the time of the largest conference of the year for the cult, and the campus was full. This time, however, no one came near us. No one except Ari.

Over the previous several months, several of our staff had been drawn into conversation with this blond, curly haired young fellow. He claimed to be Jewish, but said he had been involved at some time or other with the Moonies. And now he was a devoted member of Summit.

I was a bit annoyed the day he walked into the lobby and interrupted me in my work. "Why are you against us? We believe in Jesus, just like you do," he began.

With a wrench, my mind came back from the

intricacies of editing, and I prayed inwardly for wisdom and grace.

"It is not enough to believe in Jesus. You must also obey Him," I said.

"Oh, we do that," he answered casually.

"No, you don't. The Bible says you are not to go to mediums, nor to speak with people now dead. And Mrs. Prophet does that all the time."

I pointed out to him the story of Saul's visit to the witch of Endor, and God's rejection of him as king because of it. "It's all in your Hebrew Bible, I said. Go home and read it."

Three times he made a trip across the street to get an answer for one of my comments. Three times he recognized how inadequate those answers were.

By then others had joined me in the lobby, and one suggested that he allow us to pray for him.

"Sure, why not?" The answer was too flippant.

When we started to pray, immediately he began to call upon Buddha, Krishna, St. Germain, and Kali. Even Kali—the Hindu goddess of murder!

"Stop!" I commanded. "That is blasphemy! You are *not* interested in the truth. Your mind is closed. And we will not pray for you when you are like this. Now go and don't come back!"

I was surprised at my own words; I had never done anything like that before.

"Can't I come again?" he almost whined.

"Not until you are ready to search for the truth. It will do no good unless you really want to find the true God! When that time comes, we'll be glad to help you."

That was our last personal encounter with the cult, but only the beginning of years of testing which the Lord would put us through. To believe that He would provide was not easy when the money wasn't coming in. To endure when accused, betrayed, and deserted was even harder. It was the same story of the journey in the wilderness

137

which Moses and his people went through. I so much
wanted to avoid that.

But God saw we needed the wilderness too.

28

SUMMER 1978

"WHAT DO YOU HOLD IN YOUR HAND?"

(Exodus 4:2)

What do you hold in your hand today?
To whom or to what are you bound?
Are you willing to give it to God right now?
Give it up, let it go, throw it down!

Through blinded eyes I searched frantically in my purse for a handkerchief and ended up embarrassedly catching my tears with the back of my hand. High up front on the platform, Pat Taylor was singing *Moses*, a sermon in song written by the blind composer, Ken Medema.

It was June, 1978—a little less than two years from the time we had embarked alone on this great adventure. As I listened, I relived with Moses that helpless sense of loneliness in a job that was just too great. And with Moses, I again dedicated the little we had in our hands to His use, for His purposes, for Him to somehow multiply to fit that awesome need.

For a long time I had been trying to write the story of the early days of the U.S. Center for World Mission. I felt very inadequate for the job, having published nothing but one article. But because there was no one else to do it, no one else who had been with us from the very beginning of the project, the task was left to me.

So I had turned my "rod"—my pen—over to God, asking that somehow I would be able to tell the wonders He had done in our midst and thereby, hopefully, bring glory to His name. In writing, I had again walked in memory around the campus, climbed the heights of victory and wept in the valleys of despair.

By June 1978, the book was almost done, but the memories were still fresh. And listening to Pat sing, I felt related to Moses in a new, painful, yet joyous way. We too had stood on holy ground. We too had heard the "voice" speaking to us. We too had turned over our own inadequacies to God and had seen Him use them to work His miracles.

The book returned from the printer barely six weeks before our $650,000 was due. At that date we had only $30,000 toward that payment. But we had repaid the loans we owed, helped greatly by Campus Crusade, which had made $80,000 of their loan a gift.

When the book arrived, we sent copies out across the country almost immediately, first laying hands on them and praying that God would use them. So much depended on them. They were the only detailed explanation of our hopes and dreams.

"Is it too long?" I fretted. "Will people bother to read it? Why didn't I finish it sooner? There is so little time before our payment is due. Oh, dear God! Please use it!" In spite of the fact that I was a first-time author, I had several hopes for that book. I hoped that as people read it, God would touch their hearts and they would respond to our need. I prayed that those struggling with faith would, through our story, be reassured that their heavenly Father always provides for His children who dare to trust Him. And I prayed that maybe, somewhere, someone far from the Lord—perhaps even one of the cult members across the street—would pick up my book and be attracted to the Christ of whom it spoke and come to know Him. I well knew what a flimsy tool it was. Yet I had done my best. God would have to make it adequate for His purposes.

We had another tool, equally unlikely, equally flimsy. It was our "grapevine" letter.

Ever since adopting the one-time, small gift plan, we had known that our biggest problem would be getting in touch with a million people. We knew our approach was too unorthodox for most people. In fact, we were a bit embarrassed when one of our friends reported that at a conference of professional Christian fund raisers, our small, one-time gift approach was used as the classic example of "how *not* to do it." Humbling!

We never claimed that our way was the only way, nor even the best. We merely felt that it was God's way for *us at that time*. More important than getting the money we needed was for us to inspire hope and spread vision. We would not be satisfied until American Christians by the hundreds of thousands responded to the challenge of the final frontiers.

"How can fifteen people ever reach a million?" Ralph wondered. "Somehow we must depend on the good will of others all across the country to help us. But how?"

We did a lot of praying and thinking before Bob Coleman suggested a pass-on-able letter—the "grapevine" letter. We knew that it had to be short and readable, yet say enough to give confidence and motivate its readers to make an immediate response. We also reasoned that it had to be printed in black ink so that friends at a distance could photocopy it on their own and send it to other friends. And, it had to allow space for a personal note at the top

In July, Ralph was invited to speak to a large gathering of the evangelical wing of the Yearly Meeting of Friends. They were meeting in Denver, and I was invited to go along. We took with us a few boxes of my book, plus a stack of the newly-printed grapevine letters.

141

It was very warm in the gymnasium where they met. But our hearts rejoiced when we found so many of these wonderful people eager to help us. It couldn't have been more than a week or two later before the mail started flowing in from Oregon. Each letter had a check for $15.95. (Our instructions had suggested a gift of $15 plus an additional $.95 to cover the costs of mailing back a copy of my book, the *Hidden Peoples* pie chart, and a six-month subscription to our monthly bulletin, *Mission Frontiers*.)

We must have received at least a thousand letters from Oregon alone. The superintendent of the Northwest Meeting of Friends, we found out later, had printed enough copies of the grapevine letter for all the members of every congregation in his district. What wonderful people! How we thanked the Lord for them!

About the same time, Dr. Donald McGavran, perhaps the foremost missionary strategist in the world today and a dear friend of ours, at his own expense, sent out a letter similar to ours. This one asked missionary subscribers to the *Church Growth Bulletin*, which he edited, to request each of their prayer supporters to send the Center $15.95.

This request was so unusual that one lady, who regularly sent out the prayer letter of a Worldwide Evangelization Crusade missionary, decided she should check us out. She lived just a few miles away but had never heard of the U. S. Center for World Mission. And, she later admitted, she was frankly a bit annoyed at Dr. McGavran's suggestion.

When she visited us, she wasn't one bit impressed . . . at first. Our building was unpretentious, and the furnishings old and a bit shabby. Our receptionist seemed very young. Tricia, our youngest daughter, was newly graduated from high school and, as the receptionist, was alone in the front lobby.

Tricia started to talk with her. She showed her our literature, explained our purposes, spoke of our dreams, and asked for her prayers. I crossed the lobby just as Tricia thrust my book into our visitor's hands, saying, "Oh, before you read the other literature, you ought to read this book. It explains us better than anything else."

The next morning, in the middle of our staff prayer time, Tricia was called to the phone. She returned beaming. "That was Mary," she said. "You know, the lady that was asking all those questions yesterday?

"Well, guess what! She's already called the headquarters of Worldwide Evangelization Crusade. They told her she could send a letter to more than just this one missionary's supporters. They're sending her a large list today. And she will personally pay the postage if we will do the mailing. She's on her way right now with a draft of her letter and a $500 check!"

Some of the missionaries who received Dr. McGavran's letter complained that we asked too little. "God is not honored when there is no sacrifice," they observed, and backed up their words with $1000 checks. Many other checks also poured in, no doubt the result of Mary's generosity and WEC's.

God also gave us another tool—a film called *Penetrating the Last Frontiers*. It was narrated by Pat Boone and explained our vision beautifully! That film, too, ,was a miracle. It had been conceived by three business friends in Oregon and produced almost without any effort on our part. They hired a professional to write the script and another to film it, but were at a loss for someone to narrate it. Once more Pat Boone came to our aid. He had only ten days between trips, but he volunteered a number of hours to help us with the film.

Several copies were made and shown all over the country. The first showing was only a month before September 1st at a Nazarene church close to the campus. As before, the cult sent a contingent of six or eight of their top staff. I worried that they would publicly object to what we had said about them, and prayed hard as I watched. Aside from a few mechanical difficulties, however, all went well, and we praised the Lord.

A film, a grapevine letter, a book: as fund raising tools, they weren't much. But God blessed them, and hundreds of people used them to help us.

Ralph's father, 83 years old at that time, took three copies of the book to the retirement center where he lived and circulated them, asking every three days if the person "borrowing" his copy was through. "They can't just put the book down and forget about it if it's borrowed," he told us with a smile. Every week he brought in another stack of checks from his friends.

Mission Aviation Fellowship, Bill Bright of Campus Crusade, Jack Hayford of Church on the Way, World Opportunities, Young Life—they all lent a hand to help us make the payment. Some sent out our grapevine letters. Bill Bright and Jack Hayford gave out thousands of copies of my book and asked those reading it to send us $16 or to mail out grapevine letters. Hundreds responded.

Many churches quickly booked the film to show in Sunday school classes, prayer meetings, Bible studies, evening services, and even some morning services. Some sent in offerings they had collected. Others urged their members to each send us $15.95, immediately.

Those on staff were as busy as ever. Yet in a strange way, it was as if we were standing still, watching while God worked. What we had to use had seemed so inadequate, so flimsy by fund raisers' standards. Yet they were our only "rods," and we had committed them to God.

I remember thinking that if He could part the Red Sea with a shepherd's crook, if He could kill a giant with a boy's slingshot and a pebble, if He could feed 5,000 with five loaves and two fish—then wasn't it just possible that in His hands what we had would be enough? We could only trust and pray.

144

29

"FOR THE HONOR OF HIS NAME"

(Eze. 38:23, 39:7)

Even in the face of the onrushing $650,000 deadline on September 1st, our spirits were considerably strengthened by an important event: the end of Summit's lease on the campus. Starting the last week in July, we watched truck after truck load up, then pull away from the other side of the street. It took nearly two months for the cult to move out completely, and the buildings they left behind had to be thoroughly cleaned, both physically and spiritually.

As so many times before in the previous two years, we claimed Christ's victory through His shed blood on Calvary, and commanded the evil spirits to depart. If we hadn't personally experienced so much spiritual warfare, we would have scoffed at ourselves for doing what could seem like a superstitious ritual. But we knew only too well it was not. Even to come near certain rooms gave one a very eerie feeling, and it wasn't until some time later that we learned those were the rooms which Mrs. Prophet had occupied when she stayed overnight in the dorm.

When September 1st arrived, it seemed to be an ordinary day filled with the rush of work and prayer.

145

Though we had done our very best, time had run out. If God truly wanted us to have this campus, He would simply have to provide.

With so much at stake, it was hard not to be distracted, but except for those in the accounting and administration offices, we continued in our day-to-day tasks, pausing every now and then to get the new tally which Ralph and our accountant kept current as the gifts came in.

For the past five days, a farmer in Canada had been calling each day to see whether we would come close. He said his wife had read the *Jericho* book and had insisted that he do the same. He had just finished it when he first called and wanted to know how we were doing.

"How much money do you lack?" he asked.

The first day he called, the answer was $190,000. The next day it was $150,000, etc.

Looking back, I don't really know how God put it all together. I remember that on the final morning we still lacked just over $50,000, and were driven to earnest prayer. "In a pinch we can run around and borrow that much," Ralph told our Canadian friend when he called. "I think we'll be okay!"

But the man insisted, "How much should I wire you?"

How do you answer a question like that when you don't know the resources available? Anyway, it was up to God to tell him.

"Let's just say," Ralph answered, "that a small *gift* is better right now than a loan. And don't pay the cost of wiring. We'll cover somehow until it gets here!"

"All right. I'll be sending you . . ." But the words were muffled, and Ralph was reluctant to ask him to repeat it.

"What did he say?" Ralph asked himself when he got off the phone. "Was it $1600 or $16,000?" We didn't find out for several days, then praised the Lord when it turned out to be the larger of the two. God knew how much we needed it!

It was wonderful to watch God work that day . . . people walking in asking if they were too late, but would we please take their money anyway? Phone calls, telegrams of money. . .

Once again we had a frustrating delay with a bank in San Francisco that wouldn't release to us the money that had been deposited there to be transferred to Pasadena for our use. The branch bank had held it for a number of days, and nothing we did seemed sufficient to get it released. It was a large sum, and we desperately needed it.

About that time a Nazarene realtor who had come weekly to our prayer council, learned of our problem and talked to the bank in San Francisco. She identified herself and warned the lady responsible that it was illegal to hold money so long in branch bank. "If you do not release that money immediately, I am going to report your conduct to _____," and she named the president of the home office, which happened to be in Los Angeles. Within two hours, just in time, those funds were in our hands. Again, just before the bank closed at 3 p.m., we had the money we needed, the $650,000 to complete our down payment!

Strangely, I didn't feel like jumping up and down. I was glad, deeply glad, inside. Yet I felt that it was God's honor that was at stake, not ours. We had come onto the campus in response to His call, to do His work in obedience to His last great command. Unexpectedly, there we had run into conflict with a religious group which was diametrically opposed to everything we believed and thought. In the names of their own personal "godhood" within, they had determined to make this place a missionary center to spread their philosophy of self-realization.

We, in turn, had claimed the property in the name of the historical Jesus of Calvary in order to make it a missionary center from which His ambassadors would go to the ends of the earth, proclaiming, "There is no other name under heaven whereby men can be saved except the name of Jesus!" (Acts 4:12)

Now, more than ever, we realized that God intended to receive honor in this place. He was not interested in our merely acquiring a piece of property. The campus was of value only as we would bring honor and glory to Him through how we lived and what we did.

The road ahead, however, was long and rough. Instead of sprinting to a close goal, we still had the wilderness to face with its temptations, trials, misunderstandings and hurts. It could not be crossed in a day, nor in a month, nor in a year.

30

WINTER 1979

"FIRST FORGIVE"

(Mark 11:25)

We were over the Jordan—or was it just the Red Sea? The cult was gone. The campus was ours—at least, that is, in name! Stretching before us, however, were five years of mortgage payments—$175,000 due every three months—followed by a balloon payment of many millions. After our financial struggles of the previous year, I dreaded even these smaller payments. But God had so obviously led thus far, He would have to see us through.

Up until then we could have backed out without much financial loss. After completing our down payment, however, we were legally and financially committed. To pull back then would mean we would lose most of the $1.5 million we had already paid. We were, therefore, very much like the Children of Israel on the other side of the Red Sea: there was no way to go but forward.

In the two years we had reluctantly shared the campus with the cult, we had been very aware that we were involved in spiritual warfare—from without. Once they were gone, however, and we could see the way forward, Satan attacked in new but equally vicious ways. This time it was from within. Almost before we were aware of what was going on, the harmony and peace of our little team was destroyed, and we almost went under as an organization.

Basically, it had to do with who was really in charge. Typically, when a new organization starts, those who follow are excited and challenged by the vision of the leader. But the very characteristics which make him a leader, especially his willingness to risk, often make those in authority under (or over) him nervous. Before long, convinced that he is making a terrible mistake about something, they may begin to pull back, make demands and eventually pit themselves in direct opposition to him. Sometimes without even realizing it, their actions jeopardize the very vision which attracted them in the first place.

As in every time of trouble, the Bible was a tremendous comfort to us in this time of stress. We appreciated especially the great detail to which it goes when discussing situations similar to ours. Over and over Ralph read the struggles Paul had with some of the leaders in the churches to which he wrote. It was obvious that Paul was very pained and embarrassed to have to defend his God-given authority over them, but he felt that the future of the church depended upon his doing so. (See chapters 8 to 13 of II Corinthians.)

As Ralph's wife, who all too readily (and unwisely) took on his hurts as my own, I urged him to assert his authority as Paul had. But to confront was extremely difficult for Ralph. He much preferred to "turn the other cheek" by waiting patiently to see if, with time, things wouldn't work out on their own.

I could see the storm clouds gathering, and fretted that Ralph didn't "*do* something." Meanwhile, I began again to read about non-confrontive Moses.

I felt so sorry for Moses! In Egypt, the Children of Israel saw their enemy as Pharaoh. Once safely over the Red Sea, however, they forgot the cruelties of the past. Now they remembered only the pleasant things they had left behind, and compared their present hardships with those. And they turned on long-suffering, patient Moses. *He* was now their enemy! Every little problem was *his* fault. Instead of trying to help him find solutions, they grumbled and complained until his patience was tried to its limits. They forgot the marvelous victories through which he had led them, and even talked of stoning him on more than one occasion. Amazingly, all too often those responsible were leaders he himself had appointed! (See Numbers 12 and 16.)

Sometimes even Moses couldn't take it. In Numbers 11:11-15 (LB) he complained bitterly to the Lord: "Why pick on me? . . . The load is far too heavy! If you are going to treat me like this, please kill me right now; it will be a kindness! Let me out of this impossible situation!"

Curious, I thought I'd check to see if other leaders in history had gone through similar experiences, and I was amazed. Not one, it seemed, was exempt. All experienced battles from within their little group, challenges to their leadership which almost overwhelmed them in intensity. Often these occurred right after tremendous victories!

William Carey and his fellow missionaries, Marshman and Ward, made up the famous "Serampore Trio" in Northeastern India. They lived and worked harmoniously together from their earliest days there until they died. Over the years, the Lord crowned their work with tremendous success, and they came to be recognized, even by secular authorities, as gifted, capable men.

After twenty-some years, however, back home in London the members of the original board which had sent them had all died. In their place were several well-meaning, godly younger men, who, nevertheless, were all strangers to the veteran missionaries and to their work.

Without consulting those on the field, as had been the pattern, at a very inopportune time, the new board sent out two new missionaries who were unable to pass the British government's requirements for residence and had to return home. Disgruntled, they blamed Marshman, and so sullied his name that the new board peremptorily fired him.

Asserting further authority, the board demanded control of all the properties in India even though they had been bought with personal funds earned by the Serampore Trio in the absence of salaries from home. They also announced that from then on all decisions would be made from the home office. No longer would those on the field have any say in recruitment or field policies.

Carey was appalled, but powerless. Marshman was like a brother, and his closest fellow worker. How could he dismiss him when he was innocent of all wrong? He remonstrated with the board, which refused to yield, and the mission split. Compounding his personal distress, Carey's own nephew, newly arrived, was one of the ringleaders of the opposing group, who established another station just ten miles away.

For ten years Carey, Marshman and Ward agonized over what to do, then finally, for the sake of harmony, yielded all rights, at enormous personal cost. The rift was healed in the surrender of all the property demanded, even the house which Carey, Marshman and Ward had bought and had lived in together all those years. Nevertheless, the agony of the dissention never quite left Carey for the rest of his life.[1]

Hudson Taylor was another. When he started the China Inland Mission, the recruits who sailed with him and his family seemed a real answer to prayer. Nevertheless, before they even got to China, the first symptoms of trouble appeared. Three people in particular decided that they really didn't have to follow Taylor's lead. Within a year they had split the mission, produced misunderstanding with other missions in China, and caused such resentment on the part of the Chinese that the work of the entire mission was threatened, almost before it started. Again, the pain all this caused Taylor was almost more than he could bear.[2]

When our own situation came to a crisis, we were equally perplexed and hurt. Even more difficult to heal was the turmoil on our staff. Before peace could be restored, even partially, the staff spent long hours, on several occasions, in repentance and prayer.

Though Ralph was deeply hurt, I was amazed at how readily he forgave. "They just don't understand," he would tell me. Or, "They honestly think it would be better their way." But I saw what had happened as a direct challenge to his authority, an attempt to force things their way. And while Ralph forgave, without really realizing what I was doing, I assumed his hurts as my own, and as a consequence struggled with forgiving.

All my life I have tried to keep "short accounts" with others. But this time I really struggled, wanting with all my heart to forgive—knowing that according to the Bible I had to—and yet feeling a tremendous barrier between myself and those who had caused us pain. It was easy to put my arms around the ones who said, "I am so sorry." But try as I would, I found it terribly difficult even to greet those who had told Ralph that, given the chance, they would do it again. With all my *will*, I forgave. But my *feelings* did not seem to recognize that. I longed for the sense of perfect harmony; still the hurt persisted.

Over and over I examined the Biblical passages on forgiving. I read what others wrote on the subject. I forced myself to be friendly. And in despair, when in honesty I still recognized the barrier, I questioned: "Did Jesus forgive the unrepentant Pharisees? How could He have when he spoke such condemnatory words against them?" Yet I had to recognize that his harsh words were not because of the way they treated Him but because of the stumbling block they were to others. Did Jesus excuse us from forgiving those who were unrepentant? Or, can we truly forgive and yet feel deep pain and alienation?

I envied Ralph for his ability to say, "Just think how

much the Lord has blessed us! Our family is all healthy. Our children all love the Lord dearly and are working with us. We have two wonderful sons-in-law. (Only two daughters were married then.) How many other people do you know who have fewer problems than we have?" Out of strong conviction, Ralph refused to judge their motives. I, by contrast, felt that if he had not so determinedly closed his eyes to what was happening, things would not have come to that impasse in the first place. Yet he had peace; I did not!

In fear and trepidation, I went several times to the one I blamed most, seeking reconciliation. Because I felt we were the ones wronged, however, I found it hard to say "Will you forgive me?" For what? For being terribly hurt? For resenting the pain? With all my will, I forgave him, and told him so. "Yet," I thought, "how much easier it would be to *feel* I had forgiven him if he would just ask Ralph's forgiveness."

Day after day I prayed, "Oh God, take this bitterness from my heart somehow. Show me what to do. I have done my best; you know I have. Now do a miracle in me. You will just have to do the forgiving for me, through me. I give you my permission. Indeed, I beg you!"

Little by little, He began to show me what I could do. First, He told me to pray for those who had caused us so much anguish. All right! I could do that! I could even pray that God would bless them and fill them with His love.

Then in a very excruciating process, God began showing me that down through the years I hadn't actually been so expert at forgiving as I had thought. He showed me how many offenses I still harbored—usually offenses which were really not mine in the first place, offenses against my husband which I, in my "more discerning," (less forgiving!) spirit, had decided to make my own. (Wasn't I simply being the loyal wife?) Unfortunately, I didn't realize then that our Lord does not promise grace to cover "borrowed" offense!   But He showed me how He had been trying to get this message through to me for years, but I would only learn so much.   "That is why I keep bringing it back," He said, as I wept.

He showed me how "prickly" I could be sometimes— how unwilling to give up "my rights," even though He (how could it possibly be?) was the One who was asking me to. And one by one I went over those past hurts and forgave, as best I could, each unkind word spoken about Ralph, or to him, as well as those to me.

I began to realize that by championing my husband's cause through taking on his offenses, I wasn't really helping him. I was only hurting myself. Also, gently, the Lord began to show me how that by so doing I might actually be doing Ralph harm. Did I really want him to struggle with bitterness, like I did? And I began, once again, to yield up "my rights," chief among them the right to feel bruised for Ralph's sake. God could take care of Ralph. In that simple act I found peace again. The bitterness against which I had struggled was gone.

I have often pondered about forgiveness. I know that without repentance of the wrong done, the happy relationship cannot be restored. (See I John 1:6-7.) But it is possible, even necessary, to forgive even if there is no repentance, even if the relationship is never restored. A mother does this all the time with a rebeliious child. But even as she forgives, she waits longingly for the child to repent. She knows instinctively that even though she forgives that child, until that child repents of its wrong, it is impossible for her to shower on her child the same kind of happy love she so wants to give. No matter what, there is an undercurrent of pain, a disruption of fellowship, until repentance is complete.

Probably the most important lesson for me, however, was one which it took even yet more time to fully understand: *that to bear another's burdens does not mean I also take on his grievances*. Since then I've recognized how those who feel they have the gift of mercy often take on the offenses of others, thinking this is a godly thing to do. But in so doing, they become bitter, angry, resentful, and a source of disunity to the whole community. In the end, God cannot use them until they release to Him this offense that should not have been theirs in the first place.

I do not mean to say by this that I should be insensitive to wrongs, nor less discerning. Nor should I be less loyal to my husband. What I am trying to say is that even though hurts are sure to come, I must look at them in a different way. My part is to keep my heart pure and my hands clean by forgiving, by praying for the unrepentant, by refusing to take on the offenses of others (no matter how much I love them and hurt when they hurt), by confronting where necessary, in the spirit of meekness, and if I cannot do that, to pray.

I do not know why learning to forgive, even when it is unrequested and, perhaps, undeserved, is so essential to the development of our Christian character. But there is something in the process which teaches us humility and breaks our pride. It is not easy. We do not learn the lesson once and for all. When we think we have perfected this skill, then, suddenly, some other occasion arises when once again we must call on God's grace to help us forgive.

The alternative is to live with bitterness and to become hard, unloving, and eventually unloved. Jesus promised to be with us, even in this difficult lesson. He has grace that is sufficient to help us, even though our own resources are inadequate. He is making us like Himself, willing to take abuse and scorn, and to take them meekly and with patience.

One would hope that by middle age, forgiving would not be hard to do. Or better yet, nothing would ever happen that would require forgiveness.

Unfortunately, life is not like that. To live, at least as unto the Lord, is to forgive and forgive and forgive, "seventy times seven," as Jesus said.

But the One who gives us the grace is the one who from the cross looked on those who were mocking him, laughing that He considered Himself the Messiah. In the agony of death, bearing the terrible oppressive guilt for the sins of all mankind, to right then forgive those who scoffed at Him for claiming to be what He really was must have been hard. He it is who gives us grace when we find forgiving difficult. He it is who gently, but firmly, prods until we do.

O Lord, because You have forgiven us so much, we also forgive.

---

1. See pp. 162-195 of Mary Drewery's *William Carey, A Biography*, (Grand Rapids: Zondervan, 1978).

2. See pp. 262ff of Vol. 3 of A. J. Broomhall's *Hudson Taylor and China's Open Century: Survivor's Pact* (Robesonia, PA: The Overseas Missionary Fellowship).

31

"STUDY TO SHOW THYSELF APPROVED"

(2 Timothy 2:15)

"Are you crazy? To have a university you must have thousands of students and hundreds of courses! And a $100 million!"

Ralph sighed and patiently answered, "No, that's not true. What determines whether or not a school is to be called a university is if it is authorized to give Ph.D. degrees."

"As to the number of courses and different departments, haven't you ever heard of Dropsie University? It is one of the most prestigious universities in the world in the field of Hebrew Studies. But it has only one building and a handful of students. It is a specialized university, as we plan to be."

The shock some of our friends expressed is still clear in my mind eight years later. Those who knew him best couldn't easily have expected Ralph to be conventional. But perhaps they didn't realize that he had more than the usual amount of experience in designing educational programs.[1]

Typical of an engineer, when Ralph recognized a problem, he first looked at what the desired end product should be, then worked on how to reach it. Universities are constantly having to rethink their courses in order to satisfy the demands of society. They have to produce engineers, teachers, doctors, computer scientists, etc. If the courses are too far off, industry refuses to hire their graduates.

Most schools (even Christian colleges) are essentially oblivious of the needs of the mission world. They haven't really stopped to ask what kind of product the mission societies need. But this question was uppermost in Ralph's mind when he set out to design the William Carey International University.

Several streams led into Ralph's thinking:

During his ten years of teaching at Fuller Seminary, over 1,000 missionaries went through his classes, contributing quality research. Right there he recognized the economic significance of students paying for the supervision they receive while pursuing advanced degrees. Their tuition fees become income, not expense, to the school, and a positive benefit to the agencies involved.

Then, Ralph's experience with Theological Education by Extension convinced him that an on-campus program often does not enroll the most capable students. Real leaders are usually too responsibly involved to take off several years to get a Ph.D. If the object of a school is to facilitate advanced degrees for "movers and shakers," then the extension pattern must be considered.

For years Ralph had noticed how clumsy and even destructive the traditional Ph.D. educational pattern was for missionaries. The year they are allowed for furlough is inadequate to complete the degree. Yet if they take a leave of absence for a year or two in order to finish, they have to find some other means of support and their work on the field is drastically interrupted.

"Why can't we take advantage of the fact that there are missionaries with Ph.D.s in almost every major city of the world today? A Ph.D. is basically a one-on-one tutorial situation anyhow. Why can't these Ph.D.s overseas serve as graduate mentors for candidates who live and work in their areas?" Ralph wanted to know.

He saw other serious problems on the undergraduate level. It was the rare college that had any courses at all on missions. It was a miracle, really, that any students ever ended up as missionaries. Often, after speaking, Ralph would be engaged in conversation by some student who eagerly announced, "I feel the Lord is calling me into missions!"

"That's just wonderful," he would answer. "With what mission are you going?"

"Well, I don't know yet. You see, I am graduating in June, and before I can go overseas I will have to pay back $8000 (or $15,000 . . . or $30,000) in student loans."

It was hard for Ralph not to say what was on his mind: "Forget it. You'll never make it! When you took out those loans, right then you decided not ever to become a missionary!"

Instead he advised, "Yes, you'll have to pay back those loans first. No agency will even look at you with a debt like that." But he always wondered if any of these would still want to go into missions once they were solidly ensconced in well-paying jobs, married (perhaps to spouses who were not interested), buying their homes —essentially getting settled. They would be gaining gratifying skills, security and seniority, but drifting further from their original call.

Increasingly Ralph realized that, without intending to, Christian colleges were keeping young people from becoming missionaries simply because, like every private school, they encouraged their students to take out loans to complete their education. But the typical missionary salary is basically a "living allowance." It is not intended to be sufficient to repay huge student debts.

From its founding, Ralph planned that the William Carey International University would always be on the edge of innovation. His avowed intent was that it would not duplicate existing programs elsewhere but would develop programs other schools were not pursuing, at the same time maintaining high traditional academic standards. Ralph hoped that in meeting the felt needs of the mission industry, our university would also set a pattern that Christian colleges could follow.

Early in 1978 we gained permission from the State of California to grant a Ph.D. degree in International Development with concentrations in the fields of Hindu, Chinese, Muslim, and Tribal Studies, Communications, and Religious Studies. Actually a Ph.D. in International Development could specialize in any problem a developing country might face.

We also were given permission to give an M.A. in International Development (with its various special fields) and also in Teaching English to Speakers of Other Languages (TESOL).

It was this latter program which developed the most quickly. The University was founded in 1977, before China once more welcomed visitors from the West. In our earliest promotional film that year, Ralph had prophetically asked, "Should the day ever come when China opens her doors and asks for, say, 50,000 teachers of English, would the Christian world be ready?"

Just two years later China opened her doors wide. One of her first requests was for 100,000 teachers of English! And we found, to our amazement, that not a single U.S. Christian college or university offered a master's degree in Teaching English to Speakers of Other Languages (TESOL).

Our program was already two years old, under the capable hands of people with field experience. We found to our surprise that we had almost as many students in this program as the University of California at Los Angeles, which boasted the largest in the U.S.—only fifty students.

In 1981 Dr. Herbert Purnell, a linguist and former missionary, came to head up our program. With a Ph.D.

from Cornell University, he was a rigorous academician. As a result, our students involved in practice teaching so impressed their master teachers throughout the Los Angeles area that some of these inquired about the possibility of taking some of our courses. And we were very pleased when, in 1982, the TESOL program not only received the "approval status" from the state of California, but was also highly commended by the examining committee. This status took the university a long way toward the private type of regional accreditation.

In 1980, Dr. James Buswell from Wheaton College became our Dean of Graduate Studies. Then in 1981, Dr. Virgil Olson, newly retired, came for a few years to help us out as President and, fortunately, stayed five. Both men were highly qualified in the academic world, but both also were deeply involved in missions.

Then Dr. Bob Pickett, formerly of Purdue University and for three years a consultant to World Vision, Inc., became the head of our Department of International Development. In no time he developed a periodicals library in his field that was so complete that students from surrounding colleges and universities began finding their way to our campus to use it.

Soon Dr. Buswell was in touch with dozens of missionaries and national church leaders who were interested in our doctoral program. Because most of these were very busy people, we expected them to take longer than the usual three to five years to get their degrees. Seven years later, the first was already graduated.

It is a blessing to the university to have various specialty organizations on campus. International Films, for example, teaches graduate courses on film production and communication. The Zwemer Institute offers several relating to the Muslim world. The Institute of Chinese Studies teaches Mandarin and several other courses. The Institute of Hindu Studies has a remarkable summer program. FACE (Fellowship of Artists for Cultural Evangelism)

162

Ralph and Roberta Winter
Founder and General Director, U. S. Center for World Mission

Art and Elaine McCleary
General Manager, USCWM & WCIU

Dr. James O. Buswell III, Dean of Graduate Studies and Greg Livingstone, President of the Board of Directors of the William Carey International University

Director's Advisory Council
Darrell Dorr, USCWM Coordinator; Bruce Graham, Assoc. Director for Fnance; Wesley Tullis, Chairman, Mobilization Division; BobColeman, Associate Director for Planning; Dr. and Mrs. Winter; Art McCleary, General Manager

You don't send out missionaries?

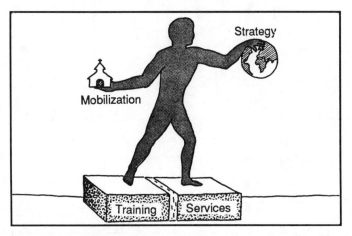

People ask us what 300 full time workers here actually DO each day. They speak 40 different languages, come with experience in 60 different countries, and with backgrounds in 70 different mission agencies. We have a lot of ordinary people, too, who don't have such exotic credentials. Lot's of eager, committed young people, and a powerful treasure of senior citizens (we are short on people in between!).

Basically, every person here, including all separate offices (involving 42 different corporations), function in one or more of FOUR DIMENSIONS, which we call "Divisions."

STRATEGY: Reaching out the the ends of the earth to help clarify the task is our Division of Mission Strategy.

MOBILIZATION: Reaching back to the U.S. churches to mobilize individuals, congregations, student groups is our Division of Mission Mobilization.

TRAINING: a support division, the Division of Mission Training, helps people find training opportunities—the Perspectives course (taught all over the country), and our own university which offers highly unique undergraduate and graduate training all over the world, geared in with the mission enterprise.

SERVICES: this final division covers everything else, library, publishing, computer services, the Global Mapping Project, for example, or International Films, Frontier Media, typesetting, and on and on.

CAMPUS OF THE U. S. C. W. M.

The campus is shaded to show the properties owned by the U.S. Center for World Mission in a residential neighborhood. The Xs indicate residential rental units, where most of the staff live. In the future, many of our residential properties will be redeveloped to provide more apartments, parking, and office space. For example, the soccer field will become a 40-unit apartment building for retired missionaries who will be working here.

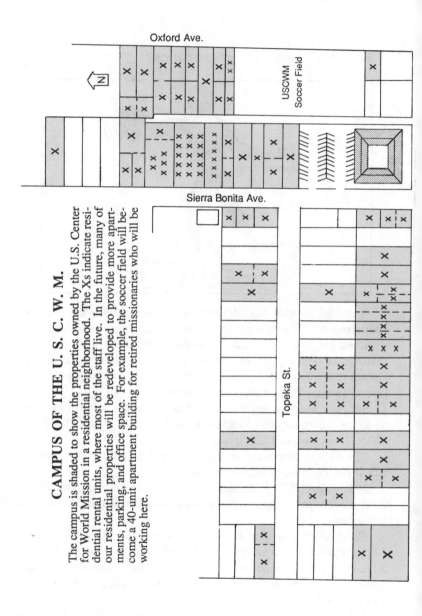

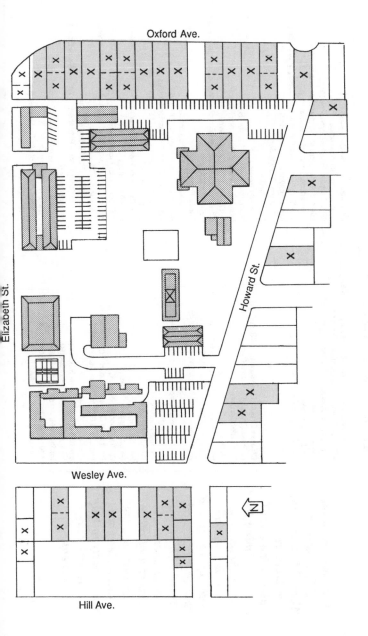

Oxford Ave.

Elizabeth St.

Howard St.

Wesley Ave.

Hill Ave.

N

AGENCIES / DEPARTMENTS OF THE USCWM COMPLEX

The ministry of the U.S. Center for World Mission is the combined result of 300 fulltime staff coming from 70 mission agencies, working both separately and together in the 57 listed offices and departments. The majority of these staff also live in houses related to the USCWM.

The ministry of the U.S. Center for World Mission is the combined result of 300 fulltime staff workers, coming from over 70 mission agencies, working both separately and together in the 57 listed offices and departments. A handful of other activities occupy available space temporarily to help us with our expenses.

Africa Inland Mission - Western Regional Office (L)
AL/TESOL (Applied Linguistics / Teaching
  English to Speakers of Other Languages (A)
Armenian Bible College (B)
Asia Agape Association (L)
Asia Evangelical Mission (L)
Bibles for All (L)
Caleb (L)
China Ministries, Inc (L)
Chinese Church Planting in LA - CBHMS (H)
Chinese Church Research Center (L)
Computer Center (H)
Dataserve(H)
East-West Center for Missions Research &
  Development - U.S. Office (L)
Episcopal Church Missionary Community
  1567 Elizabeth St.
FACE—Fellowship of Artists for Cultural
  Exchange (L)
Frontier Fellowship (L)
Frontier Media (B)
Frontiers (E)
Global Mapping Project (I)
Global Opportunities (H)
Institute of Chinese Studies (H)
Institute of Global Urban Studies (H)
Institute of Hindu Studies (H)
Institute of International Studies (B)
Institute of Japanese Studies (H)
Institute of Latin American Studies (H)
Institute of Native American Studies (H)
Institute of Tribal Studies (H)

International Films / Center for
  International Communication (I)
IFMA Frontier Peoples Committee (I)
International Journal of Frontier Missions (L)
International Theological Seminary (C)
InterVarsity Christian Fellowship S.C. Regional Office (H)
Korean International Mission (L)
Maranatha Mailing Service (F)
McGavran Library (I)
Mission Frontiers (L)
Missionary Strategy Agency (H)
Mobile Missionary Assistance Program
  1736 N. Sierra Bonita Ave.
North American Commission of Chinese Evangelicals (L)
Operation Sound (L)
Panda Prints (H)
Perspectives Study Program (B)
Pioneers-Western Regional Office (L)
Presbyterian Center for Mission Studies (L)
Presbyterian Order for World Evangelization (L)
Trinity Press (F)
U.S. Center for World Mission - Administrative Offices (L)
USCWM Strategy Division (H)
U.S. Society for Frontier Missiology (L)
William Carey International University - Administrative &
  Academic Offices (A)
WCIU Press 1705 N. Sierra Bonita
William Carey Library Publishers 1705 N. Sierra Bonita
Winter Library (I)
Youth with a Mission / Frontiers People Project
  1612 N. Hill Avenue
Zwemer Institute of Muslim Studies (E)

Staff associated with the USCWM/WCIU complex.
Some of the 300 staff who work with the agencies which are part of the U.S. Center for World Mission

Radio Spots from the Global Prayer Digest, sample listing. Write for the complete list of more than 500 stations.

(Note: times per day is the final number)

ALABAMA
Birmingham,WBYE,1370
Auburn,WFRC,88.9
Birmingham,WMBW,95.3
 +Cable
Birmingham,MBN,100.1
ALASKA
Fairbanks,KUWL,91.5
Nenana/
Fairbanks,KIAM,630
Petersburg,KRSA,580
 *Satellators
Anchor
Point,MBN,107.1
Dillingham,MBN,100.1
Homer,MBN,104.9
Juneau,MBN,93.3
Kenai/
Soldotna,MBN,97.7
Kodiak,MBN,107.1
 +Cable
Anchorage,MBN,93.3
Cordova,MBN,98.1
Kenai/
Soldotna,MBN,98.3
Kodiak,MBN,103.1
Nome,MBN,98.1
Petersburg,MBN,98.1
Valdez,MBN,98.1
Wrangell,MBN,98.1
ARKANSAS
Hot Springs,KSBC,90.1
 +Cable
Jonesboro,MBN,93.9
N. Little
Rock,MBN,99.1
ARIZONA
Lake Havasu
City,KNLB,91.1
Phoenix,KFLR,90.3
Phoenix,KHEP,1280
Tuba City/
Flagstaff,KTBA,1050
Tucson,KFLT,830

Bullhead City,KNLB,88.7
Kingman,KNLB,91.1
Yuma,KNLB,91.3
COLORADO
Denver,KWBI,91.1
Grand Junction,
KJOL,90.3
Colorado Springs,
KWBI,89.5
Delta/Montrose,
KJOL,100.9
Meeker,KJOL,91.7
Paonia/
Hotchkiss,KJOL,91.7
Rangely,KJOL,91.9
Rio Blanco/
Garfield,KJOL,89.9
Steamboat Springs,
KWBI,89.3
 +Cable
Colorado
Springs,KWBI,96.5
Dilton,KWBI,91.1
Fort Collins,MBN,102.9
Frisco,KWBI,91.1
Glenwood
Springs,MBN,103.1
Grandby,KWBI,91.1
Kremming,KWBI,91.1
Paonia,MBN,102.5
Tabenash,KWBI,91.1
Vail,MBN,102.1
Winter Park,KWBI,91.1
CONNECTICUT
Hartford,WCTF
Danbury,WFME,90.1
Westport,WFME,91.9
DISTRICT OF COLUMBIA
Washington,WRBS,780
Washington,WFSI,107.9
Washington,WJYJ,90.5
FLORIDA
Boynton Beach/Ft. Lau-
derdale,WRMB,89.3
Jacksonville,WNCM,88.1
Melbourne,WCIF,106.3
Miami Christian College,
WRFJ

Miami/Ft. Lauder-
dale,WMCU,89.7
Orlando,WTLN,95.3
Orlando,WTLN,1520
St. Peters-
burg,WGNB,1520
St. Petersburg,
WKES,101.5
Sarasota/St. Peters-
burg/
Tampa,WJIS,88.1
Key West,
WMCU,102.3
Sebring,WKES,95.9
 +Cable
Ft. Myers,MBN,91.1
Gainesville,MBN,95.0
GEORGIA
Atlanta,WYNX,1550
Columbus,WFRC,90.
Toccoa
Falls,WRAF,90.9
Albany,WFRC,89.9
Atlanta,WMBW,100.
Atlanta,WMBW,105.
Atlanta,WMBW,107.
 +Cable
Dublin,MBN,101
Quincy,MBN,91.7
IDAHO
Bonner's Ferry,
KMBI,94.3
Kamiah,KMBI,90.9
Lewiston,KMBI,100.9
ILLINOIS
Chicago,WMBI,1110
Chicago,WMBI,90.1
Davenport/E. Moline/
Rockford,WDLM,960
Davenport/E. Mo-
line,WDLM,89.3
Joliet,WJCH,91.9
Peoria,WCIC,91.4
Springfield,WIBI,91.1
Freeport,WDLM,88.
Rockford,WMBI,91.1
 +Cable
Decatur,MBN,93.1
Quincy,MBN,91.7

teaches its students to recognize various art forms within other cultures which can become a bridge to evangelism.

Our "central" staff do not have to be responsible for any of these programs. We only have to ascertain that the professors are academically qualified to teach and that their courses meet all University requirements. We also help package the courses into academic degrees, and, of course, provide the necessary classroom space. It is a marvelous system.

By 1983 it seemed time to inaugurate our undergraduate program, which we knew would be the most non-traditional of all, and thus the most controversial. As Ralph envisioned it, there would be several non-negotiables:

1) At every step of the way it would be a work-study program so that the students would not need to take out loans.

2) The students would be required to study six months of every year in this country and six months of every year overseas, each time on a different continent in association with a different mission agency and supported during that time as a "short-term missionary." In today's world it is perfectly possible to study in English in a university in Hong Kong, India, South Africa, Singapore, Manilla, Nairobi and in many other places of the world.

3) Before we would accept a student, he would have to be recommended to us not only by a church but also by a mission agency under whose supervision the "work" aspect of his study would be done while overseas.

4) Our degree would be rigorous. We were not interested in students who were merely passing time or looking for an easy degree. Indeed, we hoped that most would eventually go on for their Ph.D.s.

Being so non-traditional, the B.A. program has taken a bit longer to get started. The weight of its development has fallen on Corinne Armstrong, a very capable educator who joined us in 1982 after significant experience overseas. Already two student groups have spent six months in North Africa. They admitted that the experience was demanding, but they were extravagant in their praise for what they had learned.

Perhaps the most well developed educational program we offer is our four-unit course titled "Perspectives on the World Christian Movement," which operates under the name of our Institute of International Studies.

From its beginning in 1974, two years before the Center was founded, this program was envisioned as enrichment to the basic college curriculum, especially for students in secular schools. By now at least 8,000 students have taken it, almost 3,000 in 1986 alone in 62 extension centers throughout the U.S. and the world. The text compiled by our IIS staff (especially Steve Hawthorne) bears the same name as the course and is used as a major missions text in almost every evangelical seminary and college in the U.S. today, selling 10,000 copies in 1984 alone.

The Perspectives course has been truly life-changing for the students. Even we are amazed at its impact. The early core staff of the USCWM would not have been available were it not for this course and its transforming effect. Many of its alumni are now members of the missions committees in their local churches. Hundreds have gone overseas. Several have started mission-promoting organizations such as Caleb Project, which, as a team, monitors almost a thousand college students, helping them keep their mission vision alive.

Not only young people enroll. Nowadays pastors and mission committee members also take the course. In some extension centers grandparents sit alongside their grandchildren, each learning things they hadn't dreamed of previously. Even missionaries on furlough comment, "I thought I knew all about missions, but this course has really opened my eyes."

The William Carey International University is moving

ahead, but it is still very young and faces many unresolved problems. For example, it is not easy to get well qualified professors whose orientation is missionary and who can, like the rest of the Center community, raise their own support. Ralph says he is content to let the University be no better or worse than the quality of people in what he calls "the mission industry." For him, those are quality people!

It is even more difficult to get people who can work with something so non-traditional, still in the process of development. It is not always easy to explain why we are doing what we are doing, even to our own staff. At such times, even Ralph sometimes wonders, "Is it worth all the effort?"

Then we look at the lives that are being changed. We look at the organizations that are beginning to mobilize for a massive push to the final frontiers. We recognize the impact that our courses are making on the lives of students, even those studying at a distance. And we have to say, "Yes, God does want this done; we must persevere. Now, Lord, give us the strength to go forward and the vision to see how."

---

1. Ralph's involvement in educational design includes the following :

a) One of three founders of the InterAmerican School in Quezaltenango, Guatemala, a K through 12 school for the children of missionaries and national church leaders.

b) Founder of the Junior High school for the town of San Juan Ostuncalco, Quez., Guatemala. Ralph started this at the urgent request of the town's leading citizens.

c) Founder of an adult education program, approved by the government of Guatemala, which in three years graduated over 3,000 rural church leaders. Many of these have gone on to seminary or to university and now hold prominent positions in the national church or in civic life.

d) Member of the founding board of the Universidad Mariano Galvez, the prestigious Protestant university in Guatemala City.

e) One of two designers and founders of the Theological Education by Extension Movement. This program has been adopted by almost every mission society and enrolls more than 100,000 students in theological education around the world. The third section of *Theological Education by Extension*, (Ralph D. Winter, ed., Wm. Carey Library publishers, 1969) is Ralph's explanation of the logistics, academic and financial, of how to inaugurate such a program. Unfortunately, the book is out of print, but may be found in many seminary libraries.

f) Between 1966 and 1969 Ralph was the Executive Secretary of the Latin American Association of Theological Schools, the accrediting association for all the theological schools in the northern half of Latin America.

g) While a professor at Fuller Seminary, he served on U.S. accrediting teams, examining other schools either applying for or upgrading their accreditation.

2. Since his work experience overseas would be in the role of a "short-term missionary", he would be supported by his church or friends at home or by some task there such as teaching English.

32

NOVEMBER 1980

"LORD, DO IT AGAIN"

(Daniel 9:15)

"Would you like one of these buttons?"

The Fuller School of World Mission faculty had come well prepared to Billy Graham's Congress on World Evangelization in Lausanne, Switzerland in July, 1974. Pushing through the crowded halls between sessions, we'd watch for former School of World Mission students or missionary friends and press into their hands little red buttons which Dr. Arthur Glasser, our dean, had secured. They said "World Missionary Conference 1980," a date six years off!

Two years before, in 1972, the outgoing president of the Association of Professors of Mission had suggested that it was time for another world level conference of missionaries, mission professors and mission executives. "The last one, as you know, was in 1910, and with all that has happened since, we have a lot to discuss."

Not since 1910, indeed! The telephone, the airplane, two world wars, the nuclear age, the computer—1910 was like several centuries ago! Even more significant, most Western missions by then had outproduced their homeland sending base. (For example, there are today three times as many Baptists in India as in England!) And in that time mission strategy had gone through a number of significant changes. Could anybody doubt it was time to meet again?

But missions professors are not usually conference organizers. Neither are mission executives and missionaries. And though the interest in such a conference began to build up around the world, nobody did anything very effective to organize it. It could well be the most important conference in history, and *yet it almost didn't happen!*

Ralph was very concerned that the meeting actually take place. As Professor (at Fuller) of the Historical Development of the Christian Movement (a description of his own making) he knew a great deal about that earlier meeting. In fact, his final exams often asked his students to list how it was unique. The answer he expected was as follows:

1) It was a delegated meeting. Participants were not invited but were chosen by the mission agencies which sent them.

2) It was a working conference. The delegates didn't come merely to listen. They came to strategize together, to work out plans for finishing the Great Commission.

3) By design, no church leaders as such were present, only those who were also mission professionals.

4) The theme was "going where the gospel had not gone." Mission agencies working exclusively in countries where the Christian faith was well established were specifically *not* invited to participate in 1910. This caused some consternation, especially when none in Latin America were included. In 1910!

During the next four years after Lausanne, Ralph wrote several articles describing the hoped-for conference in 1980, and he watched anxiously to see if anyone would accept the challenge to help get it started.

Early in 1976, he approached the other faculty members. "My sabbatical is due this fall. How about letting me use it to help plan the 1980 conference?" he asked. And they agreed.

But the Lord had other plans. That spring He began to

talk to Ralph about something far bigger and far more difficult than planning a world conference. And instinctively, Ralph knew it might cause misunderstanding. He took months to make his decision, and when we moved to start the U.S. Center for World Mission, all of a sudden we were very much alone, cut off from former associates and friends.

Under the circumstances, even I assumed that now someone else would have to plan the World Missionary Conference. Ralph couldn't!

That year he was the president of the American Society of Missiology, and in his presidential address he stressed the conference being planned for 1980. That fall he gave the keynote address to the triennial joint meeting of the IFMA (Interdenominational Foreign Mission Association) and the EFMA (Evangelical Foreign Missions Association), the two largest associations of mission agencies in the world. His address, "The Grounds for a New Thrust in World Missions," emphasized the unfinished task and again urged the need for a world level meeting of missionaries in 1980.

Still nothing happened!

In November we moved onto the campus of the USCWM. By December we had begun negotiations for an option to buy the $15 million property and became aware of the first flickerings of opposition from the Summit Lighthouse cult, renting most of the space on campus.

After much prayer, complicated legal procedures and stress, in mid-April (finally!) we had the option to buy. It required us to pay the first $850,000 on our down payment by September, only four and a half months away. And our staff numbered fifteen!

Obviously, we were incredibly busy. But Ralph continued to be concerned about that very strategic conference which, through inattention, seemingly wasn't going to be. As with the old adage, "What's everyone's responsibility is no one's responsibility," no one seemed inclined to take the lead. And time was rapidly passing.

Providentially, however, the School of World Mission at Fuller asked Ralph in the spring of 1978 to teach the main (mission history) course he formerly taught. After teaching it for ten years, he wouldn't need to spend much time in preparation, so he agreed. His classroom was packed; the seventy or so students were all experienced missionaries.

On the last day of classes, Ralph spoke about the 1910 World Missionary Conference and the need for a followup one that, like it, was strictly limited to mission leaders. His closing words were an all-out plea that at least one of those missionary students before him would take a two-year leave of absence in order to organize the conference suggested six years earlier for 1980.

"I'll stay after class to talk to anyone about it," he added. "If you feel at all inclined to help, please come and talk to me about it right after class."

Only one student came forward, and Ralph plunged into discussions of what would be involved. Leiton Chinn was not the one Ralph at first would have chosen. Quiet and rather deliberate in his manner, he didn't seem visionary enough to initiate something new. He had never before organized a conference of any sort. Could he manage a world level one? Moreover, since his mission, International Students, Inc., was not one of the "standard brand" overseas agencies, Ralph wondered how the executives from the other agencies would respond to him. Amazingly, however, just then his assignment was very flexible, and he was willing.

Years later Leiton confessed to Ralph, "After class that day I had already forgotten your plea and had no intention of volunteering. I had come forward to talk to you about something entirely different." Ralph was flabbergasted —and then laughed. The conference was now history, and more than anyone else, Leiton's willingness to help had allowed it to happen.

In just a couple of weeks, Leiton moved into an office we offered him on campus and had already called together a meeting of mission executives in the Los Angeles area. Larry Allmon, Executive Director of Gospel Recordings, Inc., became the head of this Steering Committee, which would be meeting almost weekly for a long time to come. Center leadership decided to loan a young couple just coming on staff to help out in Leiton's office. In no time they had the office organized, and in just a few weeks their letters began arriving in the offices of mission agencies around the world.

In the meantime, unknown to us at first, two other widely divergent groups thought that, in the evident vacuum of leadership, they themselves should volunteer to sponsor the proposed 1980 World Missionary Conference. One was the World Council of Churches, in one sense one of the indirect products of the 1910 conference. By 1978, however, the WCC had become so vastly different (both in theology and mission strategy) from the mission group that had preceded it that it would definitely be unacceptable as sponsor to most evangelical mission leaders who might want to come.

The other group was the new Lausanne Continuation Committee representing the 1974 Congress on World Evangelization where all of us had passed out the buttons. Theology here was no problem, but its constituency was almost entirely churchmen, people with little connection to mission agencies. Even the individuals on their committee, drawn from "mission lands," were church leaders, not people who had ever done missionary work. They had no experience in planting a church in a culture different from their own, certainly none where no church already existed.

By the time Ralph heard about these two other conferences, their leaders had moved far into the planning stages. The WCC conference would in no way overlap.

From previous experience Ralph knew their topics of discussion would likely be justice and liberation—basically political concerns such as apartheid, guerrilla warfare in South America and Africa, etc.

But we had dear friends on the Lausanne Committee that we didn't want to offend. Yet those they had invited to come were mainly church leaders, not mission leaders delegated by their agencies. Because of this, we felt their meeting would be vastly different from the one so long hoped for, something which had not taken place since 1910. "Is it too much to ask that mission leaders be allowed to get together by themselves once every seventy years?" Ralph asked rather plaintively.

The Edinburgh 1910 meeting had been so historic that everyone, it seemed, wanted the honor of sponsoring the conference that would commemorate its anniversary. Before those who had proposed this follow-through meeting were really aware of what was happening, both the WCC and the Lausanne Committee had shifted the dates for their next world-level meetings back a year or more so they would fall in 1980, 70 years after Edinburgh. And they were a bit surprised to learn that some of the mission professors involved in the original suggestion in 1972 still felt it was necessary to hold a conference after the *pattern* of 1910—namely, one composed of delegates from mission agencies with a special concern for unoccupied fields. But by then the other two groups had already announced their change of date to 1980.

It took some juggling to get three world level mission conferences in one year. The WCC decided to meet in Australia in March, 1980. At first, the Lausanne Committee planned their meeting for January. (At that time the Edinburgh meeting was being discussed for July.) When, instead, it settled on June, the date for the Edinburgh Conference was moved to August and then to November in order not to conflict. Edinburgh's weather in November was not ideal for those from warm climates. Also, the change of dates was confusing and, no doubt, hurt the attendance somewhat. Yet, being so exclusive in those it allowed to come, Edinburgh II, as it came to be called, was nevertheless a success.

Less than a year before the conference was to begin, David Bliss of our Pat Boone concert days, got into the act. In the fall of 1977, he had gone with African Enterprise as a missionary to South Africa. The next time we saw him was at Inter Varsity's Urbana Missionary Convention at the end of December, 1979. He had brought with him 25 South African students. Some were East Indian in background, some tribal blacks, some Afrikaaners, some British. Two were older—one a dear, deeply spiritual black missionary to Madagascar and the other an equally wonderful seminary professor of British (or Afrikaaner?) stock. After Urbana, as a group they came to the Center to take our month-long "Perspectives on the World Christian Movement" course.

While the group from South Africa was with us, the Steering Committee of the Edinburgh Conference met in our cafeteria. David was very excited about their plans. "Going to Urbana and then coming here has been a wonderful experience for these young leaders from South Africa," he told Brad Gill one day. "Do you suppose we could somehow figure a way to get a youth contingent like these to Edinburgh?"

Brad, then editor of our Center news magazine, *Mission Frontiers*, had been sitting in on the meetings of the steering committee. He also was deeply interested in this upcoming conference.

"Well, Dave, you know this is a conference for mission executives and missionaries. I'm afraid people like us just don't qualify."

"That's certainly understandable for the strategy working sessions. But the younger generation is going to have to carry out the strategy planned by the older one," Dave

173

insisted. "It seems to me that we've got to be there."

"I agree," said Brad.

"I know! Let's hold a simultaneous conference for students interested in missions." Dave suggested. "We could have our own sessions during the day and then join the other conference at night. Wouldn't that work? Even this late we could get mission-minded young people from all over the world to come. We'd have to lay out some strict requirements to be sure to get the right ones, not just young people interested in excitement, but I think it would be worth it. What do you think?"

"I tell you what I'll do," Brad answered. "I'll talk to the Steering Committee about it and see what they say."

They had barely eight months to get organized, and had to work across an ocean, sometimes by long distance telephone with no previous mailing list of students. To a great extent they depended upon the various student groups like Inter Varsity, Campus Crusade, Navigators and their European, Asian and African counterparts to get the word out. Unavoidably and unfortunately, some key student groups, such as one in India, were missed.

Nevertheless, under far less than ideal circumstances with inadequate time and resources, David and Brad pulled together the first-ever International Student Consultation on Frontier Missions.

In order to insure that only students dedicated to frontier missions would come, every application carried a "Statement of Purpose" which the applicant had to sign before being accepted. It was quite rigorous, some said too much so, but because of it, the group that came was a highly selective one, ready to work and pray in earnest.

Even with such a short lead time and so little help in organization, 243 sent in applications. Mainly because of expense, however, only 180 from 26 countries actually came. A last minute gift from a wealthy Christian business-man enabled some from Asia and Africa to come who would not have been able to otherwise.

The conference of the executives was also a first in a very critical sense: fully one-third of those in attendance were heads or executives of mission agencies founded in non-Western countries. As seen from today, one of the "scandals" back in 1910 was the fact that only a handful of delegates were citizens of non-Western countries. These were invited merely as observers, representing the national churches. Interestingly, one of them, Bishop Azariah of India, had already started two mission agencies and should have been there as a fully participating mission executive! Evidently this thought never crossed the minds of those planning that conference.

It was not easy for many from non-Western agencies to get to Edinburgh. Those from hot climates didn't have the proper clothing for Scotland in November. Mary Frances Redding of our staff begged or borrowed as many warm coats as she could find to solve that problem.

Then, there was the problem of expense. Many of those who came were able to only because of a small, last minute miracle. Two months before the date of the two conferences Larry Allmon, Executive Director of Gospel Recordings and head of the conference Steering Committee, had dropped a birthday card to Anthony Rossi, former owner of Tropicana Orange Juice and one of the wealthy supporters of his mission. A couple of days later he was amazed to get a phone call thanking him for the card. "Do you need any help with anything?" the caller asked.

Larry took a deep breath and told him a bit about the Edinburgh Conference and its accompanying student contingent. He added that many of the delegates from the non-Western world couldn't come for lack of funds. "Maybe I can send you a bit to help out," this man said, and hung up.

A few days later, Larry came beaming into the office, waving a check for $100,000. Ten thousand dollars were given immediately to those running the student conference.

The rest rippled around the world and probably doubled the delegation from Third World countries.

I'll never forget that first night in Edinburgh: the beautiful Scottish hymns, some so different from our own; the welcoming address from the mayor of Edinburgh . . . and then those flipping pages! George Cowan of Wycliffe Bible Translators brought a five-inch-thick stack of "fanfold" computer pages listing the tribes yet to be reached. He placed the printout on a stand, then gently tugged the first sheet, and the rest of the pages began to flip over, one at a time, automatically. For ten minutes, it seemed, those sheets flipped, one by one, down to the floor as he talked. I confess I don't remember anything he said, but the impact of those flipping sheets, each page representing 30 or more unreached people groups, was unforgettable.

Every day was full of exciting discussions on how to penetrate unreached cultures with the gospel. I smiled to myself when I saw Erik Stadell of the early days on our campus go to the platform to pray. With the headquarters of his young mission agency now in Sweden, he participated mainly in the Youth Consultation. Still gangling, still beaming, still unpredictable, I wondered how the more staid British delegates would respond to him . . . even his prayers. On one occasion, when asked to pray from the platform, like a cheerleader at a football game, he first led us over and over again in shouting the theme of the conference: "A Church for Every People by the Year 2000." And we all breathed, "May it be so, O Lord, we pray."

The third or fourth day at Edinburgh, as Ralph and I came out of the meeting of the executives, we found our daughter Beth, Brad's wife, standing outside, looking very sober.

"What's wrong?" I asked Brad.

"Well, it's been sort of a hard morning," was his cryptic answer.

Just then I caught sight of our second daughter, Becky and her husband, Tim. At that time Tim was our Center Coordinator at the USCWM in Pasadena. I hoped that his experience in management would give him an increased understanding of the dynamics of the Student Consultation so as to explain these sober faces.

"Whatever is going on?" I insisted.

"Well, we have a lot of things, feelings, really, to resolve among the students. The number of Americans here is sort of overwhelming to the rest—more than twice as many as everyone else combined. Then a lot of us are from the U.S. Center for World Mission, and Brad, of course, has a key role, being one of the planners.

"We also have the different student groups with their own interests, and fears. To weld us all together is not easy. And because Brad and David are in the limelight, they sometimes get a few barbs."

"Like what?"

"Well, you know, to Europeans, Americans always seem to rush in and take charge. They sort of resent that."

"But somebody had to call the meeting. Anyhow, David is from South Africa."

"But he's still an American, and they know that."

I thought of the long months of hard work both the Blisses and Gills had put in to make this conference a success. And I felt very sorry. "Missionaries go through this kind of accusation all the time," I warned them. "In a sense, it's a part of culture shock. Sometimes the charges are completely unfounded. But still they hurt."

Even so, it was a great five days (nine for the students).

Ralph planned to leave Friday noon, the last day of the executives' conference, because he was scheduled to speak in Philadelphia the following Sunday. I had to stay behind to take care of unfinished business in London left by the video cameraman. And I also hoped to visit the Island of Iona where scores of Celtic missionaries had trained in the centuries between 500 and 1000 A.D.

In the main conference, that morning was given over to evaluation. Had it been worth the time and expense? Had it really been that crucial?

The answer was a resounding "Yes!" Some added, "Why haven't we done this before? We should have been consulting like this all along. How long will it be before we can get together again? We simply must!"

There were two rather negative comments, which surprised me a bit. One delegate complained, "We don't have enough church leaders here." Another added, "Why aren't we discussing the problem of justice or the tensions that arise between the national church and the missionaries?"

"Who is that?" I asked the person seated beside me.

"He's a theology professor from somewhere here in Europe—Norway, I think."

"If he's not a missionary or mission executive, how did he get here in the first place? I thought only mission executives or mission-related people were allowed. Doesn't he realize our *only* topic is unreached peoples? Can't he understand that the subject of church-mission tension pertains only to well-established fields, not to pioneering situations? He should have gone to the other conference in Thailand. That's where those other issues were discussed."

But I had to smile as I reflected on the situation. Before we came to Edinburgh, several of our missionary friends who had gone to the conference in Thailand had complained to us that at Pattaya the issue of the unreached peoples hadn't even *come up* until the very last day. Like our theology professor, they simply were at the wrong conference. They should have been at Edinburgh. In a sense, for the Norwegian theologian to participate at Edinburgh was like an interior decorator attending a conference of construction engineers. How could we talk of church-mission tensions if there were not yet a *church* in that culture? And how could the ordinary pastor or seminary professor understand the problems of presenting the gospel in a relevant way to a culture, a people group, which had never heard? The problems were vastly different.

After Ralph left, I moved into one of the youth hostels with Linda, our third daughter. The youth consultation still had two days to run, and remembering the early adjustments the students had to make to each other, I was eager to see firsthand just how they were getting on now.

They were meeting for those last administrative sessions in the basement of a church a few blocks away from the convention hall where the older group had met. Paul Graham, a very gifted young leader from South Africa, was moderating. Brad Gill and David Bliss sat at a table taking notes and, I noticed, carefully refrained from imposing their views so that the students would participate more fully.

"We must meet together for another conference." It was the common feeling among them all.

"But when?" someone asked.

"Whenever the executives meet! There must always be a student contingent. That is very important," another replied.

And I thought, "Yes, it is. But just when will that be?"

Then the question naturally arose, "Who will call our next meeting?" All week long they had skirted around the problem of an ongoing structure of some sort with authority to act. Some felt that to hold together and move forward, at least a skeletal organization was necessary. Others insisted that they had enough organizations already; one more would be one too many.

It was obvious even in that final meeting that vested interests still confused every issue. Inter Varsity was there, with delegates from several countries; Navigators also and Campus Crusade. Also, several mission organizations and schools had sent fairly large delegations: the U.S. Center for World Mission, Worldwide Evangelization Crusade in London, Biola University. There were a number of capable seminarians—from Talbot, Dallas, Fuller and Gordon-Conwell, etc. Several students had come from secular schools, Princeton University and Penn State in particular.

They were all agreed on one point, however: whatever resulted from their meeting should not be too closely identified with any one group. As the discussion progressed, I looked at Becky and Tim and shook my head. "How on earth are you ever going to get anything of value out of this confusion? And why is everyone so scared of organizing? Organization merely gives the ability to move; it doesn't mean control!"

"I know," Becky said, "but we have to work with what we have here, and this is it!"

Back and forth the discussion went. Whenever it got a little tense, Paul Graham, as moderator, would call for a time of prayer. It seemed to me that every hour or so they stopped to pray. "I wish people our age more often would solve their differences this way," I thought. "What a wonderful habit to have learned here."

Finally, after an hour or more, the group came to a decision: 1) they would not start a new organization, but 2) they would appoint an "advocate" to contact the mission executives for them and perhaps pull together another conference when the time came. "We'll each write several names on a piece of paper. The person who gets a unanimous vote will be our advocate," the moderator ruled. And Brad was elected.

I thought back to the distress Beth had felt only the week before and wondered how she felt about this. Her husband was suddenly being asked to fill a tremendously important role, in spite of the muddled title it carried. "Oh God, help them both," I prayed as the entire group spontaneously laid their hands on their heads, commissioning them to be the spokesmen for the group.

Gordon and Sherrie Aeschliman then offered to edit a

newsletter to keep them all together, and that offer was gratefully accepted. Two years before, with Dave Dolan, a fellow student at Westmont College, they had started *Today's Christian* magazine (now called *World Christian*) and were well acquainted with the publishing process. As with Brad and Beth, the group laid their hands on their heads and prayed for them, and finally the meeting was over. It was time to go home.

Almost six years have passed since Edinburgh 1980. Most who attended the student consultation are no longer students. Many are already missionaries, some in very sensitive areas overseas.

As a group those students have been highly influential. A young German there went home and set up the German Center for World Mission. A young Pakistani, through a series of annual missions conferences which he set up, has almost singlehandedly in that country lit a fire for the frontiers which has tremendous implications for the future. The seminarians who were there are the backbone in the Theological Students for Frontier Missions, which now has chapters in many of the seminaries in the U.S. and around the world. Greg and Nancy Fritz head up Caleb Project which, on a monthly basis, monitors the mission involvement of more than a thousand college students throughout the U.S. and is helping the agencies in recruitment. As their subscription list has grown, the Aeschliman's *World Christian* magazine has attracted a staff of more than 20 writers and graphic artists. The student newsletter they started after Edinburgh has become the *International Journal of Frontier Missions*, an exciting, but scholarly, quarterly journal, the only one of its kind dedicated to the discussion of frontier strategy. Following the pattern of the consultations at Edinburgh, half of its articles are written by missionaries and mission executives and half by the young mission leadership coming up. Brad Gill is the editor, but since he is now working overseas, the weight of the responsibility falls on Darrell Dorr, another Edinburgh alumnus, who is doing a tremendous job as managing editor.

The story has yet to be told of many of those students. The data are not yet all in. We do know, however, that most of them are, in one way or another, actively involved in the cause of which they spoke at Edinburgh.

In some respects these five years have seen even more pronounced results among the mission executive delegates. It is hard to believe that ten years ago only a handful of agencies consciously worked with unreached peoples. Today almost all are determinedly pushing into new frontiers. Some, such as SIM International, are planning to double their missionary force in seven years in order to see that there will, indeed, be *a church for every people by the year 2000*.

But the question most asked those last days at Edinburgh is still unanswered: how long will it be before there is another such conference? Will it take another 70 years? Will these young leaders then be too old to participate, even as mission executives? If not, will they recall the exciting combination of age levels at Edinburgh and plan for a similar consultation?

Some might also ask, "Is there really a need for a world-level meeting of mission leaders exclusively?"

All we can answer is that William Carey thought so; he called for one back in 1810. (Unfortunately, it never materialized.) Hudson Taylor thought so, and in 1888 attended the one most nearly answering that description during his lifetime. It was not worldwide, but regional, but in its published minutes it carries his own statement on what he felt should be done with the extra wives of recently converted polygamists—hardly a topic Western churchmen would understand and appreciate!

The Edinburgh Consultation on Frontier Missions was not as large as the Pattaya, Thailand Conference in the Lausanne tradition. Yet it was an important milestone.

Among Western mission agencies, the reawakened concern for unreached or hidden peoples is now a clean sweep. And non-Western agencies are joining as never before, reaching out to unreached people groups within the borders of their own countries and also sending their missionaries to other countries, far and near.

The glorious thing is that neither Edinburgh '80, nor the U.S. Center for World Mission, nor the Lausanne Committee, nor MARC of World Vision is the prime mover of this new interest in frontiers. Rather, these things themselves are the result of the Spirit of God moving on the face of the earth in a new way. He is doing *a new thing*. He is stirring His people to band together to pray for revival and for the evangelization of the world. He is calling young people by the thousands once again, and most of them are eager to go to the frontiers. It is God who has called us all to this final harvest of the nations, and He expects us to do it as a world Christian family, in touch with each other.

Just a century ago a young man knelt at a monument commemorating an impromptu prayer meeting which had taken place under the eaves of a haystack during a sudden rainstorm. At that earlier "Haystack" prayer meeting in 1807 was born the American foreign missionary movement. Louis Wishard, kneeling in the snow at that monument almost 80 years later, prayed earnestly, "Lord, do it again." The Lord answered that prayer in a mighty way *because it was eminently within His will*. The Student Volunteer Movement, which began soon after, over the next twenty years sent 20,000 new missionaries to the inland, still unreached, areas of every continent on earth.

Edinburgh '80 could very easily become just another forgotten monument of the modern missionary movement. Its watchword can pass into oblivion, remembered by just a few.

And yet the Lord of the Harvest still yearns over those lost sheep, lost as individuals and lost as tribes, tongues, peoples which He has repeatedly insisted will praise Him around His throne one day.

Before that is to be, however, a massive new movement to the frontiers must be born. God's people in every church must once again band together, praying earnestly: "Lord of the Harvest, let your Spirit move upon the face of the whole earth. Teach us to pray as we have never known how! Let us see true revival in our day. Send *our* sons and daughters into your harvest field to reap the nations for your glory. Stir your people as we have never been stirred. Yes, Lord, do it again, we pray!"

The addresses and proceedings of the Edinburgh Consultation of Frontier Missions as well as the International Student Consultation on Frontier Missions may be found in *Seeds of Promise*, edited by Allan Starling (Pasadena: William Carey Library, 1981).

33

"BUT FOR THE GLORY OF GOD"

(John 11:4 LB)

The exhilaration of Edinburgh 1980 took some time to fade, in spite of the continuing financial crises, the heavy work load and the unpleasant criticism which we suffered from time to time. Edinburgh had been a real milestone —but in more ways than one. Before then, our staff had consisted of a few older missionary couples, sent by their mission agencies to help us, and a far larger number of young people, half of whom were newly married. Several of the older couples had children in high school, and these became the nucleus of a Bible study group which won many of their classmates to the Lord.

Then in 1981, first one then another of our young couples announced that we would have some tiny, new additions to our community. From no babies at all, we soon had five or six. Every couple of months, it seemed, another newborn was proudly displayed in staff meeting, some just hours after birth.

With all the joy from these new arrivals, perhaps we were not sufficiently on the alert spiritually, because Satan chose just this time to strike our community with serious

185

physical problems.

In the spring of 1980, within one week, three different people in the larger Center community had had serious accidents which "totalled" their cars. One of these, a godly girl in her early twenties on Central staff, suffered severe headaches for more than a year afterward, and assumed these were related somehow to her accident. Then, in the fall of 1981, she began to have other seemingly unrelated symptoms and decided to have a thorough checkup. The diagnosis: a tumor of the pituitary gland.

About the same time this was diagnosed, Mary Frances Redding, our dear, older, former-Christian-Education-director, became ill. In many respects, Mary Fran was our crucial link to local churches. It was she who started the Christian Leaders Institute of International Studies, a one-week version of the IIS program specially designed for pastors and church leaders.

Almost by herself, she organized the Athens (Missionary) Conference, which drew almost 100 people from 19 countries. For months she worked on travel and hotel arrangements as well as details relating to the conference speakers. Ralph was to be one of these, and since I had never been anywhere near the lands spoken of in the Bible, I wanted desperately to go with him, but lacked the money. Mary Fran knew this, and when a couple cancelled out at the last minute, making their tickets available to two others, she gave one to me.

It was a fascinating experience to follow in the footsteps of the Apostle Paul from Mars Hill in Athens to Thessalonica (now Thessaloniki), Philippi, and then Corinth. It was also very educational; everywhere we went, Ralph and Don Richardson pointed out Paul's missionary strategy, most of which is still relevant today.

Then, Mary Fran was the spark behind our "Southern California Annual Missions Conference." She spent weeks preparing for this event, cajoling, persuading, doing whatever she could to find the help she needed to prepare the large auditorium on our campus for the thousand guests who came.

Central to the program on the opening night was "the passing of the torch" ceremony. Within thirty miles of our campus there are at least five major missionary retirement centers: Presbyterian, Congregational, Methodist, Nazarene, and Disciples of Christ. "Mary Fran, let's have a tea for these older missionaries," I suggested. "It would be great for our young staff and students to meet them and learn what it was like when they went to the field. I would guess that many of them were Student Volunteers in the early days of this century." So Mary Fran added that to her list of things to do.

One hundred of these retired missionaries came. Some were in their nineties and walked with canes. I was not the only one with tears in my eyes when, one by one, they marched or hobbled (as the case might be) down the aisle, accepted a burning candle from the large lighted torch, then crossed the platform and handed the candle to a young person preparing to leave for the field. A long line of young candidates stood waiting, unfortunately numbering more than those now retired. The older ones could hardly believe the enthusiasm of the young—so many so eager to go. And the young who didn't receive candles were extremely disappointed that there were not enough retired missionaries present, so that each one could receive a lighted candle.

In many respects, Mary Fran represented the heart of the Center. In her sixties, she was energetic, cheerful, always forward looking. It was a real blow, therefore, when on a short vacation in the fall of 1981 she suddenly became unconscious and was rushed to the hospital. Even after two surgeries, she never fully recovered from the aneurysm of the brain she had suffered, and finally died eight months later.

Meantime, the Lord was gradually healing the pituitary tumor. After a year of many tests, the tumor suddenly, (inexplicably, the doctors said) disappeared.

But Satan was not through with tormenting us. Some of the problems that beset us during those months were so severe and painful that even yet it is difficult to speak of them.

One situation in particular I prayed earnestly that God would protect us from. Over and over in my heart I went through the promises of scripture. I reminded Christ of His promise that if we would abide in Him and obey, we could ask what we would and it would be done. (See John 15:7.) Every night I fell asleep with a cry on my lips that God would protect and take care.

Yet God allowed the thing I most dreaded—in spite of my prayers. Why? Didn't He hear? Didn't He care? Even more devastating, Satan insistently whispered that I really couldn't trust the Bible to mean what it said.

One night when I was especially distressed, I was drawn like a magnet to the story of Mary and Martha and Lazarus in John 11. I had always loved those three, especially Mary, and as a teenager had tried to pattern my life after hers. But as a young, overburdened mother years later, I reluctantly came to realize that I was probably more like Martha.

I knew Jesus loved Lazarus—they were best friends, weren't they? And who wouldn't love gentle Mary? But I didn't particularly like Martha. She was irritable, jealous, anxious—the one Jesus had to rebuke.

That night as I read, however, I noticed, amazed, that John said, "Jesus loved *Martha* and her sister and Lazarus" (Jn. 11:5 NIV). The Bible didn't say "Jesus loved Lazarus and Mary and their sister!" Overburdened, anxious Martha's name came first! He loved *her!* How comforting!

But it was the next few words to which my eyes became glued: He loved them, "*so* when he heard that Lazarus was sick, He stayed two more days in the place where He was" (Jn. 11:5-6 LB).

As I mused on what I had read I thought to myself, "If I had been Martha or Mary and knew that He deliberately stayed away when I needed Him most, I would have found it hard, indeed, to believe that He really loved me."

But they didn't know that His absence was deliberate. They must have wondered, however. They evidently knew where to send the messenger. Their words when he finally came showed they felt a bit betrayed: "If You had been here, my brother would not have died!" Underneath was the agonizing question, "Why didn't you come? We sent for You in time."

Then, both Mary and Martha must have known that Jesus could have healed him, even from a distance. But He had not? Why?

What they did not know was that Jesus had another, far more important agenda than simply healing Lazarus. And his agenda would involve them in agony before it would bring them joy.

But they couldn't know that. All they could cling to was their confidence of Who He was and the fact that He loved them. And when He came, and in tears each sister fell at His feet, their only comfort was His quiet, steady voice saying, "Trust me. I have everything under perfect control, no matter how it seems!"

As I read through my tears, I was riveted to His earlier comment to the disciples: "The purpose of his illness is not death, but for the glory of God. I, the Son of God, will receive glory from this situation" (Jn.11:4 LB).

And I noticed how gentle, yet firm, were His words to Martha: "*I* am the one who *raises* the dead . . . Do you believe this, Martha?" (vs. 25-26 LB).

Through my own anguish, I saw things in this passage I had never seen before. Jesus *did* love them, a great deal! He loved them so very much that He knowingly took a tremendous risk, one He couldn't have taken with many people. It was absolutely essential that one more time before His crucifixion the leaders of Israel be confronted, unequivocally, with the fact that He was the Messiah, the Son of the God they claimed to serve. He had to do something so spectacular, so impossible, and so public that only by the most stubborn refusal to believe could they continue to deny who He was. Their sin of rejecting the Messiah had to be without question.

Thus Jesus chose to involve this little family whom He loved so dearly. He knew He could trust them to not lose faith in Him, no matter the trial. He wept over the pain they felt, but He was glad that they would be the ones who would participate in the glory of what He was about to do. *Especially this dear family!*

Because of the serious medical problems faced by these members of our staff, those months in early '82 were full of anguish for those of us to whom they were most dear. Later, when God's purposes became more plain, I asked myself in some surprise, "Why were we so surprised when the devil attacked our community so viciously? We know that when we fight for outreach to the Hidden Peoples, we're encroaching on territory Satan has long claimed. We know we're on the front lines in a major battle for the Kingdom. Aren't there always casualties on the front lines?"

Some years later George Verwer of Operation Mobilization spoke to our staff. Without knowing all we had gone through, but knowing a bit about our ministry, he reminded us, "Satan is not trying to give you bumps and scratches. He is out to destroy you! Especially you!"

I love to think of Christ as my Shepherd—which He is, caring for the flock. But He is also the Commander of the armies of the Lord. He is very much a soldier, determined to win this battle, no matter the cost. Read the list in Hebrews 11; His soldiers across the centuries have not always come through unscathed. As verses 39 and 40 tell us, sometimes the "promise" is still ahead.

Yet, comfortingly, Jesus, as Commander of the Lord's armies, is very aware of every little scratch that we feel.

190

And He cares. He catches our tears and stores them to use not only for His glory but also for our later refreshment. This I truly believe.

It is also true that He is the heavenly Bridegroom, preparing His bride to rule with Him. Can One who came to the throne through suffering have as His bride one who doesn't even know what pain is? Is it not absolutely necessary for us also to have gone through pain if we would rule with Him?[1]

To bring Him glory through our tears—what a costly and thus precious gift! May our tears someday produce a glorious harvest in another people group, won to the Lord, is my prayer.

---

1. I am indebted to Paul Billheimer in his *Destined for the Throne* for this concept. His book, *Don't Waste Your Sorrows*, is also a tremendous blessing to those who are suffering. The first is published by Tyndale House (Wheaton, IL) and the second by Christian Literature Crusade in Fort Washington, PA.

34

DECEMBER 1983

"I WILL GIVE THEM HEARTS THAT RESPOND . ."

(Jeremiah 24:7)

It was early December, and it was cold, especially since the retreat center where our staff was gathered was at an elevation of 4000 feet. I shivered as I unlocked the door to our room, and hastily stepped inside. I had just a few minutes to prepare for our guests. We had only two chairs; where would they all sit?

That afternoon, late, Ralph had said to me, "Roberta, I want you to get in touch right away with the older couples on staff. Ask them to meet with us here just after the evening meeting, around 10 P.M. I have some heavy things I want to discuss with them."

I knew what he was referring to. After several years of financial struggles and swings up and down of staff morale, all of a sudden it seemed that we were under a new kind of Satanic attack.

In the months just preceding, several of us had spent hours, individually, praying and counselling various ones on staff having serious personal problems. It is well known that Satan always attacks us when and where we are most weak; anyone who has been a Christian for any

192

length of time at all knows this. However, rather than to submit ourselves to the surgery of God in His determination to make us like Himself, we tend to hug our weaknesses to ourselves, in effect excusing them by telling ourselves that God's grace can't be sufficient to change *that* in our personalities.

In the case which precipitated our gathering that cold day in December, change needed to come in both parties involved. Ralph and I were frankly appalled, however, at the many, well-meaning but simplistic, judgmental remedies which several of their peers (and even some recognized as Christian leaders) had suggested. Almost none of these counselors were people who had known the ones needing help even half as well as we did.

That evening in our room, Ralph mentioned the case to these older staff members, then commented: "As a general rule, our staff should not have to turn for help to people outside our community. After all, we are the ones who really know and love them. If we are ever going to be the kind of community we have envisioned, we must set up a structure to deal with personal problems, not just personnel problems related to job performance.

"I have been doing a lot of praying about this, and it seems to me that the elders in our community are those best able to give mature advice. All of you have had years of experience dealing with 'people problems' within mission structures. Would you be willing to function together as an Elder's Council to consult with and advise in these difficult situations? After all, congregations have ruling elders even though their members see each other only once a week. We work together all day every day.

"We may have to deal with all sorts of problems," Ralph continued. "We want those needing help to know they can come to us. If, for example, a particular staff member has an attitude problem, theoretically Art (McCleary, our General Manager) and I together could deal with it, but I can't help but think that the weight of a group

193

of elders behind us would be better. Will you help in this?"

Someone asked, "How will the younger staff respond to this? Will they resent us?"

"We don't really know. But sometimes they have really severe problems that ordinarily they should share with their parents. But most of them are far away from home, and I believe that God expects us, in the absence of their parents, to function in that role, to a certain extent."

"What if they refuse our advice?"

"Well, I've thought quite a bit about that. And I've decided that if they refuse to follow what we say, we have no alternative but to ask them to leave staff."

The room was very quiet as all of us considered the implications. The years of working with a mainly younger staff had shown us that their basic orientation to life and ours were quite different. We had gone through the World War II years when yielding to proper authority was not only stressed, it was absolutely essential for the common good. By contrast, from their high school years on (or maybe even before), they had been urged to exercise independent thinking in choosing courses, choosing colleges, choosing friends, choosing lifestyles. To many of them *authority* all too often implied dictatorship, which they felt justified in refusing. Would they be willing to understand and trust us? Would they accept our decisions regarding things that pertained to them personally? All of us felt like we were taking a gamble with young people whom we highly respected and dearly loved. The feeling wasn't particularly comfortable!

We attacked the large problems first, and were shocked to find out how many there were that we had not known about. We took months, meeting weekly or even more often, to consider and pray over some of the problems. Even so, we did not always agree among ourselves at first as to the correct diagnosis of the situation nor the best way to resolve the problem. However, as time passed, the feedback from the younger staff on the whole was very heartening, "We are so glad you have set up the Elder's Council. We have needed something like this for a long time. Now we feel we have someone to go to."

Some of the counsel we gave reflected our own missionary experience. After just a couple weeks' acquaintance with a young mission leader from another country, one young staffer announced their engagement at morning staff prayers. As older couples who had all known similar situations on the field, we were concerned. We felt they didn't know each other well enough; they couldn't even speak a common language! But what to do now?

"Have you met each other's parents?"

"He's met mine, but I can't meet his. You know that they live . . ." and she named a country at quite a distance.

"We realize that. Nevertheless, we believe that before you officially announce your engagement, you must get acquainted with his family and his culture. We would like for you to visit his parents for at least a month. Then, if your families are happy with your plans, you can announce your engagement.. You're very wise to wait almost a year before getting married. Cross-cultural marriages involve a lot of extra adjustments, and we think you need at least that long to be really sure."

The young couple were very solemn. Instead of the congratulations and hugs they might have expected, we required them to check further, at great personal expense. We realized that the girl could have rebelled—and left staff. Instead she chose to stay with us and to follow our guidelines. (Today they are happily married.)

As a group, the elders breathed a sigh of relief. We didn't want to seem like ogres to the wonderful younger staff. But many of us were thinking, "What if they were our own children, living at a distance? Wouldn't we appreciate it if some mature couple gave parental advice if it were needed?"

We could have said, "Do what you want. You're an

adult now." Most Americans would respond thus. But we felt that when we accepted these young people on our staff, we also accepted a certain amount of responsibility for them, especially if they were far from home. As Ralph pointed out, "Nowhere in the Bible does it say that grown children can ignore their parents' wishes. Indeed, Jesus had some rather strong statements to make about religious leaders who encouraged children to forget their parents and give their money to the temple." Also, we realized that one of the typical indications that a group is a cult is that its leaders encourage those who join to ignore their family relationships.

We were surprised at some of the problems which came to the attention of the Elder's Council. Some involved hidden moral sins. Had we been a church, we would have done our best to lead those persons to repentance without breaking their relationship with our community. But we were a community involved in missionary outreach. As such, we felt we could not condone sin by allowing those persons to remain on our staff any more than a church can allow a pastor guilty of moral sin to continue his ministry uninterrupted. A necessary trust bond had been broken, and those concerned had to give up this particular ministry. Even so, various of the elders spent weeks counselling and praying with those involved.

The Elder's Council is only one aspect of the Center community. It is not an administrative group, but rather one which advises. From the very beginning the USCWM was deliberately structured like a mission agency. Staff are not "hired." If we feel God has called them here, and if they feel they can agree to the Biblical Covenant ("Love the Lord . . with all your heart, soul, mind, and body. .") as we understand it, they are invited to become a part of the USCWM family. They understand that we are choosing them; they are being invited into a mission community. Membership is a privilege, not a right.

A missionary overseas is a missionary 24 hours a day,

not just from 8 a.m. to 5 p.m. That is also true of our staff. On several occasions we have called for after-hour work parties where all are expected to participate. Though it is never convenient to have our busy schedules interrupted, almost always these work parties have proved to be times of great fun, even though we might be only stuffing envelopes or unloading donated used furniture.

Because we are a mission community, wives as well as their husbands are given job responsibilities. Mothers with young children are given what we call "home assignment," meaning their primary job is to take care of their own small children at home. Nevertheless, because they are a part of the team, the wives in their own names receive half of their salary as a couple. Since her time is paid for, even though a mother with small children may be on home assignment, she is not free, without special permission, to take an outside job, nor even, for example, to teach Daily Vacation Bible School in some local church as though only her husband were employed. That is, what time she has available already belongs to the Center.

As a regular mission society, we expect all staff members, if at all possible, to take part in certain gatherings: the weekly staff meeting, the morning prayer time, and the Thursday night Frontier Fellowship meeting, for example.

Outsiders do not always understand the function or the value of these family times. It may seem at first that we are as regimented as IBM or the army. But we feel that in missing a year of these required meetings, the staff member would lose an education in missions of incalculable value.

For some months we had noticed that fewer and fewer staff were coming to the Thursday night meeting. One morning, at prayers, Ralph asked us all to jot on a piece of paper why we were not there the evening before. Several days later we had our Board meeting. One who was sitting in as proxy for a Board member spoke up, "I would

197

never join an organization which required me to go to a prayer meeting. You should at least warn people before they become staff."

Ralph looked up, rather amazed. "It so happens we do," he said. "And those who cannot agree are not invited to join us." He noticed the puzzled look and explained further, "What we require is not that strange. All mission agencies have certain requirements and lifestyle expectations. Their staff are not merely employees of a Christian organization."

He could have told how missionaries "covenant" to abide by the long established guidelines of their mission. And that it is such covenants which separate mission agencies from other Christian organizations. He could have pointed out that even the Internal Revenue Service recognizes this distinction and on that basis allows Protestant mission societies the same benefits it gives to Catholic orders.

When Ralph told me about that exchange, I thought back to the early days of the U.S. Center for World Mission. At that time we had only five staff members, and I thought Ralph was getting ahead of us a bit when he asked Prudence one day, "Do you think Campus Crusade would let us use their Staff Manual as a resource in writing our own?"

Before getting married, Prudence had been one of the top regional staff of Campus Crusade for six years. As a result, besides her other obvious gifts, she became for us a tremendous resource on anything having to do with institutional organization. "They usually won't let their manual out of the hands of staff members," she told Ralph. "But since you and Bill Bright are good friends, I'll ask."

Actually, we could have asked almost any mission agency for such a manual. All have them. Most of these, however, are written with overseas personnel in mind. While not altogether the typical mission agency, in its personnel policies Campus Crusade still operates like one, and we felt we could learn from them.

Quite commonly, after their initial adjustment to a missionary lifestyle, missionaries become so accustomed to it that they are basically unaware just how different it might seem to outsiders. A *missionary lifestyle* involves far more than living on less. Instead of merely working *for* an organization, a missionary actually joins a mission *family*. The other members become "aunts" and "uncles" to his children in a very real sense. And, as is true with a family, there are certain unwritten assumptions which everyone in the mission family understands, at least after the first few years.

The written guidelines are what constitute the "manual." Ours is simply a careful attempt to interpret Luke 10:27: "Thou shalt love the Lord thy God with all thy heart, with all thy soul, with all thy mind, and with all thy strength . . . and thy neighbor as thyself." Practically speaking, however, just what does that mean for our community?

We have set up four basic staff committees to oversee the various aspects of love to the first half of Jesus' summary. To help us to love Him with all our heart is the task of the Spiritual Fitness Committee. At morning staff prayers, our small groups help us to be faithful in our private devotions and to keep fit spiritually.

To help us love Him with all our soul, we have the Psychological Fitness Committee, which encourages us in staff meetings both to "order our private worlds" (Gordon MacDonald's book title) and to discuss honestly any complaints we may have with management decisions.

The Intellectual Fitness Committee helps us love Him with all our mind. Each staff member is encouraged to upgrade his (or her) formal education by taking one class every quarter. Then, all are expected to participate in informal discussions about mission strategy at our Monday noon missiology meetings and our Thursday night Frontier Fellowship meetings, both open to the public. Each of these meetings has proven to very stimulating, spiritually as well as intellectually.

In order to better love God with all our strength, the Physical Fitness Committee sets general standards for rest and exercise and also suggests foods that are natural and nutritious, even for the menu of our cafeteria..

We also take seriously the second part of that verse: "and thy neighbor as thyself" in four other committees which we have set up. These encourage us in our responsibilities to: 1) our families, including parents, grandparents, aunts and uncles, etc.; 2) our immediate, accountable community, including our fellow staffers and our church; 3) our existing relationships with still other people we have known, are near to, or grew up with, for whom there is, in effect, a "given" responsibility, and 4) those other relationships we may optionally establish with individuals and people groups throughout the world to the "ends of the earth."

Each committee has met for extended periods of time, trying to decide what disciplines we need to help each other build into our personal lives so that we can truly love the Lord in the way He has outlined.

In 1985, we added several hours per week of what we call "Staff Development." This is actually a type of discipleship training for our staff, where invited authorities speak to us on such subjects as the fatherhood of God, living together in community, intercessory prayer, spiritual warfare, obedience, forgiveness, etc. These lessons have all been extremely helpful to us.

Sometimes a committee becomes quite personal in checking up. For example, one day Prudence asked one who seemed discouraged, "How are your daily devotions? Are you having them faithfully?"

"I need help," she answered.

"Okay. What is the best time for you?"

"About 5 a.m., before the kids wake up."

"That's my favorite time too. All right, I'll call you at

5 a.m. to see if you're up yet. Is that okay?"

Or, in the physical fitness realm, the head of the committee asked Ralph one day, "Will you back me if I start implementing our exercise standards?"

"Absolutely!" Ralph was waiting for that.

At first there was a great howl when we were told we had to report how many aerobic points we had earned that week (as students, and even faculty, do at more and more colleges, we are told). But in a few weeks several, rather sheepishly, admitted that they felt better than they had for a long time.

As might be expected, it is in the psychological fitness realm, as we interpret it, where we have the most struggle. In America we are all too often taught to first watch out for Number One. All through school everything we do brings credit (or blame) to ourselves alone. Except in the realm of sports, we do not learn to work in teams. And only rarely are we required to redo something until it is perfect. All this may make for easy grading, but it is a very poor preparation for life.

Adding to this is the "old nature" of which Paul spoke, namely, the uncrucified self which refuses to be stepped on. Therefore, it is not surprising that merely learning to be responsible to those with whom we live and work is quite a spiritual (and psychological) struggle.

I remember that as a young missionary in Guatemala, I suffered under what I felt was an unjust, unfair situation. I complained to everybody who would listen that *I had some rights, too!* I felt very justified in my misery, and it took the Lord a long time to get me to understand that if I were *His* servant—His *slave,* really—no, I didn't have any rights, any rights at all! I had voluntarily given them all to Him. (Or had I?) I did a lot of crying and praying .

and yielding . . before finally I was able to say, "Yes, Lord, I have no rights!"[1]

The crux of the matter was that I really didn't want to believe that He was the One who had allowed the situation

201

which was so unbearable for me. I knew I could not fight Him, but didn't I have a right to fight the situation? No! Not unless He told me to. I was under His orders. And that unbearable situation was part of his training for me!

I wish I could say that I never had to be taught that lesson again. That would not be true. I have had to learn it again and again, but each time the yielding is "clearer," if not easier and quicker.

The comforting thing is that God is trying to make us like Himself. He is a tremendously creative God. No two flowers are exactly alike, and no two disciples will be either. He hand tailors for us all the lessons we need to learn, but usually we learn them in community, not on a mountain top alone. Always He is gentle with the one who really wants to follow; but He can seem almost harsh to the rebellious soul.

In Guatemala the little Indian church which we attended was right on a major street leading to the market where 20,000 Indians brought their produce on Sundays. Sunday after Sunday I would smile when our services would be interrupted by a squealing piglet. Outside, in the dusty road, a boy would be literally dragging the animal to market to be sold. Typically, the piglet had dug his hoofs in, determined not to go a single step. But he went anyhow, pulled by the neck.

We can be like that piglet. We can be dragged, kicking and screaming. Or we can go happily, if we will just yield to the Holy Spirit. We don't have to make things hard for ourselves. We can trust that He knows why things are happening the way they are and simply trust Him.

Community living, missionary community living, is one way to help us. It is not always pleasant, although much of the time it is full of joy. But it is one way which the Lord has ordained and used over many centuries. It is tried and true, and the disciplines are not heavy for those who want to obey Him.

Jesus said, "If ye love me, keep my commandments."

Paradoxically, by yielding our rights, we come to love Him more and more.

---

1. One book which our staff has read together is very helpful in understanding the victory Christ intends us to have through dying to self.   This is Paul E. Billheimer's *Destined for the Cross* (or *Spiritual Warfare*, by which it was earlier known.)   It is available from Tyndale Publishers in Wheaton, IL.

35

"DELIVER US FROM EVIL"

(Matthew 6:13)

"Mrs. Winter? Am I speaking to Roberta Winter?"
"Yes."

"My name is _____. I just finished reading your book, *Once More Around Jericho*, and thought I would call you. I was a member of Summit," she continued. And immediately I was on the alert.

"You say '*was*.' I responded. "Does that mean you are not now with Summit?"

"Yes. I left about two years ago."

"Then you must have been with the cult when it was on our campus," I suggested.

"Yes. I was the personal assistant to Mrs. Prophet But I didn't know anything at all about you then."

"That's strange," I thought, and decided to probe further.

"I grew up in the Salvation Army," she told me, "but at a critical time in my life, I got involved with Summit. The members seemed so warm and loving . . ."

"The same old story!" I mused. "How many lonely people join cults because they appear at first to be close-knit, loving communities? But how could one who had grown up in the Salvation Army be so deceived?" I wondered. "Surely she should have seen through them!"

I was very cautious as I listened. Could I trust what she said? Or was she only trying to find out information from me? Then I realized that I had been the only one asking questions. But I had one more still burning within me.

"Please forgive me, but I must know. Why did you decide to leave Summit?"

She told me a long story about a freeway breakdown at Christmas time as she was on her way home from picking up her children at the airport. She had called Summit headquarters for help, but was told to fend for herself. That lack of real concern when she most needed it caused her to look more critically at what was happening around her. She left Summit soon afterward.

Every now and then since the Church Universal and Triumphant left our campus in the fall of 1978, we hear from someone formerly connected with this group. Once a brother and sister of a cult mem-ber came asking advice on how to get past the barriers so they could talk to their sister. Someone had given them my book and they came to us, almost in tears, hoping that we had some answer.

Another time, along about 1982, one of our daughters noticed a young man intently studying a bulletin board on campus. Thinking he was a student she hadn't yet met or perhaps was someone interested in one of our classes, she stopped for a moment to chat. Immediately he began asking all sorts of questions. "Are all the buildings full?" "Do you have many students?" "Are you making your payments?"

"Are you a new student here?" Linda asked.

"No, but I used to study here."

"Oh. With the Nazarenes?"

"No. After that."

With a start Linda realized he had to have been with Summit. As graciously as possible, she avoided answering any further questions and made her way to our office across the street.

"Why would someone from Summit be here?" she asked me. I wondered the same, myself.

Only two weeks or so after the call from Mrs. Prophet's former secretary, I received a call from an elderly Methodist minister on the East Coast. He also had read my book and was wondering if I could help him locate his grandson who had gotten involved with the cult.

I gasped when he gave me the name. His grandson was none other than one of the top leaders of the group! When Summit had been on our campus, this old gentleman had tried to see his grandson, he told me, but had been refused admittance.

I was able to answer only a few of his questions concerning where the cult had moved, and decided to call the woman who had spoken with me two weeks before.

"I understand he's in Panama with his wife's parents," she said when I phoned. "I don't know whether he's been kicked out or was sent there to open a new branch. Either one is a possibility."

My heart ached for the elderly minister. How many more people were in his position?

One day I got a letter in the mail. It was from a lady who had battled to make contact with her son, a member of the cult. She enclosed a copy of a letter written by one of the cult leaders, warning of the need to chant mantras against their enemies. Out of ten people named as enemies, I wasn't surprised to see the name of Walter Martin, a well-known writer on the cults. But Ralph's name and my own were there as well! I knew the danger of their chants, and determined to pray all the harder, claiming our authority through Christ over the powers of the Evil One.

At about the same time, the *Los Angeles Times* ran a series of articles warning against the cult. It mentioned that Summit had bought a large tract of land in Montana, a former ranch. "Good," I thought. "Now maybe they'll leave *people* alone."

Several months later I mentioned the cult when I was

teaching a Perspectives class at the state university in Bozeman, Montana. "Oh, that's the group that is not too far from here," one of my students commented. And I sighed. True to form, they had settled near a university campus where they would be able to woo more students to their way of life.

Then, in the fall of 1984, I mentioned the cult in a talk I gave at a large church in Northern California. After the meeting a woman said to me, "My daughter is with that group. I've been letting them meet in our home for their prayer meetings, but I'm not going to do that any more."

Usually the newspapers said very little about this particular cult. Every now and then some item would show up about Scientology. But I was surprised when one morning a staff member announced that according to the *TV Guide,* a major news broadcast was giving five minutes each night for a week to an "expose " on the Church Universal and Triumphant. Evidently the leader of the cult, Elizabeth Claire Prophet (King), had had a falling out with her second husband, Mr. King, who was suing her for money which he claimed had been enticed from him by fraud. His statements about the group were quite revealing, but the pictures shown on television even more so. I wondered how the cameraman had been able to get them.

Our latest "contact," however, occurred in late January, 1986. One morning when I drove to work, I noticed a pickup truck just ahead of me which stopped beside our building. I didn't think much about it until I noticed the bumper sticker, which said, "I (heart symbol) St. Germaine."

"Oh, no!" I thought, and looked closely at the two men who got out. They went to a car with the hood raised which was parked on the university side of the street and bent over to look at the motor. I watched them for a few moments, then went in to staff prayers.

A couple of days later, Rhonda, who works with our

Perspectives staff, came to morning prayers with two posters which she had taken off the bulletin board in the university administration building. The afternoon before she had stopped to look at the bulletin board and began reading these new posters. In typical, Summit, four-color design, they announced the next major conference of the cult. "How did they get on *our* bulletin board? Inside our locked building? What nerve!" I said. Then I remembered the two pickup trucks with the Summit bumper stickers.

Most of our present staff were not here when the cult was across the street. They may believe there *is* such a thing as spiritual warfare, but I sometimes wonder if they think those of us who were here from the beginning see spooks behind every tree. They know very little about Summit and its teachings. We don't often think of the cult ourselves anymore. But every now and then something happens to remind us to continue praying for those who are caught up in such groups. Some are truly seeking after God, but have been deceived by the Evil One. But God is faithful. He will not allow those who truly want to find Him to be forever led astray.

Those of us who have sensed the power of occult forces in our country are appalled by the casual, almost careless, attitude young people (sometimes even Christian ones) have toward such things. Americans pride themselves on being tolerant and open-minded. Therefore they usually don't realize the danger there is in "playfully" investigating such things as Summit, Hari Krishna, tarot cards and fortune telling. Even karate, transcendental meditation, and yoga, which might seem perfectly innocent to the unaware, are not only based in Hindu philosophy but carry as an integral part of the "course" this philosophical system which is really in opposition to Biblical Christianity. Those who are much better acquainted with the occult than I often warn that Satan uses such seemingly innocent beginnings to get a foothold in young lives—a foothold that it may take years to break.

Even secular psychologists admit that the game "Dungeons and Dragons" not only warps the mind but seems to exert a strange, evil influence on adults as well as children.

When our children were young, I used to let them see TV programs which playfully deal with "witches." Knowing what I know now, I would stay a long way away from such things. They make things that are either of the occult, or border on it, seem so innocent that young people are later lured on to dangerous involvement. As Christians, we need to be less naive, more aware that "Satan walks about like a roaring lion, seeking whom he may devour," as the apostle Peter warned (1 Pet.5:8). We may think we are getting exercise, or simply playing a game, or learning to relax, but Satan is preparing us to accept philosophies which are diametrically opposed to the Bible.

The daughter of one of our staff members one day picked up a sheet left by accident in the copying machine at the university she attended. It was addressed to members of the Satanist cult and told how they were infiltrating local evangelical churches, claiming to be born again Christians.

Several months later the pastor of a prominent local church happened to be sitting on the airplane next to a man who was fasting. When he asked if his seatmate was a Christian, he replied, "No, I'm a Satanist. We're fasting and praying that the marriages of Christian leaders will be destroyed."

Here in California we hear of all sorts of gruesome activities by occult groups, some almost too evil to believe. And yet, responsible Christian people assert they are true.

Even more dangerous are the subtle influences which are contrary to Biblical teaching but which can masquerade as wonderful psychological truths which all Christians should employ. We must be on the alert!

Christ has given each one of His children authority over the Evil One. James told us to resist Satan, and he would flee from us (James 4:7). As Christians today, we must keep close to our Lord. Parents must keep their own hearts and lives pure in order to protect their children from spiritual forces that they may never see, just sense. And if, inadvertently, ground has already been given to Satan, in the name of Jesus we can renounce his hold over us and reclaim what we yielded. How wonderful to know that! Rarely a day goes by when I do not pray as Jesus said we should, "Deliver us from the Evil One" (Matt. 6:13).

I believe with all my heart that we are in the end times, and should therefore not be surprised at the surge of evil. But I also remember the scripture which says, "When the enemy comes in like a flood, the Spirit of the Lord raises up a standard against him" (Isa. 59:19). We can expect great victories in the name of Jesus because Satan is launching an all-out war.

It is easy to become frightened and to focus on Satan. That is dangerous. Paul says, "Don't let this happy trust in the Lord die away, no matter what happens . . . His coming will not be delayed much longer" (Heb. 10:35). God is still on the throne, and the affairs of men are still under His control. We must remind ourselves of this fact.

This is the time for us to go on the offensive. Not only against the evils in our society (that is defense), but against the strongholds of Satan, where He has full control over entire people groups. We need to claim them in prayer and then move out to reap the harvest already prepared by the Holy Spirit.

36

"NOT ONE DETAIL WILL HE MISS"

(Isaiah 34:16)

"We need your prayers today. Bill Dickson and I have to go to the house of strangers and ask to rent a square foot of the back wall of their house. I went there yesterday, but no one was home, and when I tried to leave a note, I was scared off by a huge black dog. Pray for me. Will you?"

We all laughed. Rent a square foot of wall? What was Bob up to now? And scared off by a dog?

Bob is our "resident St. Francis"—the kind who picks up wounded birds, takes in stray cats and dogs (and humans!). He is also a Caltech grad, with a major in computer science and in neurobiology and one of our resident genuises.

Bob seems always involved in something new and unusual. It was Bob who heard that a Catholic college in the area was closing down and selling its library. He had grown up a Catholic and was comfortable approaching the sisters for a favorable price. When they learned about our goals from Bob, their price dropped fourfold! A real answer to prayer!

Even earlier, Bob had worked out the initial papers for the William Carey University to send to the State Board of Education. He had compiled our first catalog of studies. He got our computer center going, and persuaded a number of his Christian friends at Caltech to come on staff. He worked out the arrangements with the government surplus office so that we could get equipment free or at low cost. He persuaded World Vision to give us their 200-line phone system free when they bought their new one. He developed the initial concept for the Frontier Fellowship. And wrote the first *Daily Prayer Guide* (now the *Global Prayer Digest*). And "The Plot," a little booklet which explains in humorous cartoons the idea of daily saving our loose change for pioneer efforts to unreached peoples. He was the person who interacted with Bob Waymire of Overseas Crusades when he was deliberating locating his Global Mapping Project office on our campus so as to be able to take advantage of our computer staff and equipment.

You might say that Bob Coleman is a very useful man to have around! He is what secular, scientifically oriented companies call "a skunk"—brilliant, creative, unpredictable, the kind of person who needs his own den to work in if he is to dream up ideas which just might prove to be extremely valuable. But, they warn, no one company can handle very many.

The U.S. Center for World Mission already had a 40-terminal computer which we had bought at low cost, again through Bob's services. But the research offices on campus, especially the Global Mapping Project, would require very sophisticated computer equipment in order to build and hold a comprehensive database of the Hidden Peoples of the world and the missionary force available to reach them. Bob knew exactly what they needed, but it cost five times more that what we could even imagine being able to afford!

Bob is not one, however, to let such little problems

stop him. Somehow he learned that the Lake Avenue Congregational Church (where a number of our staff attend) was in the process of buying a computer. Bob, typically, saw unusual possibilities in the situation. "Keeping track of a wide range of information about how church members are involved in a large, active church," he thought, "is the same kind of problem as keeping track of the wide range of information about the characteristics of Hidden Peoples. I wonder if we could share a powerful machine to do both?"

At Ralph's suggestion and after a few days of careful research and proposal writing, Bob appeared before the church's Computer Search Committee. "Do the packaged computer systems you've been looking at effectively store all the information you need for as many people as you have in your church?" he asked.

"No, not really!"

"And do you have skilled programmers to write your programs?"

"No, but I suppose . . ."

"Well, it so happens that the kind of computer we need for our research could also handle all the data you need. And we have on staff highly skilled programmers who could program that computer to fit your specifications exactly. If we could somehow work together on this, we could save you immense programming costs which you, in turn, could put into a better system of benefit to us both. With your money up front to buy the machine and our manpower to program and maintain it, we could both have exactly what we need. What would you think about that?"

It took several months to persuade these seasoned, cautious businessmen and church leaders. But at last they agreed, and asked our computer center to help them find the equipment necessary for all they (and Global Mapping) needed to do. They had $45,000 available for the shared computer—no more!

Forty-five thousand! Wonderful! But like the youth

that is delighted with his gift until he sees something just a bit better, Bob groaned. For $20,000 more they could get a model that would more easily expand to keep up with our research programs. Sigh!

Nevertheless, Bob contacted a company in Silicon Valley (in Northern California) and ordered a sophisticated "data base management machine." Then he sat back and waited to hear when it would be available.

Weeks went by, then several months, and everyone concerned was beginning to get restless. Finally Bob called the company near San Francisco.

The salesman was most apologetic. "We're terribly sorry, but we've been unable to fulfill your order. Look, I'll tell you what we'll do. We have another model which is not exactly the same. . . really a bit better. But it's the only one available just now. We'll let you have it for the same price."

"Just which one is it?" Bob asked, and held his breath. After so many months of delicate negotiations with the church officials, he didn't want problems now!

"It's a 500 model."

Bob gasped inwardly. It was exactly the machine he had prayed for.

"God had to be in that shortage," Bob reported to our staff when it arrived. "The name plate says the machine is the cheaper model, but they obviously put on a new label just before they shipped it. The insides are essentially the machine that costs $20,000 more. It's a miracle!"

"But we still have one problem," he added a couple of mornings later. "The computer will be housed here on campus so we can care for it. In order for Lake Avenue Church to use it, we will have to run a special phone line between the church and the Center. Unfortunately, the telephone company says that the church and the campus are in two separate exchanges, and the interchange circuit we would need to buy will cost us an additional $8,000. We simply can't afford that.

"But I've checked around," he continued, "and found out we can avoid that expense if only we could rent some space on the border between the two telephone districts and install a small piece of equipment there. I've looked all over the area, and there is only *one* house that answers all the requirements.

"That's the house with the big black dog . . . and I wouldn't want to tangle with him!"

So we prayed. For Bob and Bill Dickson, who was the computer expert in charge of making the computer link work. For the occupants of that house. About the square foot of their wall which we needed. About their dog.

The next morning Bob had an update. "We went to the house before breakfast this time, hoping to catch the people before they left for work. I was really dreading it. How do you tell people that you want to rent a piece of their wall? Sounds pretty silly, if not downright suspicious.

"Well," and he breathed a big sigh, then smiled. "We noticed right off that their car had an "Ichthus" bumper sticker. We felt better right away. 'Hmm. So they're Christians . . .'

"When I told them I had been there the day before, they said they had gone to a Bible study." Again he smiled, took a deep breath, and continued. "We wanted to maké friends before asking our outlandish request, so we asked where their Bible study was. Do you know what? They attend one of the new churches that meets right here on our campus! Imagine that!"

We all laughed at God's goodness. "And they'll rent us as much wall space as we need. Isn't that wonderful?" he finished.

Within a few months the dream became a reality: Lake Avenue Church acquired one of the finest church computer systems anywhere, the Global Mapping Project moved its office to our campus, and Bob Waymire and his team began to collect and store vital data on the world's

Unreached Peoples. The first color-coded map that showed up on the screen was indeed beautiful to see.

The sample maps they are producing are advancing mission strategy many years into the future. All because a local church was willing to take the risk of collaborating with a campus whose future was still uncertain. That, perhaps, was the greatest miracle of all!

37

VICTORY IN DISGUISE

September 1st, 1983. For five years we had looked forward to this day when the balloon payment of $6 million would be due on the campus portion of our property. For five years we had prayed for the day when we would be able to "enter the land" and make the campus wholly ours. We had worked long and hard and had prayed as never before in our lives. And yet, when the day arrived, we were not ready.

It had been a constant struggle to make our mortgage payments of $175,000 every three months for five years. We had fallen behind several times, once almost to the point of foreclosure. But the Lord had miraculously brought us through again and again.

Because of that strain, however, it was hard to believe that God would really give us the $6 1/2 million all at once. We felt we had been in the wilderness and hoped that in the future it would be easier, somehow. But we had no idea how much work the Lord still had to do on *us*.

Though often tempted otherwise, over the years, we had continued to believe that if we gave first priority to Kingdom concerns, God would indeed supply all these other things we needed, money included. (See Matt. 6:33.) Thus, our "fund raising" plans always included the larger Kingdom concern of mobilizing the church for new mission outreach.

217

We tried many approaches: our *Hidden Peoples Chart*, our *Penetrating the Last Frontiers* movie, articles in various magazines, radio interviews with missionaries, the *Year of Vision* program for pastors, as well as a heavy speaking schedule for some of our leaders. As vision producing programs, every attempt produced results, some much more spectacular than others. But they did not bring in the money we needed for our mortgage payments.

One idea, however, came close to a promise of not only spreading the vision but bringing us financial help as well.

In the spring of 1981, Pastor Vuta from Burma told our staff a fascinating story. Shortly after World War II his country had expelled all foreigners, including missionaries. At that time his tribe, the Lushai, were still unreached. But the Mizo tribe from India which, years before, had been reached by missionaries from Wales, had crossed the "closed" border to reach the Lushai.

Barely 25 years later, the Lushai were themselves taking the gospel north to other unreached Burmese tribes. "We already have 16 missionaries," Pastor Vuta proudly told Ralph.

Ralph was amazed and pleased. "Just how do you support them? Do they have to pay their own way?" he asked.

"We have the handful of rice!"

"What?" Ralph wondered if he had heard right.

"The handful of rice. Every meal our wives set aside a handful of rice for missions. At the end of the week the Women's Missionary Society collects the rice and sells it in the market. That's the way we support them."

"Hmm," Ralph thought. "I wonder how much a handful of rice is worth in their economy."

It turned out to be substantial, really a sacrifice because they were all poor. Unknown to himself, this humble pastor from a little known tribe in Burma became the inspiration for a new movement of prayer and giving in America.

Increasingly Ralph was convinced that the answer to mission mobilization had to be something that *daily* impacted the lives of hundreds of thousands of Christians. If the Burmese Christians could give a handful of rice per meal, what could American Christians give? Bob Coleman on our staff suggested loose change, but was almost embarrassed to do so. For the Burmese, a handful of rice was a sacrifice, but the amount of loose change an American has at the end of each day tends to average about 27¢, hardly a sacrifice except for the very poor. But it was a place to start. And asking for more might seem to threaten local church budgets.

"How can we inspire Americans to do even that much?" someone asked.

Just a few weeks earlier Ralph had spoken at a meeting of Navigator leaders in Colorado Springs and had picked up their customized version of *The Daily Walk* prayer guide. "Why can't there be a *missions* prayer guide. also used on a daily basis?" he asked himself.

Several weeks later we sent Brad Gill, one of our younger staff leaders, to confer with leaders from Campus Crusade, InterVarsity and World Vision about such a guide. Each was enthusaiastic.

Bob Coleman, our Director of Planning, was thrown the task of design as usual. For several weeks in the fall of 1981, he and Koleen Matsuda, like him a Caltech grad gifted in writing, worked over the basic design and wrote the first issue of what they called *The Daily Prayer Guide*. Every day had an inspirational Bible reading which looked at the Bible as a missionary book. The rest of each page was given over to a missionary biography, the exciting report of a new missions breakthrough, or the story of a Hidden People group still waiting to be reached.

The little booklet was good--very good, everyone said. But we now had the problem of marketing. We knew how to sell books, but our goal now was nothing short of starting a movement of prayer for missions. Thus we

219

were thrilled when first ten, twenty, then thirty or more denominations and mission agencies began to promote the use of the *Global Prayer Digest* (as it later came to be called), many requesting their own customized versions.

This development was very wonderful and really crucial. Meanwhile, however, the date for our $6 1/2 million balloon payment on the campus—September 1st, 1983—marched nearer and nearer.

When we designed the Frontier Fellowship *Global Prayer Digest*, we had hoped that, as with World Vision's love loaf, the agencies or churches participating with the Frontier Fellowship Movement would help pay the start-up costs by sending the Center the first $15 collected by every new participant.

But to keep track of all this was a burden both for the participating agencies and our own little office, which was already overloaded by the task of producing the *Digest*. Almost immediately we discovered that this arrangement seemed to get in the way of vision sharing, so we decided to bear those expenses alone.

Among some groups the plan was immediately successful. For example, in its first year of participation, the Presbyterian Church (USA) received $120,000. That amount doubled the second year and continues to grow. This hardy group of evangelicals in the Presbyterian Frontier Fellowship has a goal of getting 100,000 Presbyterians involved (that is, 1 out of 30 members), which will produce $10 million per year for outreach to unreached peoples.

What a thrill to know that through our efforts, a substantial number of dollars per year were being raised for new mission work! But it was a bit discouraging to realize that, once again, one of the programs we had initiated to help the entire missions cause would not likely help us! Who then would help *us*?

One day in April, Ralph said to our staff, "I think we're looking at this situation in the wrong way.

Our problem is not to learn how to *get* but rather how to *give*—to give the most valuable thing we possess—hope!"

"Hope?" I thought. "That's what *we ourselves* need about now!"

He continued. "One reason why the church as a whole is so lethargic about missions today is that Christians have lost hope for the world. Just look at the newspapers."

I thought back to the suicide bomb which not long before had killed a number of marines in Lebanon. At the time my first reaction was quite typical: "What are we doing over there anyway? *They* don't want us. Why risk our necks?"

I really can't blame U.S. Christians for their lack of interest when all they know about missions seems so unrelated to the real problems of the world--the civil wars in Central America, the kidnapping of diplomats, the upswing of pornography and abortion! "Perhaps we ought to be grateful that they dutifully continue to support a cause they feel is rather beside the point," I thought.

"If we could just tell the churches why we have hope," Ralph added, "then I think they would be able once again to get seriously involved in missions. How many church people, for instance, know that since the Sandinistas took over in Nicaragua, the evangelical movement has grown five times larger, right under the noses of a Marxist government and against its wishes? Or, how many have ever heard of the missionaries working with the thousands of so-called "street children" of Manila? How many realize that there are entire communes in China which are now Christian? Or that entire villages of high caste Hindus are finding Christ in India? Do American Christians understand what a difference these facts are already making, even in the politics of these countries?

"We who are part of the staff of the U.S. Center for World Mission are very fortunate because we work where we find out the facts. But we owe it to the members of our churches to tell them, too."

221

It was that challenge which brought us once more to the drawing board. What sort of thing could we do that would not only bring a truly rejuvenating hope to American Christians but would also, we hoped and prayed, encourage them to help us survive as an organization?

Somewhat after the pattern of our earliest "Grapevine" (pass-on-able) letter, we decided to send out a brief, inexpensive "Invitation to Hope." On one side of the sheet it described some of the exciting things which we knew God was doing around the world. On the other, we told what He was doing through our efforts at the U.S. Center for World Mission.

Ten of these letters were put in a packet so that a person who had already given to us could send copies to ten friends, inviting each one to embrace our hopeful outlook on the world. In a handwritten note which he added at the top, he then suggested that his friend register his own hope for what God was doing through us by sending us a one-time $15 gift. These letters were our only propaganda for our "I'll Touch Ten" campaign.

I'll never forget the massive work party it took to get all those letters ready to mail out. Everyone on staff (as well as a number of the staff from member organizations on campus and volunteers from local churches) worked all day long for three days in Pasadena's largest auditorium, which happened to be on our campus.

It was already into the summer, and the auditorium was without air conditioning. At least 100 people were seated around tables placed on the only level area--the basketball court in the center near the stage. Several of the young men were assigned as "runners" to keep each table supplied with "Invitations to Hope," envelopes, rubber bands, and explanatory literature which accompanied each packet of ten letters, all of which had to be bundled together before being packed into mailing boxes.

Staff mothers brought their babies and young children,

and every now and then a child would laugh, or cry, or be caught up in the air by one of the single girls or guys. We were all one big happy family, singing as we worked, trusting that the Lord would bless our efforts. Every now and then the group around one or another table would stop to pray. These fragile letters were our lamps and pitchers (see Judges 7) that we felt the Lord had told us to use for our need.

For some years each of our Central staff has been assigned as the personal correspondent for a certain area of the United States (or the world, as the case might be). Thus, every person who contacts the U.S. Center for World Mission receives back a personal letter from someone on staff. For several weeks previous to our work party, most of us had arrived at work at 6 a.m. in order to call "back east" on midnight rates to individuals from our own particular assigned areas. We were pleased at how many were eager to help with our "I'll Touch Ten Campaign." Eventually 500 offered to be responsible for an entire "Hope Chest"—a hundred packets of ten invitations each. That meant 500 x 100 x 10—or 500,000 invitations!

Many pastors took several "Hope Chests" and encouraged their entire congregations to send our invitations to ten friends each, adding a personal note to each one. Some individuals on their own passed out at least a hundred packets.

Besides bringing hope to people in the pew, the wonderful response from all over brought tremendous hope to us, right when we needed it most. The letters started to pour in, and we scrambled to answer our mail.

In just two months surrounding September 1st, we had 14,000 new donors and in addition had received enough unsolicited larger gifts to make over $900,000.

But it was a subdued victory in view of our need for $6 1/2 million. We were extremely grateful to all who had given, but I would be less than honest if I did not say that we were also very disappointed. We had wanted so much to be *over* the Jordan. Instead we merely stood on the bank, looking across. I think it is true that, deep inside, many of us had become tired of having to trust the Lord! We were tired of not knowing until the last minute if we would go under or not. We felt that we had had enough education in the school of faith. And it took us almost a week before we could truly rejoice over that victory in disguise.

Our contract with the former owners had stated that if we failed to pay the entire $6 1/2 million, we could continue two more years at higher interest and almost double payments: $300,000 per quarter. Furthermore, the new date for our balloon payment would be two years later, coinciding with the $2.8 million balloon payment which would come due then for the off-campus housing! We had always dismissed this option as one which would surely crush us, and had prayed earnestly that we would be able to avoid it

But God evidently had other plans. Perhaps we still needed pruning. It was true that, in spite of all our efforts, most American Christians were still completely ignorant of the unreached peoples. We had tried, but we had not yet accomplished that goal. Was that why we could not get out of the wilderness through which we had wandered for five long years? Or did God know that we might claim the victory ourselves? Was the victory He wanted to give so great that He knew we were not yet ready for it?

Or was the discovery of how to reach 14,000 people with new hope more valuable than getting in the money just then? Did God feel we should have the additional opportunity (necessity!) to continue to reach new people?

I do not know. But I do know that in only six weeks God had provided almost a million dollars. We couldn't make the $6 1/2 million balloon payment with that, but we could catch up and pay the next two quarterly payments besides. God had not forsaken us. Apparently, He was just leading us by a different, longer way.

The twice-as-big $300,000 quarterly payments looked impossible—but at least the principle would be reduced faster! [1] But how ever could we meet those payments and two years later a combined balloon payment of $8 1/2 million.[2]

God had promised He would *never* leave us nor forsake us. He had promised to be *with* us and to give us all that we would *need*. He had called us to this work for His kingdom's sake and had led us by a path to bring glory to His name. Therefore our problem was His! He would have to find the solution! We only needed to push on in faith.

Still, with mounting pressure upon us from all sides, one question troubled many of our staff and board members: did God *really* want us to concentrate so much on giving hope rather than on getting the money we so badly needed? Was there no easier, more sure way?

---

1. It may seem strange, but it is true: when we were paying 8% interest and $175,000 per quarter, we could count on only a little over $60,000 going to reduce the debt. Later, paying 12 1/2%, but much higher payments of $300,000 per quarter, we were actually paying more than $120,000 per quarter against our debt. Moreover, with each payment, the percentage paid against the principle actually increases and the proportion eaten up in interest definitely decreases.

2. Although the balloon payments were set at $6 1/2 million (for the campus proper) and $2.8 million (for the houses), because of the increased payment schedule, the combined figure two years later would be only $8 1/2 million.

38

HIS, FOR BETTER OR WORSE

I walked into Ralph's office early one day in 1982 and saw Ralph and Bob Coleman poring over a computer magazine. It seemed at first glance that, as two engineers, they were engrossed with some new computer marvel. "This is the way I think we should go," Ralph was saying, to which Bob agreed. "People have become so used to the ordinary kind that they don't pay much attention anymore. They're more likely to read something that is different."

I wondered mildly what they were talking about, but since I was also quite busy, I soon forgot all about it.

Several days later they were again deep in discussion and, I noticed, looking at the same page. "What on earth are you two doing?" I asked as I glanced over Ralph's shoulder. "Whatever is so fascinating about that page?" At first glance it looked like any other page of text except, as Ralph pointed out, it had a small notice right under the title which said, "This is a paid advertisement." Now I was really curious.

"Pastor _____ has offered to pay for a full page ad about the Center in one of the major Christian magazines. We're trying to figure out the format to use, and have

226

decided to follow this design. We both feel that an ad which doesn't look like one may actually be more likely to be read. I've been working on what it should say, and Bob is working out the design. Tomorrow afternoon, we have to ship it by overnight express mail. That's really rushing it, but that's their deadline."

The next afternoon I saw the finished product just as they were putting it and the check in the mail. It consisted basically of seven astounding statements about the vigor and growth of the world Christian movement. In large handwriting scrawled across the top was the arresting phrase,

The Lord Thy God in the midst of thee is mighty!

Because of the text format, however, I frankly wondered if the ad would seem exciting enough to attract attention. "But," I reasoned, "a full page of anything is hard to miss!"

Several days went by, and we heard nothing. Finally Ralph called, asking if we had made the deadline.

"We're not accepting your ad," the editor told him.

"What? You're not accepting it?" Ralph wondered if he had heard right. "I thought you said you had space."

"Well, we do. But we have some problems with your ad."

"Just what I feared; the format must be too unconventional," Ralph thought. But he asked, "Can you tell me just what is the problem?"

"We don't believe what it says is true! To print it like it is would only embarrass you, and us!"

Ralph was stunned. And he thought, "What do we do now? What do you do when someone simply doesn't believe you, especially if you're speaking from your own area of expertise?" But he only said, "Can you give me an example?"

"Well, for one thing, you say here that there are at least a million Christians in most of the larger countries in the world. We can't believe that!"

"Then you also say that a thousand new churches open their doors every Sunday in Africa and Asia. How can that possibly be true?"

"And. . ." He was ready to go on, but Ralph interrupted.

"Just a minute! I can understand how you might find these things hard to believe. But that is the "punch" of the ad—most people don't have any hope, and can't easily believe such things. Nevertheless, they are true! Do you happen to know Warren Webster, the head of the Conservative Baptist Foreign Mission Society?"

"Sure!"

"Would you believe him if he agreed with those statements?"

"Well, yes." The answer seemed uncertain. "But we've already replaced that page for this issue, and it's too late."

As he put down the phone, Ralph shook his head in disbelief. For fifteen years he had had his hand on the pulse of the church around the world. A thousand students representing every continent (and most of the countries) of the world had brought information in from their grassroots situations. He had not only gleaned available facts but tabulated and graphed them. He knew what he was talking about! Furthermore, Barrett's *Encyclopedia*[1] had just come out and was an incomparable source of raw information which underlay statements like, "87% of the people in the world live in countries where there are at least 1,000,000 evangelical Christians."

Ralph recognized that few people had access to the kind of information he received, even the editors of America's leading evangelical magazine, who had just refused our ad. But the fact remained: if *they* could not believe what he said, would the general public? Would everyone think he was exaggerating the facts—or, worse yet, grossly dishonest?

And yet, if only American Christians could believe the truth, how encouraged they would be! How motivated to push ahead and finish the job of world evangelization. Like a winning football team, we would give it all we had instead of just struggling along passively or defensively. Apart from our own survival as an institution, it was really important to get those facts out to the public in a way they would be believed. But how?

Somewhat soberly Ralph dialed Dr. Webster. "Warren," he said, "I've got a problem which needs your help." And he explained what had happened. He went on to read the offensive statements from our "bright picture" ad.

"Ralph, I see no problem with that! Anyhow, I'd have to tell them that if I had any doubt about such statements the person I'd ask would be Ralph Winter!"

That comment was gratifying but did not solve the larger problem.

Several days later the mail brought back our unused ad. We could see where the editor in chief had tried to tone down a couple of statements but evidently had been too late.

The year before, in the summer of 1981, we had learned that *Christianity Today* was running a news story about the Center. We were excited about this because we sorely needed free publicity. A few days before the magazine was to go to press, however, the main editor, a friend of Ralph's, called suggesting that he felt he should check some of the facts as written. Evidently the writer, someone we didn't know, had interviewed a person not closely associated with the Center structure who had given him all sorts of misinformation. It was too late in the publishing schedule to rewrite the entire article, so that as it finally appeared, it still contained 13 factual errors. These were minor in comparison with the three columns that had been cut, some of which could have seriously injured, if not actually killed, the future of the project.

Fortunately, as in Ezra 5:4, God oversaw the situation so that little harm was done. But one of our daughters commented that the article in its final shape seemed a bit disjointed. One part was rather critical of the Center, another section highly complimentary and the third, halfway in between.

With this kind of exposure to Christian journalism, we were a bit surprised, but not terribly optimistic, when a year or so later, Tim Stafford came on campus and wanted to interview Ralph for a possible cover article about him for *Christianity Today*.

During our daughters' high school years, we had subscribed to Young Life's *Campus Life*, and I had always been well impressed with Tim Stafford's column. Years later we met him and his wife at a missionary conference where they (and Ralph and I) were speaking. They had just returned from Nairobi where they had started a first class Christian magazine for one of the mission agencies. The magazine was a smashing success, even selling widely through secular channels. We were really impressed!

Tim spent a couple of hours interviewing Ralph, and evidently also spoke with several others in the area, then left. And we became engulfed again in our ongoing struggle to make our mortgage payments and operate the Center at the same time.

Two years passed, and this conversation was forgotten altogether. In the middle of that time, on September 1st, 1983, the balloon payment on the campus proper had come due. Thousands helped in our "I'll Touch Ten" campaign, but we were still so short of what we needed that we had to refinance at great cost to us.

About that time, we learned that the two largest associations of mission agencies in the world had accepted our invitation to have their triennial joint meeting on our campus in September of the following year. We were thrilled to be their hosts, but with little money and an inadequate staff, we had a thousand things to do to get ready for them.

In the meantime, our mortgage payments (now $300,000) came due, right on schedule every three months. By June, 1984, we had used up the very last of the $900,000 the Lord had so graciously given us the previous September. In late August we had only $100,000 toward the September 1st payment, and we wondered if Point Loma would have to foreclose on us just at the very time we were expecting the most important guests we had ever had. We couldn't be angry. Point Loma officials had been extremely patient with us through the years. We had great respect and appreciation for these officials, but how much more patience could we expect from them? Yet we didn't think we dared try another massive fund raising campaign so soon after the one of the previous year, even if we had the time and energy.

Toward the end of July, 1984, Tim Stafford called Ralph "to pursue our conversation a bit further." Ralph had forgotten about the article interview and only remembered his own point in the latter half of that conversation—about the possibility of Tim helping our university set up an M.A. program for mission field writers. Gradually it came out that Tim was calling to update the article he had written about Ralph. He explained that the article would likely be the cover story for the September issue of *Christianity Today.*

We were amazed and pleased. And yet, with the shadow of possible foreclosure, we had very mixed feelings. The magazine would hit the homes of America at a time which was very critical for us. We would have only 90 days to "cure" our situation (that is, pay up) or lose everything. If the article was friendly, it could help us. If, however, it was very critical, it could really hurt us in our present extremity. Needless to say, we waited a bit anxiously for the sample copy to arrive.

But, in any case, we really didn't have time to give

much thought to the *Christianity Today* article. In just a few days, 425 mission executives from the over 200 mission agencies that make up the Interdenominational Foreign Mission Association (IFMA), the Evangelical Foreign Missions Association (EFMA), and the Association of Evangelical Professors of Missions (AEPM) would arrive on our campus. And we still had an enormous amount of preparation to complete.

For almost a year, Darrell Dorr, our third daughter's very capable husband, had spent most of his time working out the practical arrangements for that conference. Because it would occur right after our fall semester would begin, our students would have to be housed temporarily in homes off campus. (Whose?) Broken down lounge furniture needed to be replaced with newly donated pieces. (Where would we get it?) We would need to buy more blankets and sheets. Some rooms had to be repainted, torn carpets replaced. Darrell had to decide which meetings would be where, where the conference office would be, how to furnish it, what extra phones needed to be installed, whether to install cold drink machines or set up a snack shop . . . details, details, details! But Darrell is an expert with details. He was perfect for the job.

As the time drew closer, however, even Darrell began to panic. "I just must have more help," he complained to Art McCleary one day.

"Okay. We'll have another big work party on Saturday. We'll assign everyone on staff to something or other. Some may have to pull weeds. Some will make beds. Some will have to clean bathrooms. Just make a list of the jobs, and we'll get it done."

Fortunately, Loren and Darlene Cunningham of Youth With a Mission came by the Center and volunteered some of their staff. "Listen, we have a gal who is tremendous with decorating rooms at no cost. Here is her name. Call her and see what she can do.

"Also, I think about twenty of our Olympic Outreach

team are still in the area. We'll tell them to call you and help out."

I had worried about the unsightliness of three large potholes at the entrances to two of our parking lots. Estimates on their repair ran in the thousands of dollars. We didn't have that kind of money for potholes! Providentially, one of the YWAM volunteers was a Canadian engineer who had had experience in that very kind of thing! What amazing grace!

After a few weeks of this kind of countdown, the campus looked better than we had ever seen it. It still had a long way to go to look like the Hilton, but it was neat and clean and fairly attractive though not luxurious. Dorm rooms which had lacked them now had curtains that matched the new (used) bedspreads! Staff and friends loaned potted plants which brightened up the lounges and cafeteria. YWAM volunteers rounded up travel posters for dorm walls and put together hospitality kits which they made up from donated soap, combs, razors and snacks which they had solicited from area merchants. Others may have thought how simple everything looked. To us, after getting by for so long on the proverbial shoestring, it was simply beautiful!

In the middle of all this frenzy of activity, the long-looked-for issue of *Christianity Today* arrived. Ralph's secretary looked at the cover drawing and started to chuckle. "Mrs. Winter," she called as she headed into Ralph's office. "The article has arrived. Come! You've just got to see this!"

Others in near by offices heard, and also came. They also laughed as they looked at the drawing of Ralph on the cover. It was multi-colored and, I suppose, quite good in technique since the art work took first prize at the Evangelical Press Association's annual meeting the next spring. But as Ralph's wife, I groaned. Inside it was worse, I felt. There were no photos of him, just duplicates of the same kind of spoof. "Why does it look so odd?" I asked. Then I saw it. It wasn't a clerical collar they had put on him, as I thought at first. (He had never worn one!) "That's the screw end of a light bulb! They've drawn his head to look like a light bulb!"

Everyone laughed. "I think it's rather cute!" one said. "It's a compliment, really, to show that he's full of bright ideas."

A compliment? Perhaps. Still, he looked so bookish, rather like a man from Mars might look. Where was the twinkle in his eye that I loved so much? That didn't look like the man I was married to!

Obviously it didn't bother Ralph. He was already deep into the article itself, and he waved us to other copies to read.

I found myself a bit on the defensive at first, then relaxed. "Tim is really quite generous, isn't he? It's very good!"

Ralph put it down, finally, with a smile of satisfaction. "Tim Stafford has stated some of our key ideas better than we ever have! It is really quite perceptive. I only wish it would say more about the Center and less about me." [2]

Evidently others also liked the article. Not only the artist, but Tim also, as the writer, won a prize at the Evangelical Press Association—second place!

Because of the upcoming conference which we were going to host, Art McCleary, our general manager, hardly had time to look at the article. We really leaned on Art for everything. When he left the position of Personnel Director at Bethel College in Minneapolis the year before, he came expecting the same position with us. We found when he arrived that he was the very man we had been praying for for years. Deeply devout, he had years of experience in management with secular companies as well as twenty years with Bethel College. He was seminary trained, married to a missionary daughter, and his heart was in missions. Most amazing of all, he was willing to raise his own support, like the rest of us.

When Art and Elaine decided to join us, their friends in Minneapolis told them they were crazy. They had already applied to a number of mission agencies, and before coming to look us over, they fully intended to go with another group. His comments about those first days with us made us both wince and laugh: "One thing I knew for sure: I knew I was needed. I couldn't believe the way this place was run! If ever an organization needed an experienced manager, this was it!"

We knew that. Somehow people always assumed that the reason we didn't already have a top manager was because Ralph preferred to do his own management. They couldn't have been further from the truth. We had many willing, inexperienced young people who were heart and soul with us. And we had retired missionaries. But people in the critical middle years with management experience and vitality were sadly lacking. The result was that Ralph also had to bear much of that load—responsibility which he didn't want and in which he admittedly had little experience.

"That's why I felt the Lord led me here. Of all the agencies we could join, you needed me the most!" Art told us.

The week after he arrived he became not only the personnel manager, but the manager of the U.S. Center as well. Less than a year later, after the business manager of the University had to be hospitalized, Art became both General Manager of the Center and the Vice President for Business Affairs of the University as well. This happened only one month before the EFMA-IFMA conference was to begin. For any other person, it would have been an impossible task. Art merely commandeered an old golf cart and a walkie talkie and was all over the campus, making sure Darrell's plans worked out.

All too soon the mission executives began to arrive. For the previous three weeks we had patiently waited for legal notice of foreclosure from Point Loma. It still had not come. "Why do you think it is taking so long?" Art asked Ralph.

"I can't imagine. When I called just last week, they assured me again that this was it. They said they were starting proceedings immediately. I just can't understand it! Not that we want it. I really dread it. But if it is going to come, the sooner we know it, the better. Then we'll have 90 days to do our best to "get current," as they say—90 days which legally we are given. If we can't do that, then we either have to pay the complete amount or lose everything. It just may be that the shock of foreclosure will bring a lot of people to our aid. I really don't know. But waiting to see what will happen is very difficult."

Under those circumstances it was hard to be the perfect hosts. You might say we were distracted. Ralph had to give one of the evening addresses, and I frankly wondered if he could even get his mind on the subject. And yet we knew that, if nothing else, we were pressed into prayer. God was teaching us to be completely dependent upon Him.

So far as I know, the night Ralph spoke was the first time in their history that the IFMA and the EFMA had ever taken up an offering for one of their member agencies. It just wasn't done. All of them had financial needs! The $3000 they gave us meant far more than the money itself. It was a promise that they would stand behind us in prayer at this most difficult time.

During the conference, we had already been impressed by their times of prayer. Obviously these were men and women of prayer. "Perhaps because of the prayers of such godly people, God will do another miracle for us in just a few weeks," many of us hoped. But we couldn't imagine just what it could be.

As it turned out, it wasn't a miracle just around the corner. It was a Gethsemane.

1. *The World Christian Encyclopedia* by David Barrett, published by Oxford University Press (N.Y. 1982) is now, unfortunately out of print. It is the most comprehensive treatment ever to be made of Christianity around the world.

2. "Ralph Winter: Looking for the Hidden Peoples," *Christianity Today*, September 7, 1984, pp. 14-18.

39

OCT. - NOV. 1984

"I WANT YOU TO TRUST ME . ."

(Ps. 50:14-15)

"Ralph, your money raising ideas have obviously failed—every one of them! It's time the Board took over and did things in the usual way!"

From the beginning, that October Board meeting was very painful for us. For several weeks we had been waiting for the arrival of the notice of legal foreclosure. We dreaded it, and yet we hoped that it just might rally our supporters to help us pay off, once and for all, the balance still due on the campus proper. The risk was terrible—but we knew no other option. We had done our very best!

But these words from a member of our Board really hurt. "Is it failure," I wondered, "to have raised six and a half million dollars in eight years? Most boards would not think so! Especially when starting from zero!" But we had sometimes noticed that God's many miracles, though reassuring to our faith, sometimes made those accustomed to more traditional methods of financing a bit uneasy.

The fact is, Ralph's "money raising ideas" were really vision-spreading ideas, and in terms of their primary purpose had been immensely successful. But to those for whom the purchase of the campus was most important, to waste our time on "vision-spreading" ideas when we needed money seemed most foolish.

To a great extent, however, the entire future of the Center hinged on this dichotomy. To accomplish what God had called us to do, we had to have the friendship and cooperation of the other mission agencies. Many, we knew, employ no "money raising ideas" at all. We could not place ourselves in a situation where we would tempt away their donors. Nor could we abandon our vision-spreading to secure the campus. Somehow we had to do both at the same time. That was why every plan we had followed involved both spreading the vision and raising money in a way that would not jeopardize other agencies.

We had to admit, however, that we were now facing imminent foreclosure, when we could lose everything God had given us. This member of the Board had every right to be concerned. But just what would he suggest we do?

"If we move quickly enough, he insisted, "we can sell off a number of the houses, build condominiums which will bring in higher rent, and save the campus that way."

Ralph sat there appalled. It was not as though he had not thought about the need for rebuilding and replacing the many substandard houses. The 84 separate properties encircling the campus were readily salable (compared to campus buildings). And once we owned them outright, we could quite easily borrow against them and invest that money in redevelopment that would genuinely increase the overall value of this housing. Ralph had realized that before we had ever set foot on the campus.

But there was an ominous message behind this proposal. The money that would be "raised" by selling houses would actually be spent on paying our debts. If most of the houses were sold and the balloon payment made, what was left over would be so small that we would have to borrow a great deal more from a bank in order to do any redevelopment. Even if we sold all the houses, that money alone would not pay the remaining balance on the campus proper.

Worse yet, by selling these houses, we would lose the rental income on which we depended for operating funds. Unless we owned them outright, any redevelopment scheme would inevitably involve us in a another debt which it would take at least fifteen years to pay off before we could begin to collect any real income from that improved property.

In the meantime, how could we operate without that income? We had a lot of work to do. We could not keep on raising funds forever and at the same time move forward decisively in the work God had given us to do. We needed not only the campus but all the houses fully paid off *now!*

To us, therefore, this proposal was actually not so much a money raising idea as a partial campus-liquidation plan. It was an attempt to deal with our debts by reducing our holdings—and in the process giving up on the original goal of a self-sustaining plant. It would mean that we would forever have to raise operational funds—and do so in competition with the very mission agencies we were professing to serve. To us, this plan seemed a disaster.

This Board member, personally involved in a number of real estate deals, naturally tended to think in terms of his own expertise. He knew how to work with property on a commercial basis. But, he admitted, he knew very little about fund raising, and he had long criticized our small, one-time-gift plan.

In the area of financial considerations, however, he was very influential on the Board, and before the meeting was over that day, the vote had carried. A Development Committee was named and told to start work immediately. It was directed to get estimates on all the houses, draw up plans for which should be sold first, hire a contractor to upgrade those houses, and start finding buyers.

This decision was like a blow to those of us who had started the Center. We could understand how the majority of the Board, involved in Center affairs for only one day every three or four months, could see things differently from the staff who met daily to pray over each crisis. And yet we felt very strongly that God had led us, step by step, even into the tight situations in which we sometimes found ourselves. As we read our Bibles, His ways with us were not all that unusual.

Nevertheless, we appreciated the sincere concern of these people. The questions they asked were the same that others, much closer, had also asked: "Do you really need all those houses? Couldn't the staff and students still live in them even if other people owned them?"

But they could see the logic of Ralph's answers: "Isn't the same true of the dormitories on campus? What if someone else owned them? Couldn't the students still stay there?

"Yes, perhaps! But the major difference is that the one who owns the properties gets the rent! The average college cannot survive without both the income from their dorms and, say, another 30% from donations. Those houses have always functioned as college dorms, even when the Nazarenes were here. Once we own the campus and houses outright, we don't expect to have to raise another 30% in donations. But without at least these houses, we certainly would have to be raising money forever. They are our only planned source of income, and we need all of them for that."

Interestingly, before we made our first bid for the campus back in 1976, part of the original fleece which we laid before the Lord was that if He wanted us to proceed with the campus, He would make the Point Loma Board willing to stop selling off the houses and to hold them for us, even though we could not put a penny down on them for at least a year. For them to accept such a proposition meant a loss of capital, money which they really needed. The houses were in demand and it was to the college's benefit to sell them, one by one.

Nevertheless, they agreed to our request. Later, the

elderly realtor on their board, who had managed the houses for the college all through the years, told Ralph privately, "You were very wise to insist that the houses be part of the package. It has always been true that the campus is simply not financially viable without them. Now whatever you do, don't fail to buy them. You simply must have them to succeed!"

Almost all our staff, especially those few who made up the minority on the Board (four out of twelve), were in deep distress over the board action. All of us felt like our birthright was being sold away from us, and there was little we could do about it but pray.

We thought of all the miracles God had done for us in this place. He had so definitely led us here and in unexpected ways turned the property over to us. By a series of miracles He had brought in the $6 1/2 million we had already paid. Would He forsake us now? Was the only answer to sell what He had given us, houses which were not only necessary for students and staff but whose income was essential to the operation of the overall complex? Did we have to assume there would be no more miracles? Couldn't we at least wait a bit longer and give God time to act on our behalf?

Two weeks after the October board meeting, I had the prayer watch from 7:30 a.m. until noon. From the window of the 24-hour prayer room, I could see the staff as they arrived for morning prayers two floors below. All knew that both Ralph and I felt very uneasy about the Board's decision. They knew he believed that selling the houses should be a last resort fallback plan, to be followed only in the event that all else failed.

In spite of how things appeared, we believed that God would come to our aid. Those on staff who agreed with us sent Ralph notes of encouragement; the few who didn't sent notes of rebuke. The harmony we usually enjoyed was shattered. Most didn't even know what to pray for.

Because of the situation, my heart was very heavy that

morning as I entered the prayer room. And I cried out to the Lord, "I cannot bear this. Give me something from Your Word to comfort my heart!"

The preceding May God had been talking to me about total dependence on Him. It seemed that every verse I saw, every devotional book I read, stressed the same thing. I truly wanted to trust Him completely, but I was still afraid.

"Why don't You send us a wealthy benefactor," I complained to the Lord. "Other organizations have them. Why not us? Why does it have to be so hard?"

I struggled with this, especially after the Board's decision to sell. "Lord, we could lose everything we've fought for while we're trying to learn dependence. Is that what You want?" But I felt ashamed.

That morning in the prayer room, I paced the floor as I cried out to Him. Down below all was still . I knew the staff were also in prayer, also seeking His face, and I turned to my Bible to see what God might want to tell me.

During the years, our tests had so often paralleled those of the Children of Israel on their way to Canaan that I turned to those pages once again. I examined the situation of the ten spies at Kadesh Barnea in Numbers 13 and 14. Were we likewise in danger of not trusting God to care for us? If so, would He reject us also, and send us off into a forty year wilderness? And yet, under the circumstances, just what could we do? "What is Your way, oh God?" I prayed. "Protect us from disobedience and unbelief."

Knowing that Exodus often gives a parallel account of something told in Numbers, I looked for the same story there. I couldn't find it. Still praying earnestly, "Give me a word from You," I continued leafing, idly, on through Exodus and into Leviticus. I admit that I didn't expect anything from Leviticus: isn't that all about rules and rituals and directions for building the tabernacle? What could Leviticus possibly have to say to our situation?

Suddenly my eyes were glued to the page. I read the verse once, then twice—in amazement—and started to laugh. It couldn't be! But there it was!

And remember, the land is mine, so you may not sell it permanently. You are merely my tenants and sharecroppers! In every contract of sale there must be a stipulation that the land can be redeemed at any time by the seller. (Lev. 25:23-24 LB)

"The land is mine!" it said. "You may not sell it!" Amazing!

Even the other part, "In every contract of sale must be the stipulation that you can buy it back at any time". . . Those were almost the exact words that Ralph had fallen back to in the Board meeting when he saw he could not prevent their decision.

All at once my heart started to sing. God hadn't forgotten us. There would be an answer, one that would not compromise our faith. We could wait on the Lord with confidence. He would somehow take care of us.

244

40

"DON'T THROW AWAY YOUR CONFIDENCE...PERSEVERE"

(Heb. 10:35 NIV)

My heart was at peace, at least for awhile. But Ralph's was not. The months between October and March were months of tremendous stress for him. Never have I seen him so discouraged for so long. It seemed that the decision of the Board to go against what he felt was best was like an arrow in his heart. He could no longer work with confidence that they would back him. He felt he didn't know what they would decide next, and if he could live with it. The joy left his eyes. The faith and hope which is ordinarily so much a part of him was no longer there. He said very little, but he lived with pain. Never have I seen him come so close to quitting.

As the months passed, and I saw the agony Ralph was going through, I spent a great deal of time in prayer for him personally. If he could just be distracted from the vision God had given him, if he could just spend his time fretting about problems over which he had no control, then Satan could still stop us.

Through a providential circumstance at the height of our personal distress, Bill Bright of Campus Crusade learned of the struggle we were in and called Ralph one night at midnight. He had just arrived back from Germany and was calling from Tulsa.

He recounted some of the stresses he had gone through in earlier days, times which were equally as discouraging as our own. "But Ralph," he added, "one thing is true. These men on the Board didn't call you to start the Center. God did! You're answerable to Him. Anyhow, there are some things that you just can't resign from. You can't resign from being a father to your children. And you can't resign from God's call. Just hang in, and God will see you through!"

Ralph was very quiet when he got off the phone. I could tell that he felt like he was deliberately walking back into the Garden of Gethsemane. But at least the light was clear. He knew which way to go, even though we were no nearer an answer, and we were still as desperate financially.

Just to know that founders of other Christian organizations had faced exactly the same problems was a comfort. We were in good company. Paul must have been in a similar circumstance when he wrote, "We are pressed on every side by troubles, but not crushed and broken. We are perplexed because we don't know why things happen as they do, but we don't give up and quit. We are hunted down, but God never abandons us. We get knocked down, but we get up and keep going (2 Cor. 4: 8-9 LB).

In that phone conversation, Bill Bright suggested that Ralph call Bill's own chief financial advisor, a man Ralph had known and respected for years, but had never spoken to about financial affairs. Ed Johnson is well known in the banking world, a man who has risen to the top. After discussing the situation with several on our Development Committee and with Ralph, he made some very creative suggestions. Then he turned to Ralph and said, "Ralph, I feel very strongly that whatever we do, we must be careful not to go against what God is telling the one He has especially called. What is your sense of God's leading.

What has God told you?"

From time to time in the months since October, various members of the Development Committee had contacted the officials of Point Loma College. Neither Ralph nor Art knew the content of those discussions. It was almost as if there were now two Centers for World Mission, with different ways of doing things.

In early March, 1985, prompted perhaps by Ed Johnson's proposal, we received a rather stern letter from the Point Loma lawyer outlining two options we could take. Ralph was rather surprised at the tone of the letter—it was so different from all others we had ever received from them. Later, their business manager commented that the communications they had recently been receiving from our Development Committee had seemed so much like secular "hard-ball" business negotiations, that they had decided to respond in kind. "But this is not the way we prefer to operate," he confided. "In fact, through the years we have really appreciated Ralph's open-handed, no-secrets way of negotiating, and we really prefer to deal with him."

Perhaps that was the reason that when the Development Committee requested a face-to-face discussion of their terms in the March letter, the Point Loma officials insisted that Ralph be present.

We were not at all in a good bargaining position. Since the previous September—seven months before—we had been expecting daily to receive a foreclosure notice. Lest we have no money to mount a final campaign after that came, we had withheld any further money that had come in to us, informing Point Loma as to what we were doing and why. Even though they understood this tactic, our failure to pay put them in a quandry. They had budgeted our payments for salaries and other expenses.

But they really didn't want to foreclose. Indeed, a number of their students, we were told, had been meeting together for the precise purpose of praying that God would provide for *our* needs.

Nevertheless, a legal contract is a legal contract. And, in view of their other obligations, they were no more financially able to forgive our debt than we were able to pay it right then.

Thus, they were very willing to meet with our representatives. Both Ralph and Art went, as well as two others representing the Development committee. "It was a friendly meeting," Ralph told me later. "And though the terms of their letter were very difficult for us, they were, nevertheless, very fair."

Essentially, they gave us two options: 1) they could foreclose immediately (Would we prefer that?), or 2) they could give us an extension of two more years on our combined balloon payment (which would then be roughly $6 million for the campus proper and $2 1/2 million for the houses). If we chose this latter option, they would have to increase the interest on the housing payments from 8 1/2% to 12%. We winced at the increase in interest, but realized that it would not be an insuperable problem since we were now benefitting from the rising rental income of the area in general. That additional rental income would cover the extra interest on the housing as well as property tax and maintenance costs. The interest on the central campus property had already been raised to 12 1/2%, so that was not "new."

But we were already struggling to meet the higher payments ($300,000) due every three months on the campus proper, and Ralph commented rather wryly that their offer was like saying to a drowning man, I can't pull you out, but I'll give you an extra half hour to struggle. "But we really don't have much of an alternative, do we?" he asked our staff.

"There were several other stipulations," Art told me, "none of them easy for us to fulfill, but fair. As the meeting closed, the Point Loma officials looked at those from our Development Committee and added, 'We want to make it very clear that you cannot sell any of the houses—not any at all—unless by so doing you can completely pay off both houses and campus. If we eventually have to take the campus back, we do not want it without the houses. The houses are absolutely essential to the financial stability of the campus proper. We have said that all along, as Dr. Winter can tell you.' " As Art related this, he added, "They were very pointed about that!"

This answer certainly wasn't what we had planned and prayed for. In some ways it was worse, in some ways better. Yet because we had prayed so earnestly, we had to believe that it was from God.

I, for one, felt that God had indeed answered prayer. In our helplessness, He had preserved the houses for us, and He had done so without any manipulation on our part. All we had done was pray.

Nevertheless, the road ahead would be very long. We knew instinctively that it was only a matter of time before the same problems would all arise again. Certain members of the Board were still determined to sell in spite of Point Loma's statement. Only with great reluctance were they persuaded to postpone any moves in that direction until the fall of 1986.

But that small reprieve gave us breathing space. And though our task was still as difficult as ever, the spirit of heaviness began to lift from Ralph's heart. Once again he was able to look beyond the daily pressures to the goals and vision God had given him.

I knew that God had met him in a very special way when the verses he shared at morning prayers were these:

So do not throw away your confidence. It shall be richly rewarded. You need to persevere so that when you have done the will of God, you will receive what He has promised.

For in just a little while, He who is coming will come and not delay.
But my righteous one shall live by faith.

And if he shrinks back,
I will not be pleased with him.
(Heb. 10:35-38)

"How well it fits Ralph's situation," I thought. "When you have *done* the will of God..."   It was true, we weren't *done* yet! But we had done our best. And He said *He* would come and complete *all* He had promised. He would not delay beyond His own perfect timing! We had to trust Him and wait.

For us, meantime, our survival—our very life itself—depended on faith...on taking Him at His word. We dared not shrink back, no matter what. We lived (and live) for His approval. And that is enough!

41

"TOGETHER WITH ALL THE SAINTS"

(Ephesians 3:17-19)

The cool quietness of early morning was broken only by the sound of hymns coming up from the morning meeting room. Over the edge of the roof on the north side of the central patio of Hudson Taylor Hall, the mountains were so clearly defined that, standing on the balcony outside the 24-hour prayer room, I felt I could almost reach out and touch them. In another hour the sun would clear the roof to the east, announcing with its warmth that summer had come.

Suddenly, not ten feet from where I stood, a bluebird burst into song. He sang for a half hour at least, pausing only to dart to another bush or tree in another corner of the patio. And my heart sang with him "The winter is past, the rain is over and gone. The flowers are springing up and the time of the singing of birds has come" (Song of Solomon 2:11).

Our winter—our time of deep despair—was also gone. God had replaced it with a new hope in His providence and grace. Without any dramatic miracle, His quiet hand had stayed the rush of events, giving us new trust that in our helplessness He was not helpless. He would not

251

allow His will to be thwarted if we only remained faithful. What joy!

Now that we could breathe again, we surveyed how everything was progressing on campus. In spite of all the strain of the past few months, altogether things were moving along fairly well. The production of the *Global Prayer Digest* was pretty much on schedule; just recently two more denominations (Missouri Synod Lutheran and Foursquare) plus a large evangelical Methodist group had decided to use it. Enrollment in our *Perspectives* courses across the nation was increasing; from all appearances, it looked like we might have as many as 3000 students in 63 locations during the next year. A few weeks earlier several key mission strategists, known world-wide, had met in our library to lay plans for a massive mission mobilization effort across America; all that was lacking now was the person to head it up. (We called this the "Mission 2000" plan.) Also, cooperating agencies on campus all seemed to be moving ahead, also experiencing the blessing of God on their work.

In April, in order to end the seven-month payment stalemate, at Point Loma's suggestion we had paid all the money we had. The balance still due they applied to our mortgage so we could start again with a clean slate. At our request they also slipped our payment schedule one month to the usual calendar quarters—January 1st, April 1st, July 1st and October 1st. Ralph felt this new schedule would fit our needs better and, incidentally, give us an extra month to raise the money for the July 1st payment.

Summer meant vacations for most of the staff—and a few extra four-hour prayer watches for the rest of us because of their absence. The mountains and the beach called, yet there was little time for play. Somehow, summer always seemed to be the busiest time of the year on campus.

In winter, the research and mobilization offices were visibly hard at work. But every summer, the campus swarmed with students. Not only did we have two of the 63 *Perspectives* courses on campus, we also had students for all the courses offered by the various institutes and agencies which cooperated and worked here with us. The Zwemer Institute of Muslim Studies expected its largest enrollment yet, well over 100 in its two sessions, each six weeks long. Then there were, as usual, the month-long courses taught by the Institute of Chinese Studies, the Institute of Buddhist Studies, and the Institute of Hindu Studies. Also, International Films had several courses on filmmaking and the Fellowship of Artists for Cultural Evangelism their usual course on the use of native art as a bridge for evangelism. All these besides WCIU's on-going program called "Applied Linguistics/ Teaching English to Speakers of Other Languages." (Just to pronounce the name of that program took practice!)

Anyone visiting our campus during the summer can't be blamed for assuming that the USCWM/WCIU is primarily a school. But that is far from true! The training courses given here are essential, especially since our policy is not to teach anything taught anywhere else. Yet, in our minds, the most important contribution which the U.S. Center for World Mission and the William Carey International University make is in the fields of mission research and mobilization. These may not be quite so visible but are absolutely crucial if the Christians of the world are going to pursue the completion of world evangelization efficiently .

The research done by the various institutes and by Global Mapping Project is just now beginning to flow to denominations and mission agencies around the world. And in the field of mobilizing the church worldwide, there is so much to do—and so few to do it—that we often wring our hands. I sometimes worry about all the important pieces of mission literature that go out of print and wait months (sometimes years) before someone finds the time to update them and get them back to press. Or the number of manuscripts that sit on my desk, waiting for suggestions and approval before they can be printed and added to the mission literature which is so crucial to a new missionary thrust. I fret at the lack of really up-to-date Sunday School mission materials, films, and videos. We do our best, but we need help.

I sometimes think about God's call to Isaiah (Isa. 6:8) when He asked, "Whom shall I send, and who will go for us?" From my youth I have always thought of this as a "missionary" verse. Yet the way Isaiah "went" is the way these crucial mobilizers on our team "go." The world will never be won to the Lord unless some people, equally "called," stay at home and mobilize. Unfortunately, church mission committees rarely understand this and often will not support the mission mobilizers living in the States. What a tragedy. May the Lord forgive our short-sightedness!

Always we sense the lack of enough people with managerial experience to supervise all the work here. We need at least five more like Art McCleary. If we could pay salaries, we could get them easily. But very few have the faith to trust God to supply their personal needs. Why? Aren't there at least any retired people with management experience whose hearts burn for missions?

The summer of 1985 was no different in these ways from any other summer. One experience, however, stands out.

Because of the brush with foreclosure, it was absolutely critical that we be on time with all future payments. But now that would be more difficult than ever. Instead of $175,000 for the campus itself, our new payment schedule required $300,000 each quarter. Also, our housing payments increased more than $10,000 per month.

In the stress and uncertainty of the fall and winter months, we had fallen behind in our only communication with the public—our monthly bulletin called *Mission*

Frontiers. We had long noticed that when *Mission Frontiers* went out regularly, the donations kept coming. But when it didn't go out, donations inevitably fell.

So we scrambled to catch up...while April turned into May and May into June.

"Art," Ralph said in mid-May, "we're going to have to figure out how we can meet this next payment. We must encourage staff to really be in prayer about this. As I see it, unless God provides in some unforeseen way, we're going to come up very short. According to Bruce, very little money has come in toward this payment, but we simply cannot be late. I know we paid everything we had last time, but do you suppose there are any unrestricted internal funds anywhere at all that we can tap?"

Together they looked over Bruce's financial records. Yes, there was one fund, but...

Ralph thought back to his time as a professor at Fuller Seminary. On one occasion, the faculty had had to decide between taking a cut in salary or having part of their salary withheld temporarily because of a financial crisis. "I wonder if we dare do the same here," Ralph mused. "What would happen if we had to withhold salaries for a couple of weeks? Dare we do that? Or at least keep back $100 from each paycheck? Do you think, Art, that our staff could weather such an action if it is necessary in order to save the institution itself?"

The question was not as simple as it might seem. Many had found it very difficult to "raise their support," and had struggled along for years on only part of what it should have been, which was low by usual American standards. One staff member that month had received only $105 from his supporters!

In this crisis—praise the Lord!— most of them rallied to the occasion. Moreover, several gave from their personal resources to help others in greater need.

A number of couples on our mailing list learned of this sacrifice on the part of our staff and joined them by sending a third of their own salaries for three months. One of Ralph's long held dreams is that hundreds of thousands of American Christians would adopt this kind of lifestyle and use the extra money for a new mission thrust by all agencies and churches.

Those who helped us in this way we called our *One-third Times Three* donors. Without exception, they were not wealthy. Indeed, we were surprised at how many were retired people, missionaries, or country pastors with salaries not much higher than ours. But their generosity got us through that July 1st payment and the October 1st one as well.

As it turned out, we were able to repay the $100 staff loans almost immediately. But a few of the staff left because they were so troubled about the whole episode, especially the lack of forewarning. Almost all who stayed voluntarily signed a statement that should a similar emergency arise again, up to one-third of their salaries could be considered available.

On the whole, however, the experience seemed to bond us all closer together. Certainly it forced us to think whether we were here to be served or to serve and to reconsider whether the Center really needed to exist.

Admittedly, most Americans would never be willing to give up part of their salaries in order for the organization to survive. Yet the pattern is not that strange among mission agencies, all too well acquainted with financial strains. Those among us who had served a number of years overseas did not seem distressed by this request, even though it meant personal hardship in some cases. But the the suggestion seemed scary for some who were younger—not because of the financial insecurity so much as the implication that someone else could decide such a move. This kind of team "live-or-die together" attitude had not been part of their previous experience.

Whatever was true, we saw that one of our basic weaknesses was that we had never set up a staff training program that would prepare us all for this kind of togetherness. "What you need is a Discipleship Training School," Todd, our youngest son-in-law told us. "I don't think Youth With a Mission (YWAM) would have survived without it. We have found we really can't assume that even missionary candidates are spiritually prepared for the kind of stresses they may go under just from being members of a team. They often come with old unhealed hurts which, when the going gets rough, they project onto the organization. Everyone who joins YWAM goes through this kind of training, no matter how long they have been Christians, or even missionaries, for that matter!"

"You may be right, Todd," Ralph responded. "Come to think of it, most home based agencies seem to have something of the sort. I know Campus Crusade does, and also Navigators. It gives the candidates time to either become a real part of the team, or to leave without feeling like they have failed. But we started with so few and with so much to do that we just overlooked the importance of this. And I think we have suffered because of it. Now what do we do? I'd really like for all of us to go through something like this together. But how could we ever take off six weeks, like YWAM does, to do this?

"Well, instead of the two hours of staff meeting we now have on Wednesday afternoons, perhaps we could have a shorter time on Wednesday mornings and follow it with this kind of staff development," Art suggested. "It might seem like a huge expenditure of time, but I think it will help in the long run."

Within weeks we had set up another committee to work this out. It was made up of a couple who had been with Navigators, a YWAM couple, and a couple who had come to us from Agape Force. Starting in September, every Wednesday morning we gave over to this kind of "staff development," we called it. The roster of those who shared with us was like a "Who's Who"—George Verwer and George Miley (both of Operation Mobilization), Joy Dawson (YWAM), Bilquis Sheik, Dan Sneed (Navigators), David Hunt, David Bryant (Intervarsity), Greg Livingstone (Frontiers)

On the whole, we chose speakers who were part of some other close-knit mission community. Some of their shared experiences were so typically like ours that we roared with laughter, even while we grimmaced at some of our own memories. It takes grace to live in close community, but in the process you also grow in grace.

But the experience was a wonderful time of refreshing as well as conviction and renewal and it revealed that time spent in discipleship is time well spent.

Meanwhile, Satan was on the attack again, but on different fronts.

42

NOV. 1985 - MARCH 1986

"EVERYTHING
THAT CONCERNS YOU"

(1 Peter 5:7 LB)

For years I had dreamed of the day when Ralph and I could take a vacation. At my insistence, we would squeeze in a three or four day weekend once or twice a year, but every summer I would watch the rest of the staff leave for several weeks and sigh inwardly. Would our time ever come?

I found it hard to believe when Ralph agreed (finally!) to take three weeks off to visit our two daughters and their families in North Africa. I knew he wouldn't want to be out of touch with what was going on at the Center, and since it would be difficult to phone back, I wondered if he would really relax. But both of us felt we needed to see our daughters, and they needed to see us. It was time to go.

Far more than in Europe or Latin America, there is much that seems very strange to American eyes in a Muslim country. The narrow, winding streets of the ancient market, where every few minutes you have to hug the wall to let a heavily laden donkey pass. The crowded sidewalk cafes populated only by men. The eyes of the women above their veils. The completely, and beautifully, tiled rooms—floor, walls, ceiling—and the antiquated kitchen and bathroom facilities.

Somehow in all the traveling between the two families, who lived eight hours from each other, we forgot to reconfirm our tickets for home. Our flight happened to come just after the airlines had changed their schedules, and all the way home we either missed planes or came uncomfortably close to doing so. Ralph was running a temperature of 102° from a bug he had picked up two days before, and I was having to try to make all the necessary arrangements alone. It was not the most relaxing time, to say the least.

We arrived home in Los Angeles several hours earlier than we were expected, and no one was there to meet us. Somehow, while going through customs, Ralph's carry-on bag was stolen. It contained his check book, credit cards, diary, calculator, a small tape recorder, and an accounting computer program he had been working on for weeks in his spare time. For three hours we looked everywhere then finally made the necessary phone calls to cancel our bank account and credit cards. That in itself wasn't simple since it was Sunday.

Also because it was Sunday, we couldn't locate those who were scheduled to pick us up, and ended up waiting another hour for the bus.

On arriving home, weary and frazzled, we reported in to Art, and found that our spiritual warfare had only begun. He told us that just the week before a major boiler (water heater) in the dorm had quit working and needed to be replaced—estimated cost: $16,000. Then, he said, the city fire marshalls had visited the campus and were requiring us to install a fire sprinker system in one of our major buildings, where our research offices are. (We have 13 major buildings. Why just there, we wondered, but were afraid to ask.)

Then, a 100-foot truss holding up the roof of the 3500

seat auditorium had cracked and sagged, pulling another down with it. The building had been built toward the end of World War II, when structural steel was not available. "Over the years you should have tightened the bolts holding these trusses together," the engineer told us. But not even Point Loma officials had known that. The emergency repairs alone cost $8,000. Before we were finished all of the trusses would have to be reinforced with steel, at a cost of $75,000. But the building was still worth almost a million dollars, so we felt we had no choice but to go forward! But where would the money come from?

And, of course, on top of all this we had another $300,000 quarterly payment due on January 1st.

When so many crises came at once, I thought of George Verwer's warning about Satanic attacks. Yet, in the midst of our distresses, we felt the gracious hand of our God, uplifting, strengthening, pointing the way ahead. And one by one we weathered the storms.

For example, we were able to repair the boiler at a fraction of the cost estimated.

Then Ralph's older brother, one of the most competent structural engineers in Southern California, came to our aid, donating both advice and time. He called in one of the top construction engineers in the area for this type of job, and when this man found out we were a mission organization, he dropped his price considerably.

About the same time, one of our maintenance crew noticed a small closet hidden back under the platform in the big auditorium. When he opened it, he found a large roll of papers, which to our amazement, turned out to be the original blueprints for the building, with plans clearly marked for both wooden beams and structural steel. Even the former owners had no idea where these blueprints were stored.

Then Art received a call from the business administrator of a local church. "We have a group of laymen who from time to time volunteer time in mission projects. Could you use any help?" he asked.

Could we? For several months these wonderful men came every Saturday and on several holidays (even bringing a team of young people for less skilled jobs). They installed the fire sprinkler system in Townsend Hall. And then they tackled the problem of the auditorium, climbing all over the rafters and tightening hundreds of bolts.

On several occasions several young boys in their early teens had broken in and vandalized several of our buildings, even though we always had security guards. We had always kept the doors to the auditorium locked except when the gym was being used or these men were working inside. These neighborhood boys, however, seemed determined to get in. Time and again they were run out and told to stay away. Finally, our guard caught them taking a hatchet to one of the main doors of the auditorium just as they reached through the hole and undid the lock.

This time he issued a stern warning. "One of these times one of you is going to get hurt. You must stay away." And he ran them off again.

One Saturday morning in February, the men from the church were once again climbing around on the rafters above the ceiling, tightening still more of the loose bolts. Unknown to them, four of these boys once again had sneaked into the building, found a door hidden down in the basement which opened to a ladder to the attic, and climbed up. They happen to be in an area sectioned off by firewalls from where the men were working. Suddenly one, a ten year old, accidentally stepped off the beam and fell through the ceiling to the concrete bordering the basketball court 50 feet below.

With horror, a workman below saw what had happened, called the paramedics and Art. But he was already brain dead.

We spent long hours in prayer for him and for his family. Various staff members visited the hospital room and the home and later attended his funeral. We grieved over the boy and worried about a possible lawsuit. Yet we felt so helpless.

Even here, however, God brought glory to His name. We learned that only weeks before, the boy had given his heart to the Lord at a church close by. Because of the kindness of our staff, several members of his family came to a prayer meeting on campus and found the Lord. And Art, as general manager, decided that instead of constantly running these boys off campus, maybe we should help them. He set aside a special place for a club room and encouraged several of our single young men to take them on as their special project.

In the middle of all these crises, our January 1st payment came due. The day before, after checking all our accounts, Ralph found we had at most $212,000, short $88,000. Once again, we didn't know how we could ever meet it.

But, once again, God was watching over everything that concerned us. Just as Ralph finished adding up the figures, he received a long distance call.

"How much do you lack for this payment," the person asked.,

"Well, as of right now, $88,000. We still have a few letters to open that just came in the mail. But..." Ralph was clearly embarrassed.

"Look, I have a friend here who wants to go in with me on making up the balance. We don't want you to have to borrow even in-house funds this time. Let's say we'll send $80,000 by express mail today, and if you need more, let us know. Okay?"

Ralph was stunned, amazed, thrilled at the goodness of God and of His servants. Once more, in our extremity, He had provided.

Several years ago, one of our volunteer staffers went back to Montana State University and pulled together over 100 students for one of our *Perspectives* courses. Going through the airport to teach them, I noticed a number of bronze sculptures done by two local artists. There is a small one of a miner mounted on a mule going down a trail, followed by another mule. It is called "The End of the Trail." There is one of city children trying awkwardly to mount a horse.

Most spectacular of all is a series of flying geese mounted one by one from the ceiling near the staircase that leads to the gate. There must be ten of them, large, life size, beautiful, with wings spread. The one nearest to the ground floor has its wings up in landing position.

Their attitude suggests no panic, no concern--just simple trust that the wings God gave them will not only sustain them in beautiful flight but also be sufficient for a safe landing.

God made these creatures to be beautiful on the ground, but even more so in flight. They were made for flight, from the joint of their wings to the thrust of their heads and feet.

God made us also to soar, not to grovel with our problems close to earth. It is Satan who would capture our spirits and chain them to earth—either in senseless pleasure or in untoward anxiety and pain. God would use the same circumstances to lift us higher, to teach us to soar and to trust Him.

Many times our friends at church have asked how things were going, ready with their condolences should we be in foreclosure. Each time we have not known how to answer except to say that we were in the hands of God. What else can you say?

And yet, what a wonderful place to be. The storms of life can rage. Satan can attack in all his fury. But in His Hands we are still safe.

I have always loved 1 Peter 5: 7 in the King James

264

translation: "Casting all your cares upon Him, for He careth for you." But somehow, in the Living Bible it seems a bit more personal: "Let Him have all your worries and cares, for He is always thinking about you and watching everything that concerns you."

43

OCTOBER 1986

*"YOU WILL HAVE TO SEE
TO BELIEVE IT"*

(Habakkuk 1:3)

To the casual observer, it was probably the smallest, most insignificant parade ever held in the city of Pasadena. The marchers were mainly middle-aged men dressed in business suits. There were no floats, just the unfurled flags of forty-two countries from which those marching had come. The only music was their singing. And the parade route itself was only a few blocks long. It was not surprising, therefore, that not a single newspaper reported this event. Pasadena did not even notice.

Nevertheless, as Ralph saw it, what this parade signified was far more important that the sum of all the Rose Parades for which the city of Pasadena is so famous. He doubted if in anything in the history of the city—or the United States, for that matter—could be more crucial than what these people were about.

In a formal sense, the parade was merely the closing event of the Fourth Triennial Congress of the Asia Missions Association. After meeting in Asia for its first three conventions, the AMA decided to meet this time in the U.S., hoping thereby to encourage the sizeable

Christian Asian population of Los Angeles to participate and to lend financial support. But there also was another, more surprising reason: for the first time AMA leaders had invited national mission leaders from *outside* of Asia—in particular, from Africa and Latin America.

Most American Christians, even those best acquainted with the situation overseas, are astounded to learn that the converts in mission lands not only run their own churches but nowadays head up their own mission agencies as well. At this meeting, almost all of the delegates were this new breed of mission executive. They represented more than fifty mission agencies (plus 40 other related organizations), all of which were organized and run by non-Western leaders. Many of them directed the work of at least a hundred missionaries, and Panya Baba of Nigeria, almost 600. Their organizations, together with other "Third World Missions" represent more than 20,000 non-Western missionaries who work cross-culturally today.

In a nutshell, the fact that such a meeting as this could be called made it very clear that what had once been *mission-receiving* lands were now lands from which missionaries were *sent*. That is why Ralph felt that this first world-level meeting of such leaders was the most important milestone since the Reformation. We had come full circle. The world's mission fields had become mission bases. The missionary task was almost done.

But sometimes reality is hard to believe, even when it is right before your eyes. Americans are so accustomed to thinking of missions in terms of nickles and dimes that it is hard to believe that today missions is the largest and most influential multinational enterprise in the world.

It seems incredible that in Los Angeles the 280 traditional (Anglo-Saxon) Presbyterian churches are now outnumbered by Korean Presbyterian churches in that city. As Americans, we feel a bit outclassed to learn that a local church in Korea (Paul Yonggi Cho's Full Gospel Central Church) has a membership of 270,000, while our largest is no more than 1/27th that size! Even the logistics make it hard for us to believe that (in 1980) Koreans, all on their own, could pull together a week-long evangelistic meeting that seated, at a single gathering, 2.7 million people.

We find it hard to believe that Africans hold revival tent meetings with 25,000 present. Or that in the city of Santiago, Chile a Methodist Pentecostal church not only has 16,000 in attendance every Sunday morning, but also a 2,000-member choir and orchestra besides. Or that a church sanctuary in Brazil seats 25,000.

The list goes on and on. We are so accustomed to thinking of ourselves as the teachers and the rest of the world as our pupils that it comes as a great shock to learn that they are far ahead of us.!

It used to be that when we spoke of the "unfinished task," we thought of the numbers of Western missionaries that would be needed to finish evangelizing the world. Not any more! Christians around the world are responding to this challenge, and within just a few years, we will be left in the dust.

Most shocking of all, perhaps, is to realize what the Spirit of God has done when we weren't looking. When all the missionaries left China in 1950, they left in despair, wondering where they had gone wrong and if Christianity could possibly survive the onslaughts of Communism.

Then, in 1979, the long-closed door to China creaked open again. With a certain amount of caution, followed by shock and then exhuberant joy, the former missionaries to China who were still living learned that the Chinese Christians, for the most part, had done far better than to simply endure persecution. The first report was that the million left behind were now three million. A few months later we heard it was 10 million, then 25 million. Now, the most reliable estimates indicate at least 50 million known believers in China, perhaps even twice that!

Nevertheless, these mission executives from around the world—especially those from Asia—recognized that

268

there is still much to be done in China. Besides the animistic tribal groups near the Indochinese border, there are many Muslim groups to the northwest who are still unreached—the 2.7 million Uighurs, for example. These are so culturally different from the Han Chinese, where most of the Christians are, that whoever reaches out to them will have to do so as a genuine cross-cultural missionary, whether he is Chinese or not.

The mission executives from India tell a similar story. For a number of years, now, it has been almost impossible to get a missionary visa for India. In that time there has been a resurgence of Hindu missions, such that Hindu philosophy, if not its temples, now flood the Western world. Meanwhile, in much of India itself, Hindus wanting to become Christians are actively persecuted.

Yet , they report, God has not forgotten India. In the northeast tribal areas, more than 50% of the people are now Christian believers. Many of these former headhunters are sophisticated businessmen and educators, with Ph.D. degrees. And now they are sending their own missionaries to other tribes in India and across the border into "closed" Burma.

The main body of Indian Christians, several million strong, live in South India, the area in that continent where the gospel first arrived. They also are sending missionaries—to Sri Lanka and other countries where Indian populations are large, but also into North India, where the people speak a different language, come from distinctly different racial backgrounds, and are often resentful of everyone from South India, Christian or not. In some areas, so these Indian executives report, thousands of former Hindus are asking to be baptized. Yes, God is at work.

Every Thursday evening someone who has recently come from overseas gives the U.S. Center for World Mission community and visiting friends a firsthand report on his area. Recently Emil Jebasingh, head of Trans-

World Radio in India, told us the following story.

A couple of years ago, the staff of TWR in India was able to buy a radio station in Madras. In the providence of God, their location on the dial was just to the left of that used by the "All Nation" station of the Indian government, so they decided to call theirs the "All Universe" station.

For some years, now, the government has been urging Indian couples to adopt family planning as a means of population control. For an incentive, it offered a free transistor radio to all who would promise to follow some method of birth control. About the same time, some skilled engineers working with the "All Universe" station designed a very inexpensive radio which the government is buying for these give-aways.

The All Universe station plays classical Indian-style music which sounds very similar to the music played by the All Nation station. Thousands of Hindus, by accident, get the wrong station when they turn on their radios, and for the first time are hearing the gospel of Christ.

"A Hindu priest in one village became a Christian just by listening to the radio," Dr. Jebasingh told us. "He destroyed all the idols in his temple and urged his followers to give their lives to Jesus. Now the temple is full of people worshipping Jesus."

Just as exciting is a new film about the life of Christ, perhaps inspired by the success of the Jesus film of Campus Crusade. This one, however, was produced by one of the top Indian film makers, who happens to be a Hindu. It is shown in public theaters and village squares all over India. The people clap when Christ on the screen heals someone, become angry when He is crucified, and shout for joy when he rises from the dead. Christians are amazed at its influence and rejoice that it is quite faithful in its portrayal.

A few of the Third-World mission executives came from lands which are predominantly Muslim. For years Western Christians have considered the Muslim world the most difficult of all to evangelize. Consequently, the total number of missionaries working with Muslims around the *world* is less than the number of missionaries in state of Alaska, where the population is not much larger than that of the city of Pasadena. Yet even this is beginning to change.

Most exciting, although there is a resurgence of traditional Islam, there seems to be at the same time a new openness to hear about Jesus.

An Indian mission executive at the AMA convention told one of our staff of a conversation he had with a Muslim in his country.

"Do you believe in the virgin birth?" the Muslim asked.

"Yes," the Christian answered.

"So do I! Do you believe in the miracles of Jesus?"

"Yes," the Christian answered.

"So do I! Do you believe in the resurrection?"

"Yes," the Christian answered.

"So do I! Even so, I think our faith is better than yours because we also believe in living right. We do not drink alcohol nor eat pork," he added.

Two Christian girls from Iran recently spoke at one of Thursday night meetings. "Khomeni has helped to spread the gospel," they told us.

"But how can that be," we asked.

"Well, the people see now what fanatical Islam is like, and many of them want no part of it. Now you sometimes see Muslims wearing crosses around their necks. That doesn't mean they believe in Jesus. But there is a new hunger to know more about Him. More Muslims have become Christians in Iran since Khomeini came to power than has been true in the last two centuries."

We hear of Muslims high up in society who hold extended earnest conversations with believers. They have no respect for merely intellectual Christianity, but they are hungry for a personal relationship with God as their Father. We also hear there are villages of faithful Muslims

271

which have decided that Jesus is not only a prophet (as the Koran alleges) but the Messiah.

God is not only preparing the Muslims for the gospel, He is awakening a love for Muslims in the hearts of Christian young people. Increasingly, from countries as distant from each other as Korea and Latin America, they are expressing a "call" to tell Muslims about Jesus.

Especially exciting is the response of young Latin Americans. Because Muslims controlled Spain for 700 years before the time of the *conquistadores* , their descendents in Latin America feel a special affinity for the Arab world. The Spanish language has 10,000 words which are Arabic, and other aspects of their culture—their architecture, their love of poetry and debate, even their physical appearance and temperament—reveal their common roots. It is no wonder, then, that many Latin Americans wonder if the Muslim world is not their personal responsibilty.

The churches in Latin America have long astounded the Christians to the north with their vitality and tremendous growth. But this new awareness of their role in the Great Commission is relatively new. Only in the last two or three years have there been nationwide mission conferences in almost every country of Latin America. These are leading up to COMIBAM, an international missions conference for every country of the world where Spanish or Portuguese is spoken. The conference, to be held in Brazil in November of 1987, is completely run by Latin Americans and anticipates more than 3000 invited delegates. Evangelical faith in Latin America is so strong and so vital that almost single-handedly Latin Americans could evangelize the world. No one knows what will be the final impact of the revival that is currently sweeping Argentina, for examlple.

Not all the pioneer missionary work which must be done today will take place in foreign countries, however. Like a master chess player, God has moved representatives from unreached people groups far from their homelands all over the world and has plunked them down in the midst of traditionally Christian populations, essentially saying, "You have not gone to them, so I have brought them to you. Now, tell them!" Unreached peoples by the thousand are among us: Kurds in Munich, Kazakhs in Berlin, Berbers in Paris and Amsterdam, Sikhs in Toronto, Gujaratis in Vancouver, Yemenis in Detroit, Saudis in Houston, Cambodians in Long Beach, Afghans in San Francisco.

There is a regular "pentecost of nations" in greater Los Angeles: Lebanese, Iranians, Saudis, Cambodians, Taiwanese, Koreans, Afghans, Salvadoreans, Nicaraguans, tribal people from Vietnam, from Mexico, from Guatemala... In recording each pupil's "language of the home," the Los Angeles public school system found there are at least 137 different languages spoken in that one city! Similar statements could be made for many world-class cities today.

Today, even Uzbeks and Tajiks and other Central Asians from behind the iron curtain can be found in New York, or Chicago, or Minneapolis. They are waiting for perceptive Christians to reach out in love and friendship, such as their own cultural traditions require. If ever our churches needed a course on being cross-cultural missionaries to their neighbors next door, it is now. Indeed, this is precisely the new thrust of ISI (International Students, Incorporated)—to train church people to do this strategic work.

We have to stand back in awe. God is doing something wonderful—a brand new thing. Already 370 from the city of Singapore are serving overseas as short-term or career missionaries. From one city alone! As a result, the Christians of Singapore have increased their giving to an incredible extent, even in the middle of a recession.

But this harvest of Unreached Peoples is going to be

so big that God is not depending on the "professionals" alone. He is sending Christian lay people by the hundreds of thousands to work among peoples who are otherwise shut off from the gospel. Sometimes the "sending agency" is a secular corporation. Sometimes, as in China and Russia, it is an atheistic government which as a punishment unwittingly sends Christian witnesses to Hidden People groups thousands of miles away, as happened in China's ten-year "Cultural Revolution." But still, God is behind these moves, whether we recognize this fact or not.

Many Asian Christians are going overseas—to be the Pakistani taxi drivers in Yemen, or the Filipino oilfield workers in Saudi Arabia, or Korean nurses in secular Germany or Indian nurses in some Muslim land. Like the old game of Fruitbasket Turnover, God is mixing us all up—nations with nations and Christians with unbelievers. He has a marvelous purpose in mind. He is in the mission business. He is determined to win the nations back to Himself. And He will do whatever it takes for that to be accomplished.

It is a brand new thing when the Christians who stay home also have to learn to witness to someone from a foreign culture. Who isn't called to be a cross-cultural witness today? Where on earth does he live? Not in any city. And rarely even in the countryside anymore.

It is incredible that God would transport those He wants to win half way around the world just to get the attention of His people. Or that He would use a Khomeini to awaken the Iranians to their need for a Savior. Or Mao Ze Dong not only to destroy idol worship in China but to force thousands of Christian leaders into her less evangelized areas. Or the pain of the Russian invasion of Afghanistan so that a third of her people could more likely hear of Him. Or even bring blessing out of the horrors of Cambodia so that 25,000 of these formerly highly resistant people have now welcomed Him into their hearts in the refugee camps of Thailand.

What, in God's economy and time, does all this mean? "Look at the nations and watch—and be utterly amazed," God told Habakkuk. "For I am going to do something in your days that you would not believe, even if you were told" (Hab. 1:5).

As 1986 drew to a close, we became more and more excited. All around us we saw signs that God was doing something new—something brand new. And like children on tiptoe on Christmas morning, we could barely wait.

44

SUMMER - FALL 1986

"I WILL DO A NEW THING"

(Isaiah 43:19 KJ)

The conviction had not come on us suddenly. For some years we had been looking forward to and praying that God would bring about a mighty new wave of mission outreach in our time.

But the years had come and gone, as years do. Little signs that our prayers were being answered always seemed less dramatic in retrospect than they did at the time. Still our hope didn't die, and neither did our dream.

However, 1986 was somehow different, unusual in many ways. Even secular events made us aware of the importance of remembering what had happened long before. For one thing, for an entire week in June, the city of Pasadena celebrated its hundredth birthday. We had parades of antique bicycles, anniversary fairs, and all sorts of interesting events. Then, on the 4th of July, the nation as a whole celebrated another hundred-year birthday, this one of the Statue of Liberty. The buildup for this celebration lasted for weeks.

At the Center, several of us were busily involved in preparations for still another celebration—four, actually, all commemorating just one event. July, 1986 was the

276

hundredth anniversary of a month-long Bible conference for college students which had been called by D. L. Moody in 1886. The Mt. Hermon conference became famous because, by the time it had finished, 100 young, elite college men had pledged their lives to missions.

More importantly, the organization they founded two years later, the Student Volunteer Movement, eventually turned America and the world upside down. Twenty thousand collegians went to every corner of the globe and founded hundreds of universities, thousands of colleges, tens of thousands of hospitals and clinics, and hundreds of thousands of churches. Literally!

For at least the next two generations almost every leader, secular or Christian, in most of the countries of the world had trained in those schools, been treated in those hospitals, or had been profoundly influenced in some other way by those Student Volunteers. In all of history, no other mission effort has been so massive and so influential.

Ralph is well known for his interest in their record. No doubt, that is why he was asked to speak at all four Mt. Hermon celebrations that summer. But he wanted more statistical facts, so, in May, he sent Tricia and Todd (our youngest daughter and her husband) off to Yale Divinity School to do research in the SVM archives housed there. It took four people almost three weeks to put on computer all the data they brought back.

"Bruce," Ralph said when they had finished, "can you get the computer to draw a couple of graphs for me? I'd like to compare the attendance at the Student Volunteer quadrennial conventions with the Urbana conferences that InterVarsity puts on today." Ralph knew that at their peak, the SVM meetings had only 6000 in attendance as compared to Urbana's 17,000. But there are a lot more students in college today, and to see the impact of these conventions he needed a graph showing the *relative proportion* of college students who attended.

It took a little while for Bruce to get the graph, but when he came back, we were all shocked by the picture. "Why, proportionally, they're not even *half* as big today!" he gasped. "The Urbanas look like midgets by comparison. I wonder what this means."

Because of this one graph, Ralph began to rethink all his basic assumptions. For years he had known about the constant upswing in the number of students attending Urbana and, even more important, the very striking turn-around in the percentage of students signing the decision cards indicating they were willing to be missionaries. Attendance had risen steadily during the '60s, but the percentage of those deciding for missions dropped until, in 1970, only 8 percent of the students signed. Then, suddenly, three years later, 28 percent signed. In 1976, 50 percent signed, in '79, 75 percent and then 85 percent in 1981. By 1984 so many signed that InterVarsity didn't even bother counting.

"I was convinced we were in the beginning of another Student Volunteer movement," Ralph sighed when he saw Bruce's graph, "but now I wonder."

For several days he pondered all this. Then one evening, in the middle of something else, he burst out, "How could I have been so stupid? Of course! That's the answer!"

"What?" I asked.

"I've been comparing what's been happening in the last twenty-five years to what happened *after* the Student Volunteer Movement exploded. But I've completely overlooked the period leading up to that 1886 explosion. It just may be that now, in 1986, we're still in the buildup period and the real explosion is just ahead!"

He sat deep in thought for a few minutes before continuing. "How can we check this out? I wonder..."

Within the hour we had shifted gears. Now we were looking at what had happened *before* 1886, not after. And we were especially interested to see if there were any parallels to the buildup in our time.

We were surprised and delighted by all the parallels, even in secular society.

America's self assurance in her overseas role caused the years prior to 1886 to be called "the confident years." She had the answer to the world's problems.

Also, there was a sudden rash of new millionaires, who spent their money lavishly, so much so that another term for the period was "the gilded age" which in the 1890s became "the Gay Nineties." Affluence and lavish spending is again a part of American culture, even in evangelical churches.

Cults, one after another, sprang up, many with a basis in Hinduism or pseudo-science and an emphasis on health foods. The names of many new cults today are strangely reminiscent of those back then.

Our population rolls swelled with the arrival of hundreds of thousands of immigrants, most of them refugees from political or economic oppression. Then they came mainly from Europe, now from South East Asia, the Middle East and the Muslim world.

Because of Ralph's topic, however, we were particularly interested in parallels within the Christian world. Again, we were amazed.

Those students who launched the Student Volunteer Movement followed at least three decades of genuine revival in this country, led mainly by D. L. Moody. In a very real sense, the work of Billy Graham parallels his.

Naturally arising out of these revivals was an interest in Bible study—also quite common today.

Their large Keswick conferences on "the deeper life experience" remind one of the large charismatic conferences of our times.

We thought of our international conferences on world evangelization, such as the Lauzanne conference in 1974 and the Edinburgh and Pattaya conferences in 1980. The Christians in the late 1800s also had missionary conferences, two in 1878 alone (London and New York) followed by a very crucial one in 1888.

In the decades prior to 1880, a "Concert of Prayer" movement had spread all over the nation. Once a month it brought together thousands of Christians from all the major denominations to pray for a spiritual awakening and for missions. A similar movement, initiated just a few years ago by David Bryant of InterVarsity Missions, is already very strong in some of the major cities of this country and Canada. But it is only one of a number of prayer movements which are cooperating together.

These things were all fascinating to us. But we had to get more specific. What, precisely, was it that caused those 251 students at the Mt. Hermon conference to be so interested in *missions*? We knew that the college campuses had student Christian organizations that parallel Campus Crusade, Navigators and InterVarsity today. But we were unaware how strongly the YMCA in those days stressed worship, Bible study and effective personal evangelism. Even more specifically, the Intercollegiate YMCA started in 1877 and on every college campus within three years, had missions as one of its core emphases.

When some mission-minded students at Princeton Seminary saw how fast the collegiate YMCA was growing, they called a meeting in 1880 of some 250 students from 32 seminaries and organized the Interseminary Missionary Alliance. Exactly one hundred years later, in 1980, the seminarians who went to the frontier missions consultation in Edinburgh, Scotland did exactly the same thing. This time they called their organization *Theological Students for Frontier Missions* . "I wonder if these TSFM people know about that earlier group?" I asked Ralph.

"I doubt it," he said. "Very few books even mention it."

In both Princeton Seminary and Princeton College (as

280

the university was then called), a number of students were actively interested in becoming missionaries. There were several reasons.

Still strong on campus was the local chapter of the Society for Missionary Inquiry, founded more than fifty years before after the first American missionaries sailed for India and Burma.

Then, in 1877, after Moody's return from England where he took Cambridge University by storm, he began a series of meetings in Trenton, New Jersey, just a few miles away. A group of Princeton students went to hear him and insisted that he preach in Princeton, and when he did, a major revival broke out.

And then Royal Wilder was in Princeton. Furloughed home from India because of his health, he became the unofficial sponsor for the mission group at the college, led by his son, Robert. They met regularly in his house to pray!

"He sounds like Christy Wilson, doesn't he?" Ralph commented. When Dr. Wilson returned from Afghanistan in 1975 and began teaching at Gordon Conwell Seminary, he immediately started noon prayer meetings for missions. Within a few months fifty students came, then more. Many are now overseas.

In the last five years, similar groups have begun to meet at other Christian schools. When our third daughter, Linda, was a student at Wheaton in 1976, only a trickle of students came out to the missions fellowship. Late in the fall of 1986, we were told that between 300 and 500 show up every Sunday night to pray for missions. Now they have 200 mission prayer groups on campus. "It's almost like there's been a revival there," Ralph said.

Many other campuses are experiencing this same kind of mission renewal. For example, at Trinity Evangelical Divinity School, all the students—and professors!— are now required to spend a year overseas.

This interest in missions extends to secular campuses,

even as it did in 1886. In 1985, almost 2000 took our Perspectives on the World Christian Movement class, taught by extension in more than 70 locations throughout the U.S. Now that the text is in Spanish and being translated into Korean, Swedish and Chinese, the five overseas centers will no doubt greatly increase in 1987.

I looked for a direct parallel to this broad-spectrum "Perspectives" course in the years before 1886. The collegiate YMCAs reserved the first meeting of each month for a mission emphasis, but it was probably not until after the Student Volunteer Movement was organized in 1888 that a missions course, as such, was offered. And since the SVM quickly extended to practically every campus in the U.S., very rapidly such a course was soon available everywhere.

There is also a parallel in the travelling teams. The idea of sending a team of students to visit every college campus did not begin with the SVM in 1887 but more likely with the YMCA, which had been doing this for several years. Today, such teams have been started again.

Taking the lead is an organization called *Caleb*, which began with a group of five students who took the "Perspectives" course at Penn State in 1980. As a team they went to a Muslim country, but had to leave because of political problems totally unrelated to their work. It was at that point that Greg Fritz, the leader, embraced as their calling the mobilization of the student world for missions.

Besides those who man the home offices, three or four times a year Caleb sends twenty young people in four vans to canvass the college campuses of this country for three months at a time. Some of the team members are young missionaries under appointment, assigned by their mission boards to work with Caleb for one year in order to recruit more missionaries. In the fall of 1986 the teams contacted 17,000 students and expect to meet 30,000 in 1987.

Like those students of a century ago, the Caleb teams encourage students to sign a pledge which involves them for the rest of their lives in missions promotion or missionary service. Out of the 17,000, 700 signed, promising to send a report every month of their progress to the Caleb home office. The staff go over these reports carefully, then spend three hours every day praying for these students, one by one, and writing back to them.

Today it is much easier to maintain this kind of close follow-up than it was a hundred years ago. Yet even then the students had an amazing network of communication.

There were two crucial areas where we felt the parallels were either non-existent or weak. We wondered if the SVM would have survived without these two organizations, or even have come into being. Yet in two areas, both crucial, we couldn't find the parallels we sought, and we wondered what the chances were today without something similar.

One relates to the Christian Endeavor movement. Ralph grew up in CE, as did his parents before him, and he has a tremendous respect for all it has accomplished through the years.

Founded in 1882 by a minister's wife, CE had already 30,000 members by 1886. Every major denomination in every city—and in the country churches as well—had a CE chapter. Thus, it is not surprising to hear a student at Brown University in 1885 say that all the earnest Christian young people on campus came out of CE. And he added "I think it is so everywhere."

Three standard practices of Christian Endeavor helped to produce the Student Volunteer Movement. 1) All of the youth on a regular basis were expected to be in charge of the CE meetings in the local church; adults attended only as sponsors in the back seats. The result was a host of young, capable and experienced leaders. 2) The chapters of the various local denominations met together on a regular basis, often once a month. This inter-relationship bred a true ecumenism which had a profound influence on the mission field. By the 1930s, however, many denominational leaders became concerned over this "interdenominationalism" and forced the withdrawal of their youth from the movement by setting up denominational youth organizations in direct competition. 3) CE had a strong mission emphasis, so much so that "CE Day" came universally to be thought of as "Missionary Day."

Although Christian Endeavor is still very strong overseas, in only a few areas of the U.S. is it still very influential. We do have other excellent interdenominational youth organizations—for example, Young Life and Youth for Christ. Unlike CE, however, they are not based in the local church and did not start with an emphasis on missions. In recent years, both groups have been involved in discipling Christian youth overseas. But in 1986, Youth for Christ made a monumental shift in policy, such that its overseas staff now focus on unreached peoples. This will undoubtedly affect the mission vision of the youth with which they work in the United States.

As I see it, the most serious lack of parallel between the early 1880s and today relates to the women of the church. In 1886, almost every local church had a Women's Missionary Society. There were tens of thousands of these, even as recently as the late 1940s.

As has always been true, the women were crucial to the success of the entire missionary enterprise. They kept the vision alive; they prayed earnestly and consistently for the missionaries; and they collected their coins, which together resulted in millions of dollars for the cause. Understandably, their sons and daughters became Student Volunteers.

Very few of those Women's Missionary Societies, as such, have survived to our time. Starting about 1950, their exclusive emphasis on missions was gradually dropped, and eventually the name was also changed to simply "the Women's Society."

Ralph and I once discussed why this happened and

what could be done to reverse this trend. "I have a feeling most of the younger women consider missions to be out of date," I said. "After all, for almost a generation the churches haven't really stressed missions, so now those who are in their thirties and forties consider missions to be insignificant."

"But I think this will change, especially if young people continue to be so interested in missions," Ralph said. "Actually, all it takes to make mission promoters out of the parents is for their children to decide to go. When the young people start talking about missions, praying about missions, going to mission conferences, and taking courses on missions the parents begin to ask what is going on. And then they are deeply involved."

At the U.S. Center for World Mission we are usually caught up in mobilizing the church and doing research on the world of today. Not often do we take the time to do extensive historical research. It was, therefore, an exhilarating experience for the few of us to delve into the old records and become friends with the students of the latter part of the last century. Every few weeks Ralph wrote up all we had found so far and went off to deliver a commemorative address—in Texas, Wheaton, North Carolina and finally at VISION '86, the student mission conference for all of New England which met on the very grounds at Mt. Hermon where the Student Volunteer Movement was born a hundred years ago. His closing remarks at the last three summed up why this study had so captivated those of us involved:

"We have come here to honor those students who started the SVM one hundred years ago," Ralph said. "Those students back in 1886 were convinced they could evangelize the world by 1900. And they just might have, if the church had been ready to back them fully. What about us?

"Can we," Ralph finished, "truly *honor* those students if today, with all our benefits, we are unwilling to believe that we can finish the job by the year 2000? How can we honor *their* faith and not share it today in circumstances that are a hundred times more optimistic? Can't we see that today it is infinitely more possible to finish the task of world evangelization?"

Obviously, he was right. By comparison to the road ahead of them, we have an eight-lane freeway. We can get to any country of the world in just a few hours by jet; it took them weeks, if not months, for the boat trip alone. It wasn't physically easy to evangelize the world in 1886, even if there had been no other barriers at all.

But we have other tremendous advantages. We have loudspeaker systems, slide and movie projectors, video tapes, transistor radios, television, communication satellites, and three major mission agencies with extremely powerful transmitters exclusively dedicated to communicating the gospel behind the political and religious barriers of our day. They had none of these.

Many of the missionaries in the last century died within a few months of reaching the field—from malaria, blackwater fever, dysentery, diphtheria, smallpox, polio, pneumonia. Today we have a broad range of antibiotics, sulfa drugs, and modern vaccines. Our main worries about health are related to the kinds of illness we are just as likely to contract at home—such as cancer or the diseases caused by organisms resistant to modern drugs.

Those young people of long ago went to countries where the church was non-existent or still quite weak. At best, there was only one Christian per 150 non-Christians. Today the ratio is one to fifteen. Now, there are at least a million Christians in most of the countries of the world.

Back then, the burden of evangelizing the world rested almost entirely on the shoulders of the Western nations. Today, there are more than 350 non-Western mission agencies sending thousands of their own missionaries all over the world. And they are just beginning to move.

Ever since the 1980 conference in Edinburgh, Ralph

has been talking about the significance of the year 2000, now just thirteen years away. The years come and go, as do the decades. Few humans have ever lived to see the change of a century.

I admit I was startled, however, when later that fall Ralph pointed out to me that January 1st, 2000 will be the very first time in history that the whole world will recognize the change of a millenium! Only in recent centuries, he reminded me, have most countries started to number from the birth of Christ.

For some years I have been teaching the history of the expansion of Christianity. I always start by reviewing God's concern for all peoples down through history, starting with Abraham. Two millenia before Christ, in 2000 B.C., God promised to bless him and to make him and his descendants a blessing to all peoples. Since then, four thousand years have passed. Right in the middle of that time span Jesus Christ appeared and died as our Redeemer.

As I was thinking about this, I realized with a jolt that 2000 A.D. might not be simply a nice round date to set as a goal by which to penetrate every people group on earth. Just possibly, in God's timetable, the year 2000 A.D. might be highly significant—as significant as that night in Bethlehem when Christ was born, but few were expecting Him.

"He could return in my lifetime," my heart told me. But my mind answered, "That's always been true for everyone down through history. Yet it hasn't happened so far."

And my heart said, "That's what Peter warned: *People will say, 'Where is this coming he promised? Ever since our fathers died, everything goes on as it has since the beginning of creation'* (2 Pet. 3:4). Jesus Himself warned us that He will come when least expected."

"Ah, but He gave us some signs to tell us when He would return," my mind argued.

"And almost all have been met... except one!"

I gasped in awe at the thought. *That* was it, that sign in Matt. 24:14, where He said all nations and tribes and tongues would hear, and *then* He would return. That was the challenge which called those Student Volunteers a hundred years ago to give their lives in the far corners of the earth. And that is the one which is calling *our* students to go. And the students of Europe and Australia. And of Asia and the South Pacific. And Africa and Latin America. The sense of urgency they feel is not of *our* doing. God is in it. His time has come!

Some months ago, long before we had begun the research for Ralph's talks during the summer, I asked God to give me a special verse for the title of this book. I felt particularly drawn to Isaiah 43.

Throughout the chapter God speaks of the nations and of His determination to reach them through His people: "You are my witnesses and my servants, chosen to know and to believe me and to understand that I alone am God. *There is no other God; there never was and never will be. I am the Lord, and there is no other Savior* " (vv. 10-11, italics mine).

The words reminded me of Peter's in Acts 4:12—*"There is no other name under heaven whereby we must be saved"*—and I realized again that no matter how presumptuous it sounds to modern ears, only those who follow Christ have the answer. "There is *no other* Savior." And if God's people don't tell the nations about Him, who will? And unless they hear, how can they be saved?

Once again I felt strongly convicted that what we were involved in at the U.S. Center for World Mission was exactly in the center of God's will. In a unique way He had chosen us to witness about the unreached peoples and to encourage His church to finish the job.

That call, however, involved risk and hardship. Of course! Why wouldn't Satan fight against such a witness?

Of course he would make every step of the way difficult.

My eyes swept down the page. *"For your sakes I will send an invading army against Babylon* [the forces of evil], *that will walk in almost unscathed. I am the Lord, your Holy One, Israel's Creator and King. I am the Lord, who opens a path right through the sea..."*

I thought of the struggles behind us, and those still to come. I thought of the $8 million balloon payment due in the fall of 1987, and the intervening quarterly payments until then. I thought of the miracles He had done for us in this place, and the miracles we would still need in order to survive and finish all He had given us to do.

We were witnesses of His grace and of His provision. What joy!

"But forget all that," God told His people in verse 19. *"It is nothing compared to what I am going to do."*

Forget all that! It is nothing by comparison!

I found it hard to comprehend just what He might mean. Our churches are filled with hurting people. Our pastors have little time to even consider the world beyond their parish. Our society struggles with terrorism and greed.

But God looks beyond all that. He has wonderful plans for our world—plans for renewal and healing of His people, plans for a worldwide awakening, plans for the final harvest of the nations.

"Open your eyes and look on the fields," He reminds us again. *"For I'm going to do a brand new thing. See, I have already begun!"*

45

"THOUGH IT TARRIES, WAIT..."

(Habakkuk 2:3)

It doesn't seem reasonable that God would allow us to stumble right at the threshold of the final great harvest which He called us to announce. Not after all the miracles He has done for us here in this place. We are His witnesses—both of this vision and of His marvelous grace and provision.

And yet, humanly speaking, we still have almost a year of large quarterly payments, and beyond those the final balloon payment of $8 million. As always, we continue to be utterly dependent upon the Lord to provide all that we need.

Back in May, 1986, we began preparing for this last, great financial push. Bob Coleman, as so often before, was the one to suggest a workable plan.

One day in a phone conversation with a friend, he mentioned his concern about the huge balloon payment coming due in a little over a year, and his friend suggested, "Why don't you just ask 8000 people to give $1000 each, and be done with it?"

Bob gasped in amazement, then answered. "A thousand dollars is a lot of money!" How well he knew! He had been scraping along for years on only a fraction of the support he was entitled to. "Raising his support" seemed the hardest thing he had ever attempted. So he hesitated just a moment, then audaciously challenged, "How about you? Would *you* give $1,000?"

"Well, you know," his friend answered after a pause, "I don't have a lot of money. But if I knew it was the *last* $1,000 that you needed to pay for you property once and for all, even I would give $1,000. I'd be glad to!"

The last thousand! ... The words rang in Bob's ear. "Even *I* could somehow scrape together that much if I knew it was that important—if I knew it was the *last thousand!* And there must be a lot of other people just like me."

That was the beginning of our "Last $1,000 Campaign."

We did a lot of praying about this idea and felt that God had confirmed that it was His way when soon afterward a friend of the Center called and offered a substantial sum to help fund the campaign. He knew it would not be cheap. We would need funds for brochures, for postage, for whatever it would take to make people aware of our need.

After so many years of asking only for a one-time, small gift, we wondered how our backers would respond to this plan. But not one criticized. In fact, most seemed relieved that we were asking for a larger amount at last. "We want you to be done with the financial burden," they said, "and be able to give all your energy to the things God has called you to do."

Even so, we still felt constrained to consider all such large gifts (except for those from foundations) as advances which one day in the future (as the small gifts continued to come in over the years) we would be able to return (if from churches) or reassign to some other mission project chosen by the original donor. For years we had kept a very accurate accounting of all gifts over the $16 we had requested so that we could count such funds as this type of "revolving" fund.

So that the $1,000 participants would not have to risk losing their money, should we not be able to make the final payment, we promised to put all the "Last $1,000" funds in an interest-bearing escrow account so that we could return them to the donor in that event. It seemed the only honorable thing to do.

But we felt with all our hearts that God would provide...though we didn't know just how.

As the October 1st, 1986 mortgage payment time drew near, we once again didn't have the necessary $300,000, and began to wonder if the $1,000 campaign was actually hurting our regular giving. As so often before, we prayed earnestly and long about our situation, and just in time, God once more provided for us...as usual, in ways we could not have guessed.

For one thing, in light of the Last $1,000 Campaign, Point Loma officials agreed to let us pay only the interest part of the amount due for both the October and the January 1st payments. That decision cut the amount due almost in half.

Then, unexpectedly, two large personal donations came in, neither of which was restricted as a "Last $1,000" gift.

Then, the day after receiving an unexpected $30,000 bill, Ralph's secretary opened his mail and looked in astonishment at a $35,000 check. It had been sent by the Back to the Bible Broadcast, with the following explanation. "We were recently named in a will and received a large sum of money which we want to share with you and two other agencies. We are enclosing $35,000 for you to use as you need." We were humbled by their generosity, as well as very grateful.

More importantly, the unsolicited gift showed that God had not forgotten us. He was continuing to take care of us. What a comforting thought!

Since starting the campaign, almost $1.3 million has

come in for that final balloon payment—$909,000 in cash, and the rest in pledges.

"Do you think you dare trust God to bring in the rest on time?" our friends might ask us.

Our only answer has to be, "Dare we *not* trust Him? He has always taken care of us in miraculous ways. If we draw back in unbelief now, He will have no pleasure in us. (See Hebrews 10:38.) We must live by faith. Or, stated another way, it is only by faith that we *will* live.

I have to admit that once in awhile my own faith wobbles. It is not easy to believe where you can't see and to expect something what has no real basis except your hope. Yet, when God is the One who has issued the call and when He has promised faithfully to provide all that we need, then to have faith isn't quite so difficult.

But prayer is crucial. Several years ago when I was in one of these "wobbly" stages, I earnestly sought the Lord about the balloon payment up ahead. As I prayed, my heart calmed, and I felt convinced that He had heard and would answer in His own way and time. Yet, as I often do, I asked Him for a special verse to lean on when my faith grew weak, and this is what He gave:

> ...*the gates shall not be shut against [you] anymore. I will go before you...and level the mountains and smash down the city gates of brass and iron bars. And I will give you treasures hidden in the darkness, secret riches...And you will know that I am doing this—I, the Lord, the God of Israel, the one who calls you by your name* (Isa. 45:1-3).

The gates have begun to open. That mountains which have barred us from all the provision we need have begun to crumble. But we still wait for the complete fulfillment of His promise, even as we wait with great eagerness to see the complete fulfillment of that *brand new thing which*

293

He promised two thousand years ago—*that final harvest of the nations*.

Neither has yet happened...not quite. But we believe both will, in God's time. And we believe that will be soon.

As God told Habakkuk, so He tells us:

> *The vision is yet for an appointed time;*
> *But at the end it will speak, and it will not lie.*
> *Though it tarries, wait for it.*
> *Because it will surely come;*
> *It will not tarry.*
> Hab. 2:3 (NKJ)

Appendix:

MY TURN

Ralph D. Winter

How can I be of help? If you haven't yet had a chance to get caught up in the dramatic story of my wife's book, then perhaps the questions and answers in the next section will be of value.

I confess that my most urgent concern here is that somehow in all this excitement you might miss out on the meaning behind the title of the book, *I Will Do A New Thing*. A short book title often does not tell much.

This title has to do with the remainder of your time on earth and about how short that time may be! It has to do with the quality of your relationship right now with our Heavenly Father. The New Thing, we believe, is an impending global revival which may very well lead to the end of history by the year 2000. After all, God is the one saying "I will do a new thing" (Isa 43:19).

But, what am I getting at? The point is, can this new vision—this New Thing God is doing—affect your daily life? And how can you get in touch with it?

Unfortunately most people are desperately unaware of what God is doing and is about to do. Indeed, they may not even catch on until it is too late to make any difference. As it says in Rev 22:11, "Let the one who does wrong still do wrong...": they can simply be too late. But let's all ask God to help us catch on and catch up to what He is doing. He wants to help us if we truly want to know.

I think of two examples of people missing a major move on God's part. In 1886 millions of people were celebrating the placement of the Statue of Liberty in New York harbor. At the very same time, something far more important was going on in western Massachusetts, but few perceived the meaning of it. Sure, it was a small student conference, but those people of that day simply did not realize that it was the spark that would ignite the flame of history's largest mission movement—the

Student Volunteer Movement!

But, then, a similar thing has just happened. In 1986, all Americans were once again thinking about the Statue of Liberty. Yet few people noticed that in the final 90 days of that same year Caleb traveling vans met face-to-face with 17,000 students in what is an unprecedented harvest of new missionary recruits and expect to be meeting an additional 25,000 by June of 1987. Do you see what I mean?

One way to grasp the full meaning of this New Thing God may be about to do is to know what is already true. Right now I want to list some things which may be of help. We want you to join us as we all struggle together to perceive the unfolding meaning of the New Thing God is beginning to do. None of us wants to be looking in the wrong direction when the mighty work of God is passing by!

(By the way, I am really excited to list these because we are convinced that we have something to give to you that is worth far, far more than any Founder's Gift of $16.95 which you may have given us. In fact it is worth more than any other kind of gift you might receive, short of the assurance of salvation.)

WAYS WE CAN SHARE WITH YOU

1. There is, in fact, one thing we are right now offering millions of people day after day. It is high quality excitement about the rapid advance of the Gospel around the world and the resultant fast decrease in the number of unreached populations on earth. How do we do this? You can get in on it by phoning your favorite Christian radio station to see if it is one of the 550 which daily broadcasts a page from our little devotional booklet, the *Global Prayer Digest*.. (Ask us for a list of these stations. If yours is not on the list, give the program director our address so he or she can ask for a sample tape. New stations are inquiring about this monthly cassette service each week. It is provided without charge.)

2. Remember, as we try to reach out to you, the newness of life and vision God wants to pour into your life will not show up merely in the form of a new intellectual vision. It will more likely be a growing, (daily or hourly) new AWARENESS. At first days may go by without your even thinking about the New Thing God is doing. Indeed, it may take weeks for your awareness of this new reality to triumph over the older, less-important concerns. But this is one battle we'll never win except on the basis of increased DAILY awareness. And that can be achieved more easily by listening to or reading the *Global Prayer Digest*

than by almost any other thing you yourself can determine to do. We'll be glad to send you a sample copy of the booklet itself. A new issue comes out each month with the latest events in it. Just remember: *"Nothing that does not occur daily will ever dominate your life."*

3. Equally important is to *try earnestly to give away the vision you have*, whatever you already understand of it. Your new vision will grow as you give it away. When Jesus said, *"Give and it will be given unto you"* He was not just talking about money. Write to us for the little kit, *Grandchildren are Great*, which will help you to share this vision with others—others who will be able to share with still others. You can be a vision-grandparent whatever your age! And you can feel tremendously gratified in giving away so great a gift.

4. To help you become "rich" as you give away priceless vision, we have all kinds of materials which you can use and then share with others. These range from more copies of this book to brochures, booklets, books, cassettes and video tapes. (Ask us for the "Action Check List.") All it takes in a local congregation is for one faithful person to mind a Mission Resource Table once a month. We can suggest how to do that and the things to go on it.

5. One of the main things we can offer you is our inexpensive, monthly bulletin called *Mission Frontiers*, which costs only $4.00 per year. If you receive this you won't miss anything that we hear about. *Mission Frontiers* refers to still other sources—things we have and things others have. It is the key to dozens of new books on missions and world events. (Almost all the materials we handle are at tremendous discounts. We provided these as a ministry, not for profit, since our time is already paid for.) Write for this bulletin!

6. However, before you do that, you could get this automatically. (Please don't think my primary interest is in getting you to help us.) If you are not already one of the $15 Founders of the U.S. Center for World Mission and would be willing to become one, that's great because then you'll automatically get *Mission Frontiers*. This is how it works: When you send in your one-time $15 gift (to become a Founder), we suggest you make the check out for $16.95. The additional $1.95 will get you started on *Mission Frontiers*, send you a sample copy of the *Global Prayer Digest*, a color poster giving the big picture about the unreached peoples, plus a whole list of available things and (more recently) a list of the radio stations carrying the *Global Prayer Di-*

gest. New Founders also receive a copy of this book to lend, give or keep.

7. We also have something pretty weighty to offer! It may be possible in your area to take our college credit course called *Perspectives on the World Christian Movement.* At this moment our textbook is used in over 100 Christian colleges and seminaries. But, in addition, we ourselves supervise a vast network of trained "coordinators" who each year offer it on secular campuses (and in local congregations) in more than 100 places in the U.S.A. as well as six other countries. If you have 30 or 40 people who want to take it in any one region, this will allow a different missions specialist to fly in once a week for 15 weeks. This is a potent 200-hour experience. But there are simpler versions thatn the 3-semester-unit college course.

8. Another very unusual opportunity is the Caleb organization. It is primarily focused on college students, but people of any age who sign up with them will be expected to report in monthly for a year on the various things they are doing to maintain and fulfill their mission vision. Caleb will suggest a lot of the things mentioned here plus others too. The slim office team here in their offices will pray for you by name every day. There is nothing like an accountable fellowship in becoming all that God intended. He intended accountable fellowship!

9. Along this line, perhaps the most important way we can help you is to encourage you to become part of some kind of local mission fellowship. Ideally this will be something you can start or join within your own local church. If that is not possible, then perhaps a home meeting would be possible with the blessing of your pastor or mission committee. For this type of meeting we create monthly a 15-minute *Mission Frontiers Video.* (We have a booklet telling how to set up a local Frontier Fellowship and explaining about using the *Global Prayer Digest* and setting aside your loose change each day for some unreached peoples project. This is the kind of meeting where you can turn in this loose change offering.)

OK, I could go on and on. The main thing is to realize that we would like to help you in any way we can. All of the things mentioned are available to you from: **USCWM, 1605 Elizabeth Street, Pasadena CA 91104, (818-797-1111, 24 hours 7 days/wk).**

Each member of our staff handles all the correspondence from his/her assigned area of the country. You will meet the person responsible for your area with your first letter! We are here to serve you and the mission agencies.

QUESTIONS AND ANSWERS

WHAT IS THE USCWM?

To me the U.S. Center for World Mission is simply a place where mission agencies can lend key people to collaborate on the unfinished task—in strategy, publicity, research, specialized university education, etc.—without duplication and multiplication of effort.

Others, however, have compared the USCWM to a shopping mall, a think tank, even the Pentagon. In any case we are physically a former college campus now owned and operated by a group of missionaries with an exclusive focus on the challenge of the roughly 17,000 still-unreached people groups around the world.

Although founded as recently as 1976, there are already 300 people who work here every day. Many of us are involved in research on these unreached (or "Hidden") peoples, and what strategy might best reach them. Equally, we are involved in assisting congregations in America and elsewhere to understand the challenge of the "final frontiers." We speak more than 40 different languages, have experience in 50 different countries, and have worked with, or are still related to, more than 70 different mission agencies. We intend for all of our staff to retain their ties by an "on loan" relation to us from some mission agency or other.

One dimension of our work has been the design and formation of a specialized university, the William Carey International University, which has been set up to meet the unusual needs of missionaries, mission personnel and overseas national leaders in the developing nations.

THE USCWM: WHERE IS IT?

The USCWM is located in Pasadena, ten miles northeast of the center of Los Angeles. We are thus in a major metropolitan basin having the world's largest concentration of mission agencies as well as the world's greatest ethnic diversity (at least 173 language communities). Our campus is close to a number of major universities with magnificent research facilities and lies 45 minutes from either the Los Angeles International Airport or the Ontario Airport, and only 20 minutes from the airport in Burbank.

THE USCWM: WHAT DOES IT LOOK LIKE?

The central campus is roughly two square blocks in size (quite small by today's standards for Christian colleges). Surrounding it on all sides are residential properties, 84 of which (within two blocks) are part of the campus and have for many years functioned as an essential component of campus housing.

WHAT IS ALL THIS WORTH?

In today's market, these properties, which together form a well-balanced campus whole, are worth about $25 million. Our outstanding balance, payable in the fall of 1987, is now just under $8 million, toward which as of March '87 we have $1.4 million in cash and pledges as part of the "Last $1000" Campaign. (See p. 305 for a fuller explanation.)

THE USCWM: WHO WORKS HERE?

Although I am the founder and General Director, the hundred people who work directly under my leadership on theUSCWM "central staff" as well as 30 employees of the university corporation are managed on a day to day basis by Art McCleary, who for a number of years was the personnel director of Bethel College and Seminary in Minneapolis and before that a manager in several different kinds of secular businesses. The other 200 people who work together here, making the 300 mentioned already, function within various related projects, departments and autonomous organizations on campus. Then you can add 100 to 400 students on campus (depending upon the time of year), another 2000 in a given year studying our "Perspectives on the World Christian Movement" course in 100 extension locations around the world, plus about 30 Ph.D. candidates in more than 20 countries, and you have the human dimension of this project.

The consecrated core team is no small miracle, and is as much the work of the Spirit of God here as any of the miracles connected with the funding of the campus. Yet, without the buildings in which to work in proximity with each other, much of the throbbing vitality here would be like a clam without a shell.

In North America there are three other Centers for World Mission consciously working along similar lines, plus New England and Mid-Atlantic branch offices of the USCWM. There are about 30 centers around the world of somewhat the same sort.

THE USCWM: WHAT IS IT FOR?

One of the largest multinational industries today is the "mission industry." Seventy thousand North Americans are involved overseas as well as other home-office staff making an overall cost of roughly $2 billion per year. Speaking of Protestant missionaries alone, North American missionaries are joined by about 20,000 missionaries from other Western countries, as well as an equal number of missionaries supported by the "mission field" churches of the non-Western world.

This unusual globe-influencing industry is, in a word, what the USCWM exists to serve. Our property is, thus, a vast staging ground for joint planning and for collaboration in research and specialized training. The 42 corporations that occupy our campus are all involved in this cause. Because they are next door to each other, they can work out things together without duplication or overlap and attempt projects no one mission agency could handle.

Specifically, however, we work together on whatever is necessary to promote the completion of the task of world evangelization. This task may seem large when viewed from the number of individuals who still do not know Christ. When viewed in terms of the unreached people groups, however, they number roughly 17,000 peoples still without an evangelizing church in their culture.

But there are today 150 congregations for each one of those unreached people groups. If we all work together, we can finish the work Christ gave us to do.

Part of our job at the USCWM is to make this fact crystal clear and to help the mission agencies as they pick up this challenge. Where that involves sophisticated computer demographic research, several of the offices on campus are tackling that problem. Where it involves hands-on mobilization and training of thousands of Christian congregations and students, we also give ourselves to that. If it means alerting mission agencies to some new possibilities, we try to do that. Whatever needs to be done to help finish the Great Commission we consider to be part of our agenda. But we do this in conscious cooperation with the mission agencies of the world.

In order to do all our work most efficiently , we are organized into four major divisions: Strategy, Mobilization, Training and Services. The entire university program falls under the training division. "Services" includes a mail room, computerized mailing-list management, a bookstore, a publishing house, a printing firm, a number of libraries etc., whose services are available to all on campus.

301

WHAT DO OTHERS SAY ABOUT US?

The list of well-known Christian leaders who back this ministry would be very long. To save space the National Support Committee backing our "Last $1000 Campaign" is listed on page 304. Others who have warmly supported us through the years would include the following: David Barrett, Bill and Vonette Bright, Jonathan Chao, David Cho, Evelyn Christianson, Wade Coggins, Norman Cummings, Wesley Duewel, Leighton Ford, Vergil Gerber, Billy Graham, Don Hamilton, Jack Hayford, Donald Hoke, J. Herbert Kane, Kenneth Kantzer, Dale Kietzman, Raymond Knighton, Jack McAlister, Paul McKaughan, Paul Orjala, John Piet, David Rambo, Waldron Scott, James C. Smith, Dick Van Halsema, Peter Wagner, Larry Ward, Warren Webster.

Across the years many prominent backers have made public statements expressing their confidence. A few are quoted on the first page of this book.

TELL US SOMETHING ABOUT YOURSELF

I was born into a devout Christian family in Los Angeles. For 35 years my father was the chief engineer for the design of the Los Angeles freeway system (he is now 92 and I am 62). My parents were leaders in the church (first the Highland Park Presbyterian near Los Angeles, then later Lake Avenue Congregational in Pasadena) as well as in the Christian Endeavor Movement, through which they had originally gained their evangelical faith. Both of my brothers are elders in their local congregations; one is an award-winning structural engineer and has been President of the board of African Enterprise and the other is president of Westmont College in Santa Barbara, California.

In my youth my personal walk with Christ became strong through the influence of Christian Endeavor, Youth for Christ, and Navigators (in the Navy in WW II). After graduating from Cal Tech, I taught one year at Westmont College, attended the first "Urbana" (at Toronto), helped launch a non-professional missionary effort to Afghanistan, did further studies at various places (including Prairie Bible Institute), received an M.A. in Education at Columbia University, a Ph.D. at Cornell in Linguistics and Anthropology and later a B.D. at Princeton Seminary.

Under the auspices of the Presbyterian church, my wife and I worked for ten years with Mayan Indians in Guatemala, where I helped to found the Theological Education by Extension movement (extending seminary to Indians in our case). I was elected Executive Secretary of

302

the Latin American Association of Theological Schools, Northern Region (17 countries), the last North American to hold that job. In 1966 I was invited to join Donald A. McGavran and Alan Tippett in the second year of the new Fuller School of World Mission. In 1969, my wife and I founded the William Carey Library (mission publishing house) and in the years to follow I helped found the American Society of Missiology (of which I have been both Secretary and President), the Institute of International Studies, the Association of Church Mission Committees, the Order for World Evangelization.

By invitation, I gave one of the plenary addresses at the Lausanne International Congress on World Evangelization in 1974, the opening address at the 1976 Triennial Joint Mission Executives' retreat of the Interdenominational Foreign Mission Association and the Evangelical Foreign Missions Association, as well as the opening address at the 1979 EFMA conference on Unreached Peoples. When I left Fuller Seminary in the fall of 1976, I was a tenured full Professor of the Historic Development of the Christian Movement. The September 9, 1974 issue of *Christianity Today* had its cover story an article about me and the work of the USCWM. (We will be happy to send you a copy of that lengthy treatment.)

WHAT IS YOUR THEOLOGY?

Our staff as a whole are in the mainstream of the evangelical movement. We adhere without qualification to the full inspiration and authority of the Bible, to the uniqueness and saving work of Christ, to the power of the Holy Spirit and His guidance in our lives. Specifically, we hold the Lausanne Covenant and the statements of faith of the Interdenominational Foreign Mission Association (IFMA) and the Evangelical Foreign Missions Association (EFMA) as benchmark documents with which participating individuals and organizations must be in agreement. We do not have nor do we contemplate any formal relationship with any denomination or church council, but we do welcome representatives of evangelical mission agencies to work with us in our various strategy institutes and mobilization centers. All of our staff are supported by some mission agency or other and are on loan on a short or long-term basis to us except for several of our central staff who raise their own support directly under the banner of the U.S. Center for World Mission.

Our National Support Committee

Frank Barker, Pastor — Briarwood Presby., Birmingham AL
John Bennett, Former Director — Assoc. of Church Missions Committees
Pat Boone, Singer/Actor — Hollywood Studios
Bill Bright, Founder — Campus Crusade for Christ
David Bryant, Minister-at-Large — Inter-Varsity Missions
Paul Cedar, Pastor — Lake Ave. Cong., Pasadena CA
George Cowan, Former President — Wycliffe Bible Translators
Loren Cunningham, Founder, Director — Youth With A Mission
Dick Eastman, Founder, Director — Change the World Ministries
Allen B. Finley, International President — Christian Nat'ls Evang. Comm., Inc.
David Fisher, Director — Living Waters Christ'n Fell., Pasadena
Howard Foltz, Assoc. Prof. of Missions — CBN University
Leighton Ford, Director — Lausanne Committee
Richard Foster, Professor — Friends University
Edwin L. Frizen, Executive Director — Interdenom. Foreign Mission Assoc.
Gary Ginter, Partner — Chicago Research and Trading
John Gration, Professor of Missions — Wheaton College Graduate School
William T. Greig, Jr., President — Gospel Light Publications
Norval Hadley, Director,Int'l. Intercessors — World Vision
Richard Halverson, Chaplain — United States Senate
Ken Hansen, Vice Chairman — Servicemaster Corp.
Jack Hayford, Pastor — First Foursquare, Van Nuys CA
David Howard, General Director — World Evangelical Fellowship
Ed Johnson, Retired Chairman — Financial Federation, Inc.
Patrick Johnstone, Int'l. Research Sec. — W.E.C. International
Sam Kamaleson, Vice President — World Vision International
Graham Kerr, Director, C-3 Design Team — Youth With A Mission
John Kyle, Director — Inter-Varsity Missions
Harold Lindsell, Former Editor — Christianity Today
Greg Livingstone, General Director — Frontiers, Inc.
Ralph Lord, Investment Broker — Jackson, MS
Gordon MacDonald, President — Inter-Varsity Christian Fellowship
Colin McDougall, Executive Director — Assoc. of Church Missions Committees
Donald McGavran, Founder — Fuller School of World Mission
George Munzing, Pastor — Trinity Presbyterian, Santa Ana CA
Cyrus N. Nelson, Chairman Emeritus — Gospel Light Publications
Virgil A. Olson, Professor — Bethel College and Seminary
Raymond C. Ortlund, President — Renewal Ministries
John M. Perkins, Founder, Director — Perkins Found. for Reconcil. & Dev.
Keith Phillips, Founder, Director — World Impact, Inc.
Kenneth L. Pike, President Emeritus — Wycliffe Bible Translators
Larry Poland, Fmr. Dir. Agape Movement — Campus Crusade for Christ, Intern'l
Luis Palau, Evangelist — Director , Overseas Crusades
Don Richardson, Lecturer, Author — Regions Beyond Missionary Union
Ron Sider, Professor of Mission — Eastern Baptist Theol. Seminary
J. T. Seamands, Professor of Missions — Asbury Theological Seminary
Tim Stafford, Associate Editor — Christianity Today
Clyde Taylor, Former Director — National Assoc. of Evangelicals
Kenneth N. Taylor, Publisher — Tyndale House Publishers
J. Allen Thompson, Executive Director — Worldteam
Mrs. Wm. Cameron Townsend — Wycliffe Bible Translators
Ruth Tucker, Historian and Author — Grand Rapids, MI
Abe Van der Puy, Director of Missions — Back to the Bible Broadcast
Robert Walker, Editor, Publisher — Christian Life Magazine
Matthew Welde, Executive Director — Presbys. United for Biblical Concerns
J. Christy Wilson, Jr., Professor — Gordon Conwell Theol. Seminary
Hoover Wong, Pastor — First Chinese Church, Honolulu HI
Tetsunao Yamamori, President — Food for the Hungry International

The Background of the
"Last $1000 Campaign"

We are deeply concerned to discover what it will take to enable one million Americans to discover the basic facts about the tremendous hopefulness of the world situation, viewed from the standpoint of the expanding Christian movement world wide?

How can that many people be alerted to what can be done so that Christian believers in America will do their fair share and pull their load on the world level? That is our part in finishing the task of reaching every nation and tribe and tongue with the Gospel of Jesus Christ!

Can you help? For ten years we have believed that one of our most important missions was to alert that number of people, asking them - to make sure they catch the point - to become one-time-gift Founders of the U.S. Center for World Mission.

This process has gone slowly for the most part, but also with lightning speed. Once we supplied 550 willing workers out across the U.S.A with 100 packets of 10 Founders invitations. Each of the 550 tried to find 100 people who would take a packet and mail out ten of the invitations. About 6,000 of their friends actually did it, and those 6,000 got an average of more than two responses, or 14,000 new founders in just about 30 days.

We know of course that if a Christian television program picked up this campaign we might reach a million people in a few days. But speed, and money, is not the main thing. It is rather to reach the right people.

In any case we must soon pay off these properties, and as of April 1987 we have $5.9 million to go. That is equivalent to 5,950 units of $1,000, which we need to receive as "advances" against the slower stream of $15 gifts coming in. Some congregations are pledging $10,000 and are then trying to find 667 Founders giving $15 to make up that amount. Would you like to help? We will be most grateful if you can.

COUPON

Here is an abbreviated list of the things mentioned on pages 296-298. Check off what you want, tear out or clip out this entire sheet and mail it in to the address at the bottom.

__1. List of **Global Prayer Digest** radio stations

__2. Sample copy of the **Global Prayer Digest**

__3. **"Grandchildren are Great"** brochure

__4. **Action Check List**

__5. **Mission Frontiers** (Bulletin)

__6. I want to become a **Founder.** Enclosed is my $16.95 check ($15 gift, $1.95 materials)

__7. Information on the college course, **Perspectives on the World Christian Movement**

__8. Information on the **Caleb plan** for personal accountability.

__9. Info on the **Mission Frontiers Monthly Video** and monthly mission fellowship.

__10. I want to be a part of the **"Last $1000 Campaign"** to finish paying for the property. (See over).

Here is my ___check ___pledge for $_____.

Send this sheet to:
UNITED STATES CENTER FOR WORLD MISSION
1605 Elizabeth Street, Pasadena CA 91104
(Phone 818-797-1111; a person is on duty 24 hrs every day)